Y0-DXA-850

Phonetics

DATE DUE

MAY 1 1 1983			
JUN 0 1 1986			
11/13/87			
MAR 1 1993			
MAY 0 1 2003			
MAY 2 3 2003			
MAY 1 0			
GAYLORD			PRINTED IN U.S.A.

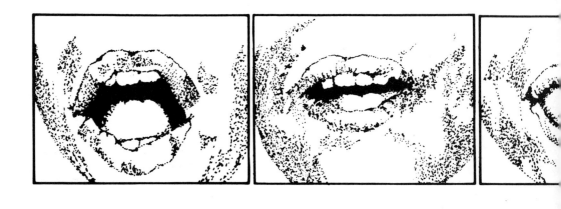

PHONETICS
Principles and Practices

Sadanand Singh, Ph.D.
Professor of Hearing and Speech Sciences
University of Texas Health Science Center at Houston

and

Kala S. Singh, M.S.
Audiologist
Private Practice

University Park Press
Baltimore · London · Tokyo

WITHDRAWN
NORTH CENTRAL COLLEGE
NAPERVILLE, ILLINOIS 60540

UNIVERSITY PARK PRESS
International Publishers in Science and Medicine
Chamber of Commerce Building
Baltimore, Maryland 21202

Copyright © 1976 by University Park Press

Typeset by The Composing Room of Michigan, Inc.
Manufactured in the United States of America by
Universal Lithographers, Inc.,
and The Maple Press Co.

All rights, including that of translation into other languages, reserved. Photo-mechanical reproduction (photocopy, microcopy) of this book or parts thereof without special permission of the publisher is prohibited.

Library of Congress Cataloging in Publication Data
Singh, Sadanand.
Phonetics : principles and practice.

Includes index.
1. Phonetics.   2. Distinctive features (Lin-
guistics)   I. Singh, Kala S., joint author.
I. Title.
P221.S53   414   75–45263
ISBN 0–8391–0822–2

4,4
Lib p

Contents

133449

Tables

Figures

Preface

This book is written mainly for students in an introductory course in phonetics and for anyone who wants a comprehensive understanding of the field for personal interest. Although the text attempts to assimilate recent advances in the various branches of phonetics, the strategy for presentation is such that anyone interested in understanding the story of American English sounds will benefit. Pictorial presentation of the production of speech sounds on the one hand, and the writing devoid of references and cumbersome footnotes on the other, facilitate the reading and comprehending of the material.

This book is also written with the following understanding: the current story of phonetics must be told in its entire and most up-to-date context; the materials must be new and stimulating; the concepts must not be presented as if they were meant merely for academic exercise, but must be put forward so that readers may apply them in solving the current and projected problems of language, speech, and hearing.

The knowledge of the various aspects of phonetics endows one with a better understanding of man's primary source of communication between his inner and outer worlds. More importantly, phonetics has been viewed both as a scientific tool for the analysis of normal and deviant speech and hearing patterns and as the art of the application of this tool in solving problems relating to the sounds of speech. This text endeavors to convey an understanding and an appreciation of these aspects.

In addition, the text tries to overcome two problems that often complicate the initial study of phonetics. First, the major obstacle in teaching the phonetic system underlying speech is that untrained ears do not listen for the same cues that trained ears do. In fact, untrained ears behave somewhat like the ears of the hearing impaired: they both miss cues. This book adopts two strategies to confront the problem: 1) the auditory exercises are accompanied by visual cues, and 2) phonetic transcription is taught fully integrated with articulatory principles. In our experience, teaching phonetic transcription is greatly enhanced when taught simultaneously with the principles of phonetic sciences.

Second, one of the problems in studying phonetics has been the difficulty in visualizing the speech production event, which is largely imperceptible to the unaided eye. This text uses an innovative approach. Sequential photographs from motion picture films of spoken words are presented along with their corresponding sound tracks, so that the reader actually can see various moments of the dynamic aspects of speech production. The photographs are complemented by schematic xiv Preface

drawings of tongue movements that occur during speech production; these further help the reader visualize the articulatory components of speech production captured in these photographs. Finally, for a more thorough understanding, sound spectrograms are given for each speech event, illustrating acoustic properties of speech production.

These three-part viewings, called "modules," and our comments regarding some of them are presented in Chapter 7, and they serve as the core of this text. Readers are advised to skim through the contents of this chapter before reading the text.

Considerable credit is due Joseph Agnello and Janice Agnello, who assisted in the preparation of the sound spectrograms for the modules; we are most grateful.

We thank Shobha P. Wagle for her affectionate care while we worked on this manuscript in Bombay and acknowledge the encouragement given to us by M. S. Wagle and V. V. Dukle. Our deep appreciation is also extended to Shaila, Punam, and Avi, who attended to us while we worked on this manuscript. We express sincere gratitude to Joanne Fokes and Marmo Soemarmo for their valuable comments on the manuscript and thank University Park Press, whose initial assistance made possible the filming of speech sound production.

Sadanand Singh
and
Kala Singh

to Bhai

Phonetics

Chapter 1 BASIC CONCEPTS IN THE STUDY OF PHONETICS

Speech is defined as the expression of thoughts by a process of articulating sounds. A speech sound is one of the simplest elements of speech. It is a significant sound made by the definite positioning or movement of the speech organs—those parts of the human body (i.e., tongue, teeth, lips, and so forth) that play a significant role in speech production.

Phonetics is the study of spoken language or speech sounds. It includes the systematic classification of spoken sounds according to the way they are produced by the organs of speech and according to how they sound to the listener. A *phonetician* is one who specializes in phonetics and uses his knowledge of phonetics to understand the systematic classification of speech sounds of the various languages of the world.

Speech sounds are comprised of consonants and vowels. *Con-sonants* are speech sounds that are characterized in enunciation by constriction or closure at one or more points in the breath channel. *Vowels* are speech sounds characterized by lack of any closure or constriction in the breath channel. Acceptable variations in the production of the same speech sound are collectively referred to as a *phoneme*. All phonemes of a given language maintain distinction from each other and yet can have acceptable variations. Thus, the /l/ sounds in "*leave*," "*feel*," and "*truly*," although slightly different in terms of their production, collectively represent the same phoneme /l/. Traditionally, a phoneme is denoted by placing a speech sound between two oblique lines, e.g., / p/.

In this text we will study the system of speech sounds of General American English. American English refers to the native lan-

1

guage spoken by the majority of persons living in the United States. The system of speech sounds can be studied in two parts: 1) the description of speech sounds as absolute and independent entities, and 2) the relationship of these members with one another.

A detailed study of speech sounds can be accomplished by: 1) studying the organs of speech and their function in producing speech sounds (physiological aspect of phonetics), 2) assessing the physical properties of the speech sounds once produced (acoustic aspect of phonetics), and 3) understanding the process by which man is able to identify the individual speech sounds he hears (perceptual aspect of phonetics).

PHYSIOLOGICAL ASPECT

Physiological phonetics is the branch of phonetics that deals with the function of the organs of speech. Man is capable of producing a variety of speech sounds by altering the movements of the various speech organs, such as the lips, teeth, and tongue. From a physiological aspect, therefore, a study of speech sounds includes an investigation of the structure of various speech mechanisms and also a thorough understanding of the function of each of the mechanisms and the part they play in producing the various speech sounds.

Oral Cavity and Tongue

The physiological aspect of phonetics includes the study of speech sounds produced as the tongue moves within the confines of the oral cavity: the lips, the teeth, and the roof, floor, and back of the mouth. For example, in the production of certain speech sounds, such as /t/ and /d/, the tongue tip plays a major role, and the sounds so produced are known as *front speech sounds*. On the other hand, in the production of other speech sounds, such as /k/ and /g/, the back of the tongue plays a major role, and the sounds so formed are known as *back speech sounds*.

Nasal Cavity

Certain speech sounds are produced when the air stream, which ordinarily travels from the lungs to the outside via the oral cavity, instead travels to the outside via the nasal cavity (nose). A study of physiological phonetics, therefore, includes a description of the nasal cavity and its role in speech production. Speech sounds produced with the passage of air through the nasal cavity are known as *nasal sounds,* and those produced without the air stream passing through the nasal cavity are known as *non-nasal sounds*. For example, /n/ is a nasal sound and /r/ is a non-nasal sound.

Larynx and Vocal Folds

The primary source of voice production, the vocal folds, is also studied in the physiological aspect of phonetics since some speech sounds are produced "with voice" and others are produced "without voice." The act or process of producing voice is referred to as *phonation.* When one phonates during speech production, the vocal folds of the larynx (voice-box) vibrate, thus causing the speech sounds to be produced with voice; these sounds are called *voiced sounds.* On the other hand, when the vocal folds do not vibrate, the speech sounds are produced without voice and are called *voiceless sounds.* All English vowel sounds are voiced.

Respiration

Respiration (breathing) is studied because the processes of inhalation (breathing in) and exhalation (breathing out) form the basis for normal voice production. The exhaled air leaving the lungs is driven past the larynx and provides the energy necessary for setting the vocal folds into vibration. During its passage through the oral cavity the exhaled air sometimes experiences obstruction. This obstruction is necessary for the production of certain consonant sounds. For example, certain speech sounds like /p/ and /b/ are possible only when the air stream is obstructed

totally and then released. Certain other speech sounds, like /l/ and /r/, do not require this obstruction. The degree of obstruction experienced by the exhaled air during its passage through the larynx and oral cavity determines whether the consonant produced will have total obstruction, as in the case of *stop consonants,* or will have partial obstruction, as in the case of *fricative consonants.*

Application

Each speech sound can be described as a physiological act. In the following chapters we will discover that we can apply physiological descriptors in fairly complete detail to compare and contrast the different sounds of English. We will see how each speech sound is produced by a specific combination of physiological actions and how a change in the physiological actions may result in the production of an altogether different speech sound. The reason for this may be that change in the physiological actions results in change in the physical properties of the sounds, thus causing the sound to be heard as an altogether different one.

ACOUSTIC ASPECT

Acoustic phonetics is the branch of phonetics that deals with the physical properties of speech sounds. In recent years it has been considered increasingly important to examine the acoustic details of the physiological categories and to focus on those acoustic details that help man to distinguish one sound from another. For example, an examination of the difference in acoustic details between the front and back physiological categories enables us to understand why people not only successfully distinguish the two categories but also are able to identify each sound within the categories. In other words, by examining the acoustic details of speech sounds, we can determine the crucial distinctive qualifications of those sounds. We can identify the unique properties of a sound, say, /p/, that prevent it from being confused with /b/ or any other sound of English.

There are three primary areas of acoustic study: frequency, time, and amplitude. As we view these areas it will become increasingly clear that their interrelationships are complex when each speech sound is described.

Frequency

Frequency, as it relates to speech, is the number of sound waves per second produced by vibration of the vocal folds. The vibration of the vocal folds depends on its mass (body). The greater the mass of the folds, the fewer the number of vibrations it is capable of in one second. Conversely, the smaller the vocal fold mass, the greater the frequency of the sound waves produced. The frequency of a sound determines the *pitch* of that sound. High pitched sounds have a greater number of sound waves produced in one second: consequently, they are high frequency sounds. On the other hand, low pitched sounds have a smaller number of sound waves produced in one second and, therefore, are low frequency sounds. It is known that women and young children sound high pitched, whereas men most generally sound low pitched. This is because the mass of the vocal folds in women and young children is relatively small, thus allowing a greater number of vibrations per second. Men, however, have a relatively larger vocal fold mass, allowing fewer vibrations in one second.

Speech sounds are made up of different combinations of frequencies. Certain speech sounds, such as /s/ and /z/, are high frequency sounds. Other speech sounds, such as /m/ and /b/, are low frequency sounds.

Time

Time is defined as a period during which a process exists or continues. As it relates to speech and hearing, time refers to the *duration* of speech sounds. Some speech sounds are longer than others, and this duration is easily identified by the listener. For example, while the production of /p/ may be completed in less than 100 milliseconds, the production of /s/ may take twice as long. Also, it has been found that a segment of /p/ 100 milliseconds long is sufficient to identify the /p/ correctly, but an /s/ segment of similar duration is not long enough for its correct identification. For /s/ to be identified correctly by the listener, the segment must be almost twice as long as that for /p/. The understanding of such temporal (time-related) requirements in the production and identification of speech sounds provides a greater understanding of the phonetic properties of speech sounds.

Amplitude

Amplitude is defined as the extent of displacement of the sounding body from its position of rest at any point in time. As it relates to speech and hearing, amplitude refers to the extent to which the vocal folds are displaced. The amplitude of the sound produced depends on the energy with which the exhaled air is propelled from the lungs to the outside atmosphere. If the energy is great, the extent of vocal fold vibration is increased, thus increasing the amplitude of the resultant sound wave. However, when the energy is low, the resultant sound wave is of a low amplitude.

Amplitude determines how loud a sound is perceived. Sounds of greater amplitude are perceived by listeners as loud sounds. *Intensity* is related to amplitude in that it is a measure of the strength or energy of a sound that produces the sense of loudness. The study of the physical properties of speech sounds must include the study of intensity as it relates to the frequency components of speech sounds. Certain consonants such as /p/, /b/, and /m/ have maximal intensity in the low frequencies. In other words, the high frequency elements of these sounds are low in intensity. However, consonants /s/ and /z/ have maximal intensity in the high frequencies. In general, vowels have intensity concentrated in the low and mid frequencies.

PERCEPTUAL ASPECT

Perceptual phonetics is the branch of phonetics that deals with the immediate or intuitive judgments people make when discriminating one speech sound from another. This aspect of phonetics concentrates on those properties of speech sounds that the listener considers important when distinguishing between sounds. Perception of speech sounds is based on the listener's discrimination ability.

Discrimination

Discrimination is defined here as one's ability to assess the differences between two speech sounds. English speakers readily discriminate between the two speech sounds /p/ and /b/ present in their language although they may experience difficulty discriminating between sounds foreign to them. It seems, then, that when one learns a language, one learns to discriminate between sounds of that language. It is known that, in language learning, a normal child learns to discriminate between speech sounds during the first few years of his life. There is little known, however, regarding the essential elements necessary for this discrimination process. For example, when a person distinguishes between the words "pat" and "bat," he uses certain clues to decide that these words are different. It is apparent that the difference between these two words is inherent in the phonemes /p/ and /b/ since the "–at" parts of the two words are identical. The perceptual aspect of phonetics concentrates on those elements of the phoneme that are used to keep it apart perceptually from all other phonemes.

Transcription

Phonemes or sounds of speech are heard in the framework of words and rarely by themselves. One of the functions of a phonetician is to represent these sounds accurately by making a written copy of what is heard. This process of writing down the sounds as they are heard rather than as they are spelled according to the alphabet is known as *phonetic transcription*. There are several established systems that may be utilized in transcribing heard sounds. One of the most prevalent systems of phonetic transcription is called the *International Phonetic Alphabet* (*IPA*). This text utilizes the IPA to provide the basis for phonetic transcription of American English speech.

EXERCISES

Fill in the Blanks

1. The parts of the human body that play a significant role in speech production are known as _____.
2. The study of speech sounds is known as _____.
3. Speech sounds are comprised of _____ and vowels.
4. Acceptable variations in the production of the same speech sounds are collectively referred to as a _____.
5. Speech sounds produced without the passage of the air stream through the nasal cavity are known as _____.
6. The _____ vibrate in the production of vowels.
7. The physical properties of speech sounds are studied in the _____ aspect of phonetics.

8. The three primary areas of acoustic study are _____, _____, and _____.
9. One's ability to assess the differences between two speech sounds is known as one's _____ ability.
10. One of the most prevalent systems of phonetic transcription is called the _____.

True or False

_____ 1. A speech sound is one of the simplest elements of speech.
_____ 2. Vowel production is characterized by constriction in the breath channel.
_____ 3. The /t/ sounds in the words "take," "Katie," and "pot" collectively represent the same phoneme /t/.
_____ 4. The study of the lips, teeth, and tongue are included in the physiological aspect of phonetics.
_____ 5. The process of producing voice is referred to as respiration.
_____ 6. All English vowels are produced with voice.
_____ 7. The greater the vocal fold mass, the greater the frequency of the sound waves thus produced.
_____ 8. Amplitude determines how loud a sound is perceived.

Multiple Choice

_____ 1. One who specializes in phonetics is known as a:
    a. speech therapist
    b. phonetician
    c. phonologist
_____ 2. Speech sounds characterized by lack of any closure or constriction in the breath channel are known as:
    a. consonants
    b. vowels
    c. phonemes
_____ 3. The branch of phonetics that deals with the function of the organs of speech is known as:
    a. physiological phonetics
    b. acoustic phonetics
    c. perceptual phonetics
_____ 4. The tongue tip plays a major role in the production of:
    a. front sounds
    b. back sounds
    c. central sounds

_____ 5. The study of the larynx is included in the:
      a. perceptual aspect of phonetics
      b. acoustic aspect of phonetics
      c. physiological aspect of phonetics

_____ 6. The frequency of a sound determines its:
      a. amplitude
      b. pitch
      c. loudness

_____ 7. /s/ and /z/ are primarily:
      a. high frequency sounds
      b. low frequency sounds
      c. mid frequency sounds

_____ 8. Amplitude of a sound wave is the:
      a. duration of the sound in milliseconds
      b. extent of displacement of a sounding body
      c. vibration of the sounding body

Chapter 2 INTRODUCTION TO THE INTERNATIONAL PHONETIC ALPHABET

The International Phonetic Alphabet (IPA) is the name for a set of arbitrary symbols designed to represent sounds used in all languages of the world. A single speech sound such as /p/ present in a number of languages of the world is represented by different written symbols. In order for phoneticians to have an easy access to the study of the sound systems of unfamiliar languages, they had to devise a system with uniform representation of all spoken sounds. The discrepancy between the written form (orthography) and the spoken form (speech) of most languages is the reason for devising the IPA.

DISCREPANCY BETWEEN THE SPOKEN FORM AND THE WRITTEN FORM

If writing corresponded directly to speech there would be no need for the IPA. The spoken form of a language is the medium of communication for the total masses (except for those handicapped persons who cannot use language effectively). On the other hand, the written form of a language traditionally has been utilized only by those persons who can read and write. Thus, while speech is the primary means of communication that keeps a community in the form of a unit, writing has been for centuries a luxury of the community. Since very early times, writing has been kept relatively obscure by certain elite strata so as to isolate themselves from the masses. The knowledge of reading and writing has been successfully used by these strata for the perpetuation of the socioeconomic classes.

In addition, in everyday speech there is immediate feedback from the listener regarding the acceptance or nonacceptance of a "new" or "modified" speech form. There is no such immediate feedback possible for the written form. Writing is "speech wrote down." It becomes frozen once written down. Whereas writing has a formal style subject to pre-scription, speech is subject to being influenced by contacts.

Speaking is perhaps as essential for the existence of a language community as breathing is for the existence of human life. The utilization of speech for expressing emotions, thoughts, and ideas within the units of the family, the community, and the culture, makes it vulnerable to alterations and changes. Fortunately, these chang-es follow specific rules and are not random. With time, these changes become so regular and distinctive that different dialects, and ulti-mately different languages, evolve.

GAP BETWEEN ORTHOGRAPHIC AND PHONETIC REPRESENTATION

Discrepancies between the written and the spoken forms of a language create a gap between the or-thography (written symbols) and its phonetic (sound) representa-tion. An unlimited number of examples from most languages may be used to demonstrate this gap between symbols and sounds.*

For example, the English vowel orthograph 'o' when preceded by the orthograph 'd' becomes 'do,' which is transcribed phonetically as /du/; however, when preceded by the letter 's' it becomes 'so,' transcribed phonetically as /so/. In the former instance the orthograph 'o' manifests the vowel phoneme /u/, and in the latter instance it manifests the vowel phoneme /o/. An analysis of other words in En-glish that also end with the ortho-graph 'o,' such as 'no,' 'go,' etc., suggests that there is no one rule to account for 'o' becoming /u/ after some consonant sounds and becoming /o/ after other consonant sounds.

There are also great discrepan-cies between orthographic and phonetic representations of other English vowels. The vowel /i/, for example, is represented by the orthographs 'ea,' 'ee,' 'ei,' 'ie,' 'e,' 'eo,' etc., as in 's*ea*t,' 'f*ee*t,' 'dec*ei*ve,' 'p*ie*ce,' 'd*e*velop,' and 'p*eo*ple,' respectively. Similarly, the vowel /ɪ/ may be represented by 'i,' 'e,' 'a,' etc., as in 'p*i*t,' 'd*e*-ceive,' and 'import*a*nce,' re-spectively. Also, the neutral En-glish vowel, called *schwa,* which is phonetically represented as /ə/, manifests itself orthographically as 'a,' 'e,' 'i,' etc., as in '*a*gain,' 'b*e*gin,' and 'intell*i*gibility,' re-spectively.

Students of English have been mistakenly informed that there are twenty-six letters in English, of

---

*From this point, orthographic symbols placed in ' ' will be differentiated from phonemic symbols placed in / /.

which five (a, e, i, o, u) are vowels and the remaining twenty-one are consonants (b, c, d, f, . . .). In reality, there are perhaps as many as nineteen vowels and diphthongs and twenty-four consonants, resulting in forty-three phonemes, each different from the other. For an adequate description of the sound system of English, all forty-three phonemes and their possible pronunciation differences resulting from context must be enumerated. The International Phonetic Alphabet makes such enumeration possible, thus "closing" the gap between orthography and phonetic representation.

PHONETIC TRANSCRIPTION

Phonetic transcription is a phoneme-by-phoneme interpretation of speech utilizing an alphabet system (such as the IPA) so as to represent all the sounds of a language without any overlap. The most frequently used alphabet in phonetic transcription is the IPA.

In this text, we utilize the IPA to provide the basis for phonetic transcription of American English speech. Before demonstrating the use of the IPA, it should be stated that this alphabet has some limitations. One fundamental problem is its inability to manifest small qualitative differences in phoneme production. For example, the vowel /i/, as in 'b*ee*t,' can be pronounced long or short; it can be produced with the tongue being

placed higher than normal, more fronted than normal, or more back than normal. There is, however, a provision for some of these qualitative differences to be represented by what are known as diacritic indicators or markers. A *diacritic marker* is a symbol that is used in conjunction with a phoneme to indicate that the phoneme has been produced with some additional articulatory effort. A detailed listing of diacritic markers is presented in Chapter 12.

In order to familiarize students with the IPA as it applies to American English, a number of key words containing each of the symbols are presented below.

Single Consonants

The traditional definition of a consonant implies that a consonant is a sound that appears with the help of a vowel. Although it is true that syllable formation requires a vowel, all consonants can be produced without the aid of a vowel. Consonants can be best defined in terms of their production. The consonant sounds are produced by creating constriction in the human breath channel.

When a consonant phoneme occurs before a vowel at the beginning of a word, it is referred to as a *prevocalic consonant* or as a consonant in the initial position of a word. If a consonant phoneme occurs between two vowels at the middle of a word, it is referred to as an *intervocalic consonant* or as a consonant in the medial position of a word. If a consonant phoneme occurs after a vowel at the end of a word, it is referred to as a *postvocalic consonant* or as a consonant in the final position of a word.

*1.   /p/ *as in* /pɪl/, /hɪpɪ/, /kip/

The speech sound phonemically represented as /p/ occurs in English as in the key words 'pill' /pɪl/, 'hippie' /hɪpɪ/, and 'keep' /kip/. This phoneme occurs in the prevocalic, intervocalic, and postvocalic positions of a word.

2.   /t/ *as in* /tɑm/, /bɑtəm/, /bʌt/

The speech sound phonemically represented as /t/ occurs in English as in 'Tom' /tɑm/, 'bottom' /bɑtəm/, and 'but' /bʌt/. The phoneme /t/ appears in all three positions of a word.

3.   /k/ *as in* /kɪŋ/, /beɪkɚ/, /bʊk/

The speech sound phonemically represented as /k/ occurs in English as in 'king' /kɪŋ/, 'baker' /beɪkɚ/, and 'book' /bʊk/. The phoneme /k/ appears in all three positions of a word. This phoneme also may be orthographically represented by 'c'; e.g., the word 'cat' is transcribed as /kæt/.

4.   /b/ *as in* /beɪbɪ/, /kʌb/

The speech sound phonemically represented as /b/ occurs in English as in 'baby' /beɪbɪ/ and 'cub' /kʌb/. The phoneme /b/ appears in all three positions of a word.

5.   /d/ *as in* /deɪvɪd/, /mɛdɪkəl/

The speech sound phonemically represented as /d/ occurs in English as in 'David' /deɪvɪd/ and in 'medical' /mɛdɪkəl/. The phoneme /d/ appears in all three positions of a word.

6.   /g/ *as in* /goʊ/, /bʌgɪ/, /bæg/

The speech sound phonemically represented as /g/ occurs in English as in 'go' /goʊ/, 'buggy' /bʌgɪ/, and 'bag' /bæg/. The phoneme 'g' appears in all three positions of a word.

Caution must be exercised regarding the orthograph 'g.' In some instances it is not phonetically represented by /g/. For example, the word 'gentle,' transcribed phonemically as /dʒɛntl/, does not include the phoneme /g/ because it does not contain the sound /g/. Also see the consonant phonemes described in numbers 14 and 16.

7.   /f/ *as in* /faɪv/, /ɛfɚt/, /hæf/

The speech sound phonemically represented as /f/ occurs in English as in 'five' /faɪv/, 'effort' /ɛfɚt/, and 'half' /hæf/.

---

*It is suggested that readers may disregard the vowels in these examples until the vowels have been formally introduced in the latter part of this chapter.

The phoneme /f/ appears in all three positions of a word.

The orthographic representation of this phoneme varies. The orthograph 'ph' is represented by the phoneme /f/ as in the words 'phoneme' /fonɪm/, 'elephant' /ɛləfənt/, and 'graph' /græf/.

8. /v/ *as in* /væst/, /hɛvɪ/, /stouv/

The speech sound phonemically represented as /v/ occurs in English as in 'vast' /væst/, 'heavy' /hɛvɪ/, and 'stove' /stouv/. The phoneme /v/ appears in all three positions of a word.

9. /θ/ *as in* /θɪŋk/, /nʌθɪŋ/, /bæθ/

The speech sound phonemically represented as /θ/ occurs in English as in 'think' /θɪŋk/, 'nothing' /nʌθɪŋ/, and 'bath' /bæθ/. The phoneme /θ/ appears in all three positions of a word.

Many students are not familiar with this symbol because it does not appear in English orthography. One way to learn the relationship of a given sound to its IPA symbol is by avoiding any reference to orthography. It has been found to be much easier to learn the IPA symbol by learning words containing that symbol; e.g., the IPA symbol /θ/ can be learned with the help of words such as 'think' /θɪŋk/, 'thin' /θɪn/, and 'thank' /θæŋk/, all of which contain the symbol /θ/.

10. /ð/ *as in* /ðæt/, /brʌðɚ/, /beɪð/

The speech sound phonemically represented as /ð/ occurs in English as in 'that' /ðæt/, 'brother' /brʌðɚ/, and 'bathe' /beɪð/. The phoneme /ð/ appears in all three positions of a word. In the English language this phoneme is not usually used at the postvocalic word position.

It is difficult to learn this sound because it does not have direct reference in the orthographic system, as do sounds /p/, /t/, and /k/. It is helpful for students to practice /ð/ in relation to words like 'that' /ðæt/, 'this' /ðɪs/, 'them' /ðɛm/, and 'those' /ðoz/. The orthographic representation of this phoneme is 'th,' which it shares with /θ/ as in 'thank.'

11. /s/ *as in* /sou/, /bʌsɪŋ/, /bʌs/

The speech sound phonemically represented as /s/ occurs in English as in 'so' /sou/, 'bussing' /bʌsɪŋ/, and 'bus' /bʌs/. The phoneme /s/ appears in all three positions of a word.

/s/ is a common sound in the English language, and perhaps this is why English is called a "sibilant language." One reason for its frequent occurrence is its usage in forming plurals, e.g., 'cats' /kæts/, 'rats' /ræts/, etc. The orthographic/phonetic relationship of /s/ is complex in that, in some instances, the orthograph 's' is not pronounced as /s/, e.g., 'ro*s*es' /rozɪz/, 'play*s*' /pleɪz/, etc. However, in other instances /s/ is pronounced when the orthograph 's' is not written, e.g., 'pla*c*e' /pleɪs/, 'de*c*eive' /disiv/, etc.

12. **/z/ as in** /zibrə/, /bʌzɪŋ/, /bʌz/

The speech sound phonemically represented as /z/ occurs in English as in 'zebra' /zibrə/, 'bu*zz*ing' /bʌzɪŋ/, and 'bu*zz*' /bʌz/. The phoneme /z/ appears in the prevocalic, intervocalic, and postvocalic positions of a word.

In addition to being represented orthographically by 'z,' the phoneme /z/ is also represented by the orthograph 's' as in 'ro*s*e' /rouz/ and 'bu*s*y' /bɪzɪ/.

13. **/ʃ/ as in** /ʃuz/, /mʌʃrum/, /buʃ/

The speech sound phonemically represented as /ʃ/ occurs in English as in '*sh*oes' /ʃuz/, 'mu*sh*room' /mʌʃrum/, and 'bu*sh*' /buʃ/. The phoneme /ʃ/ appears in all three positions of a word.

/ʃ/ is a symbol that most students are not familiar with. The phoneme /ʃ/ is represented orthographically in specific word positions by 'sh,' 's,' 'sch,' 'tio,' 'tia,' 'cio,' 'ch,' etc., as in words like '*sh*oes' /ʃuz/, '*s*ure' /ʃʊɚ/, '*sch*wa' /ʃwɑ/, 'conven*tio*n' /kənvɛnʃən/, 'iner*tia*' /ɪnɚʃə/, 'mali*cio*us' /məlɪʃəs/,

and '*ch*ute' /ʃut/, respectively.

14. **/ʒ/ as in** /æʒɚ/, /beɪʒ/

The speech sound phonemically represented as /ʒ/ occurs in English as in 'a*z*ure' /æʒɚ/, 'mea*s*ure' /mɛʒɚ/, 'plea*s*ure' /plɛʒɚ/, and 'bei*g*e' /beɪʒ/. The phoneme /ʒ/ appears only in the intervocalic and postvocalic positions of a word. It does not appear in the prevocalic word position.

Although /ʒ/ is a very infrequently used phoneme, students must learn to differentiate between the phoneme /z/ as in 'zipper' /zɪpɚ/ and the phoneme /ʒ/ as in 'measure' /mɛʒɚ/. This phoneme is represented orthographically by 'z,' 's,' and sometimes 'g,' as shown in the examples given above.

15. **/tʃ/ as in** /tʃɝtʃ/, /mʌntʃɪŋ/, /bɛntʃ/

The speech sound phonemically represented as /tʃ/ occurs in English as in '*ch*urch' /tʃɝtʃ/, 'mun*ch*ing' /mʌntʃɪŋ/, and 'ben*ch*' /bɛntʃ/. The phoneme /tʃ/ appears in all three positions of a word. It mainly represents the 'ch' letters of English.

16. **/dʒ/ as in** /dʒʌdʒ/, /dʒʌdʒɪŋ/, /fʌdʒ/

The speech sound phonemically represented as /dʒ/ occurs in English as in '*j*ud*g*e' /dʒʌdʒ/, '*j*ud*g*ing' /dʒʌdʒɪŋ/, and 'fudge' /fʌdʒ/. The phoneme /dʒ/ appears in all three positions of a word.

Orthographically the phoneme /dʒ/ is represented, in most cases, by the letters 'dg,' 'j,' and 'g,' as in 'budge' /bʌdʒ/, 'judge' /dʒʌdʒ/, and 'marriage' /mærɪdʒ/, respectively.

17. /m/ *as in* /mæt/, /hæməʳ/, /kʌm/

The speech sound phonemically represented as /m/ occurs in English as in 'mat' /mæt/, 'hammer' /hæməʳ/, and 'come' /kʌm/. The phoneme /m/ appears in all three positions of a word.

18. /n/ *as in* /nou/, /bʌnɪ/, /an/

The speech sound phonemically represented as /n/ occurs in English as in 'no' /nou/, 'bunny' /bʌnɪ/, and 'on' /an/. This phoneme appears in all three positions of a word. The phoneme /n/ is one of the most frequently used sounds in the English language.

19. /ŋ/ *as in* /dʒʌŋgl̩/, /sɪŋ/

The speech sound phonemically represented as /ŋ/ occurs in English as in 'jungle' /dʒʌŋgl̩/ and 'sing' /sɪŋ/. The phoneme /ŋ/ appears only in the intervocalic and postvocalic positions of a word. It does not appear at the prevocalic word position.

In general, when 'n' is followed by 'k' or 'g' the re-

sultant phoneme is /ŋ/, such as in the words 'link' /lɪŋk/, 'hang' /hæŋ/, etc.

20. /r/ *as in* /rɪŋ/, /kærɪ/, /kar/

The speech sound phonemically represented as /r/ occurs in English as in 'ring' /rɪŋ/, 'carry' /kærɪ/, and 'car'' /kar/. The phoneme /r/ appears in all three positions of a word.

In English, the phoneme /r/ is confused mainly with the retroflex vowels /ɚ/ and /ɝ/, which are mostly produced when the phoneme /r/ is preceded by a vowel in words such as 'other' /ʌðɚ/, 'earth' /ɝθ/, and 'bird' /bɝd/. The phoneme /r/ is clearly heard when 'r' forms a consonant cluster as in the words 'trees' /triz/ and 'free' /fri/, where it is truly a consonant.

21. /l/ *as in* /lɪlɪ/, /kɪl/

The speech sound phonemically represented as /l/ occurs in English as in 'lily' /lɪlɪ/ and 'kill' /kɪl/. It appears in all three positions of a word.

22. /w/ *as in* /waʃ/, /bɪwɪʃt/

The speech sound phonemically represented as /w/ occurs in English as in 'wash' /waʃ/ and 'bewitched' /bɪwɪtʃt/. The phoneme /w/ appears only in the prevocalic and intervocalic positions of a word. It does not appear at the postvocalic position. In the postvocalic position /w/ is pronounced as the vowel /ʊ/ as in the word 'how' /haʊ/.

23. /j/ *as in* /jɔr/, / joujou/

The speech sound phonemically represented as /j/ occurs in English as in 'your' /jɔr/ and 'yo-yo' /joujou/. The phoneme /j/ appears in the prevocalic position of a word. At the intervocalic position its occurrence in English is rare, e.g., 'joyous' /dʒɔıjəs/, 'beauty' /bjutı/, 'onion' /ʌnjən/. At the postvocalic position /j/ is pronounced as a vowel as in words like 'toy' /tɔɪ/ and 'boy' /bɔɪ/. The orthographic counterparts of this phoneme are the letters 'y' and 'u' as in the words 'yes' /jɛs/ and 'use' /juz/, respectively.

24. /h/ *as in* /haʊ/, /ınhæns/

The speech sound phonemically represented as /h/ occurs in English as in 'how' /haʊ/ and 'enhance' /ınhæns/. The phoneme /h/ appears only in the prevocalic and intervocalic positions of a word. It does not appear in the postvocalic word position.

Consonant Clusters

A consonant cluster is a string of two or more consonants. The words 'tree' /tri/ and 'street' /strit/ have double and triple consonant clusters, respectively, in the prevocalic position. The words 'country' /kʌntri/ and 'intransitive' /ın-trænsətıv/ have double consonant clusters in the intervocalic position, and the words 'fifth' /fıfθ/, 'length' /lɛŋθ/, 'fast' /fæst/, and 'wasp' /wɑsp/ have double consonant clusters in the postvocalic position. Most English consonant clusters are made of two or three consonants.

A consonant cluster is simply a way of combining the consonant phonemes in a language. Support for this contention is found in the misarticulation of these consonant clusters. When children misarticulate the double and triple consonant clusters, they tend to reduce them to a single consonant; e.g., the word 'school' /skul/ becomes /kul/, 'truck' /trʌk/ becomes /tʌk/, and 'friend' /frɛnd/ becomes /fɛn/.

The sequencing of the consonants in a cluster is governed by the phonetic rules of a language. The initial cluster /str/, for example, must occur in that fixed sequence. Alteration of its phoneme sequencing is not accommodated in the English language. In addition, only certain consonants can be used to formulate clusters. Although initial consonant clusters /sp/, /st/, /sk/, and /sf/ are permitted in English, clusters such as /sb/, /sd/, /sg/, and /sv/ are not permitted in the English language.

Pure Vowels

When a vowel phoneme occurs before a consonant at the beginning of a word, it is referred to as a *preconsonantal vowel* or as a vowel in the initial position of a word. If a vowel phoneme occurs between two consonants at the middle of a word, it is referred to as an *interconsonantal vowel* or as a vowel in the medial position of a word. When a vowel phoneme occurs after a consonant at the end of a word, it is referred to as a *postconsonantal vowel* or as a vowel in the final position of a word.

Vowels differ from consonants primarily because they are syllabic. Any time a vowel appears in a language, it forms a syllable. The consonants are primarily nonsyllabic. They differ from vowels on all major counts: in the way they are produced, in their physical properties, and in the way they are heard.

1. /i/ *as in* /it/, /bit/, /bi/

The speech sound phonemically represented as /i/ occurs in English as in '*ea*t' /it/, 'b*ee*t' /bit/, and 'b*ee*' /bi/. The phoneme /i/ appears in all three positions of a word.

2. /ɪ/ *as in* /ɪt/, /bɪt/, /hɪpɪ/

The speech sound phonemically represented as /ɪ/ occurs in English as in '*i*t' /ɪt/, 'b*i*t' /bɪt/, and 'h*i*ppie' /hɪpɪ/.* In one-syllable words the phoneme /ɪ/ appears only at the preconsonantal and interconsonantal positions.

3. /e/ *as in* /edʒ/, /vekeɪt/, /se/

The speech sound phonemically represented as /e/ occurs in English as in '*a*ge' /edʒ/, 'v*a*cate' /vekeɪt/, and 's*a*y' /se/. This phoneme occurs in all three positions of a word.

4. /ɛ/ *as in* /ɛnd/, /bɛt/

The speech sound phonemically represented as /ɛ/ occurs in English as in '*e*nd' /ɛnd/ and 'b*e*t' /bɛt/. The phoneme /ɛ/ appears only in the preconsonantal and interconsonantal positions of a word. In English, it does not appear at the postconsonantal position.

5. /æ/ *as in* /æd/, /bæt/

The speech sound phonemically represented as /æ/ occurs in English as in '*a*dd' /æd/ and 'b*a*t' /bæt/. The phoneme /æ/ appears only in the preconsonantal and interconsonantal positions. It does not occur at the postconsonantal position.

6. /ɑ/ *as in* /ɑtɚ/, /hɑt/, /spɑ/

The speech sound phonemically represented as /ɑ/ occurs in English as in '*o*tter' /ɑtɚ/, 'h*o*t' /hɑt/, and 'sp*a*' /spɑ/.**

---

*Some students disagree with the phonemic representation of the final vowel in words such as 'hippie' /hɪpɪ/, 'kitty' /kɪtɪ/, and 'baby' /beɪbɪ/. They prefer the representations /hɪpi/, /kɪti/, /beɪbi/, etc. However, it is the consensus of phoneticians that /ɪ/ is the correct representation of the vowel. Diacritic markers could be used to represent such variations that cannot be accounted for by the symbols (see Chapter 12).

**In this text, /a/, which is more fronted than /ɑ/, has been arbitrarily selected to appear in diphthongs (aɪ, aʊ). The phoneme /ɑ/, described in number 6, has been arbitrarily selected to appear in isolation.

The phoneme /ɑ/ appears in all three positions of a word.

7. */ɔ/ as in* /ɔful/, /bɔt/, /pɔ/

The speech sound phonemically represented as /ɔ/ occurs in English as in 'awful' /ɔful/, 'bought' /bɔt/, and 'paw' /pɔ/. The phoneme /ɔ/ appears in all three positions of a word. In many dialects, the vowels /ɑ/ and /ɔ/ are used interchangeably; e.g., the word 'lot' may be pronounced as /lɔt/ or /lɑt/.

8. */o/ as in* /opən/, /roteɪt/, /to/

The speech sound phonemically represented as /o/ occurs in English as in 'open' /opən/, 'rotate' /roteɪt/, and 'toe' /to/. The phoneme /o/ appears in all three positions of a word.

9. */ʊ/ as in* /pʊt/

The speech sound phonemically represented as /ʊ/ occurs in English as in 'put' /pʊt/. This phoneme appears mainly in the interconsonantal position of a word.

10. */u/ as in* /uz/, /but/, /ʃu/

The speech sound phonemically represented as /u/ occurs in English as in 'ooze' /uz/, 'boot' /but/, and 'shoe' /ʃu/. The phoneme /u/ appears in all three positions of a word.

11. */ə/ as in* /əbaʊt/, / pəteɪtə/

The speech sound phonemically represented as /ə/ occurs in English as in 'about' /əbaʊt/ and 'potato' /pəteɪtə/. The phoneme /ə/ appears in all three positions of a word.

12. */ɚ/ as in* /ɚbeɪn/, /pɚport/, /sɪstɚ/

The speech sound phonemically represented as /ɚ/ occurs in English as in 'urbane' /ɚbeɪn/, 'purport' /pɚport/, and 'sister' /sɪstɚ/. The phoneme /ɚ/ appears in all three positions of a word.

13. */ɝ/ as in* /ɝk/, /bɝd/, /bɝ/

The speech sound phonemically represented as /ɝ/ occurs in English as in 'irk' /ɝk/, 'bird' /bɝd/, and 'burr' /bɝ/. The phoneme /ɝ/ appears in all three positions of a word.

14. */ʌ/ as in* /ʌp/, /bʌt/

The speech sound phonemically represented as /ʌ/ occurs in English as in 'up' /ʌp/ and 'but' /bʌt/. The phoneme /ʌ/ appears only in the pre-consonantal and interconsonantal positions of a word. It does not appear in the postconsonantal position.

Diphthongs

Like pure vowels, diphthongs occur in three positions of a word: preconsonantal, interconsonantal, and postconsonantal.

15. */eɪ/ as in* /eɪt/, /beɪt/, /beɪ/

The speech sound phonemically represented as /eɪ/ occurs in English as in 'ate' /eɪt/, 'bait' /beɪt/, and 'bay' /beɪ/.

The diphthong /eɪ/ appears in all three positions of a word.

16. /aɪ/ *as in* /aɪs/, /baɪt/, /baɪ/ аṳ

The speech sound phonemically represented as /aɪ/ occurs in English as in 'ice' /aɪs/, 'b*i*te' /baɪt/, and 'b*ye*' /baɪ/. The diphthong /aɪ/ appears in all three positions of a word.

17. /aʊ/ *as in* /aʊns/, /baʊt/, /baʊ/ аṳ

The speech sound phonemically represented as /aʊ/ occurs in English as in 'o*u*nce' /aʊns/, 'b*ou*t' /baʊt/, and 'b*ow*' /baʊ/. The diphthong /aʊ/ appears in all three positions of a word.

18. /ɔɪ/ *as in* /ɔɪstɚ/, /tʃɔɪs/, /bɔɪ/ Ɔ̇ʝ

The speech sound phonemically represented as /ɔɪ/ occurs in English as in 'o*y*ster' /ɔɪstɚ/, 'ch*oi*ce' /tʃɔɪs/, and 'b*oy*' /bɔɪ/. The diphthong /ɔɪ/ appears in all three positions of a word.

19. /oʊ/ *as in* /oʊt/, /boʊt/, /boʊ/ аṳ

The speech sound phonemically represented as /oʊ/ occurs in English as in 'o*at*' /oʊt/, 'b*oa*t' /boʊt/, and 'bow' /boʊ/. The diphthong /oʊ/ appears in all three positions of a word.

DIFFERENCE BETWEEN PHONETIC AND PHONEMIC TRANSCRIPTION

Now that we have examined the individual phonemes as they appear in the different positions of a word, it is important to understand the difference between phonetic and phonemic transcription.

A phoneme may be defined as a distinctive unit of speech sound that maintains its inherent identity in spite of differences resulting from word context. Therefore, each phoneme of a language must have a distinct symbol to represent it. This symbol is conventionally enclosed between a pair of slanted lines, / /, as in the English phoneme /p/.

However, depending on its position in a word, the phoneme /p/ is pronounced in slightly different ways. It is aspirated (produced with a significant outburst of air) at the beginning of a word and is denoted by [pʰ] as in the first sound in the word 'pat.' It is unaspirated at the middle of a word and is denoted by [p] as in the middle sound in the word 'apple,' and is unreleased at the end of a word and is denoted by [p⁻] as in the final sound in the word 'cup.' In the event a native speaker of English releases the /p/ at the word-final position, it is considered a deliberate phonetic event and may be represented by [p⁺]. These variations in the pronunciation of the phoneme /p/ are known as *phonetic variations*. Phonetic variations are denoted by enclosing the symbol in a pair of brackets, [ ].

Whereas phonemic transcription pools all acceptable variations of a sound and represents them by one phoneme, phonetic transcription provides representation for each of the variations. Each phonetic variation caused by the phoneme's position in a word is known as an *allophone*.

Speech sounds can be transcribed in two ways: by narrow (phonetic) transcription and by broad (phonemic) transcription. *Narrow transcription* distinguishes all allophonic variations of a phoneme. *Broad transcription,* on the other hand, pools the allophonic variations of the phoneme. In addition to accounting for allophonic variations, narrow phonetic analysis also assists in transcribing dialectal differences and distortions. Students must learn to tune their ears so that they can listen to and isolate dialectal differences and distortions from allophonic variations.

EXERCISES

Fill in the Blanks

1. IPA stands for _____

   _____.

2. The written form of a language is also known as _____, and the spoken form of a language is known as _____.

3. The _____ form of a language is the medium of communication for the total masses.

4. Of the two 'a' orthographs in the word 'national,' the first is phonetically represented as _____ and the second as _____.

5. Of the two 'o' orthographs in the word 'photography,' the first is phonetically represented as _____ and the second as _____.

6. The phoneme /u/ is orthographically represented by 'oo' as in the word _____, 'wo' as in the word _____, 'ue' as in the word _____, and 'eo' as in the word _____. and 'oe' as in the word _____.

7. The phoneme /ɔ/ is orthographically represented by 'o' as in the word _____, 'aw' as in the word _____, 'a' as in the word _____, and 'eo' as in the word _____.

8. There are as many as _____ vowels and diphthongs, and as many as _____ consonants in the English language.

9. The alphabet system devised to account for all of the sounds in all languages is known as _____.

10. In phonetics, when a speech sound is enclosed in brackets it indicates that the analysis is _____, whereas if it is enclosed between a pair of slanted lines the analysis is _____.

11. The word 'pan' is phonetically transcribed as _____.

12. The same word 'pan' is phonemically transcribed as _____.

13. The two types of phonetic transcriptions are _____ and _____.

14. In the word 'paper' the phoneme /p/ does not appear in the _____ position.

15. In the word 'vacate' the phoneme /t/ appears in the _____ position and the phoneme /k/ appears in the _____ position.

16. The word 'bed' does not have a consonant phoneme in the _____ position.

17. The word 'dog,' transcribed phonemically as _____, has the phoneme /d/ in the _____ position and the phoneme /g/ in the _____ position.

18. In the word 'favor' the consonant phoneme in the intervocalic position is _____ and in the prevocalic position is _____.

19. In the word 'this,' phonemically transcribed as _____, the phoneme _____ appears in the prevocalic position.

20. In the word 'math,' phonemically transcribed as _____, the phoneme appearing in the postvocalic position is _____.

21. The name 'Susie,' phonemically transcribed as _____, is comprised of two consonant phonemes, _____ and _____.

22. In the word 'scissors,' transcribed phonemically as _____, the phoneme /z/ appears in the _____ and _____ positions.

23. When two or more consonants appear adjacent to each other in a syllable they are said to form a _____.

24. Of the following symbols—/p, ð, dʒ, s, r, ʃ, l, θ, v, t, b, tʃ, ʒ, m, ŋ, d, k/—the ones that do not exist in the orthographic system are: _____.

True or False

____ 1. Phonetic variations emerge when languages undergo changes that are essentially random.

____ 2. The written form of a language undergoes fewer changes than does the spoken form.

____ 3. Phonetic transcription is presented in brackets.

____ 4. The phoneme /t/ at the word-medial position is unaspirated.

____ 5. The phoneme consists of a group of allophones.

___ 6. Broad phonetic transcription distinguishes the allophonic variations of a phoneme.

___ 7. The word 'bobbie' is transcribed as /bɑbbi/.

___ 8. The word 'fudge' does not contain the /g/ phoneme.

___ 9. The phonemes /θ/ and /ð/ have the same orthographic representation.

___ 10. Most English consonant clusters are made of one or two consonants.

___ 11. The sequencing of the phonemes in a consonant cluster is governed by the phonetic rules of a language.

Multiple Choice

___ 1. Phonetic transcription:
   a. pools allophonic variations
   b. distinguishes allophonic variations
   c. disregards allophonic variations
   d. emphasizes distortions only

___ 2. Phonemic transcription:
   a. deals with sound substitutions
   b. distinguishes between substitutions and distortions
   c. pools all acceptable variations of a sound
   d. pools all unacceptable variations of a sound

___ 3. The phoneme /p/ at the word-initial position in American English is:
   a. silent
   b. unaspirated
   c. deliberate
   d. aspirated

___ 4. Phonetic variations caused by the phoneme's position in a word are called:
   a. allophones
   b. sounds
   c. symbols
   d. phonemes

___ 5. Students of phonetics must tune their ears so as to distinguish:
   a. consonants from vowels
   b. phonemes from orthographs
   c. allophonic variations from dialectal differences and distortions
   d. IPA from standard American English

___ 6. The phonemic transcription /bouθ/ represents the word:
   a. boat

        b. bout
        c. both
        d. booth

____ 7. The phonemic transcription /ʃouz/ represents the word:
        a. shoes
        b. shows
        c. sows
        d. sauce

____ 8. Initial consonant clusters permitted in English are:
        a. sd and kn
        b. st and sk
        c. bv and th

Phonemic Transcription

Transcribe phonemically the following words.

1. station _____
2. zoo _____
3. bizarre _____
4. taxi _____
5. says _____
6. saucers _____
7. treasure _____
8. cushion _____
9. creature _____
10. cheese _____
11. joy _____
12. badge _____
13. money _____

14. naming _____
15. ink _____
16. road _____
17. Mary _____
18. lollipop _____
19. wagon _____
20. cowboy _____
21. you _____
22. young _____
23. high _____
24. house _____
25. Ohio _____
26. three _____

Orthographic Counterparts

Write orthographic representations of the following phonemically transcribed words.

1. /wɪʃ/ _____
2. /meɪk/ _____
3. /bɪliv/ _____
4. /tʌf/ _____
5. /nid/ _____
6. /ðeɪ/ _____
7. /kʌm/ _____

8. /ɔlsou/ _____
9. /ædɪd/ _____
10. /sors/ _____
11. /feɪs/ _____
12. /hɔl/ _____
13. /wɪmən/ _____
14. /fonɛtɪks/ _____

15. /pɑlɪtɪʃən/ _____
16. /dɪgri/ _____
17. /jʌŋ/ _____
18. /dʒɛntl̩/ _____
19. /rɪkwɛst/ _____
20. /teɪbəlz/ _____
21. /wɪntɚ/ _____
22. /pʊl/ _____
23. /kaʊntɪ/ _____
24. /tivi/ _____

25. /iz/ _____
26. /lʌntʃ/ _____
27. /bʌdʒət/ _____
28. /wɛnzdeɪ/ _____
29. /ɛdɪtɚ/ _____
30. /lʌv/ _____
31. /tu/ _____
32. /eɪt/ _____
33. /mʌndeɪ/ _____

Chapter 3 ARTICULATORY ASPECTS OF PHONETICS: CONSONANTS

The focal point of this text is to understand man's ability to produce and perceive speech sounds. The study of the different speech sounds and their classification in terms of the articulatory, acoustic, and perceptual properties will help us understand this ability in somewhat greater detail. Figure 1 shows the speech process classified in terms of its source or point of origination, its property or nature, and its coding or perception by a human listener. In this chapter and the next we will see how speech sounds can be described and grouped together based on their physiological properties.

SOURCES OF SOUND PRODUCTION

The vocal folds form the source for the production of vowel speech sounds. The vocal tract, however, forms the source for consonant production. The vocal tract is a series of tube-like cavities beginning at the level of the vocal folds and ending at the lips or, alternately, in the nasal cavity. In addition to its function as the source for consonant production, the vocal tract serves as a resonator for both vowels and consonants. The nasal cavity, also referred to as the nasal tract, is an added resonator in the production of some speech sounds, such as the English consonants /m, n, ŋ/.

Vowels are produced only when the vocal folds vibrate, but some consonants are produced without the vocal folds vibrating. Consonants that are produced without vocal fold vibration are referred to as *voiceless consonants*. Consonants produced with some

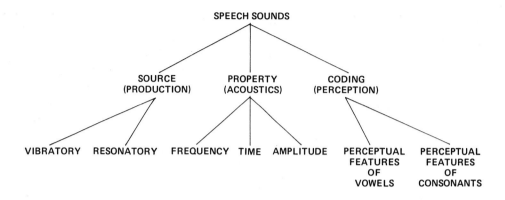

Figure 1. The division of speech sounds into the source of speech production, the acoustic properties of speech sounds, and the perceptual properties of speech sounds.

amount of such vibration are called *voiced consonants*. Thus, using vocal fold vibration as the criterion, we can categorize all English phonemes into two groups: voiced and voiceless.

In some people, however, the source for vowel production is not at the vocal folds. These persons, medically referred to as laryngectomees, have had their vocal folds removed as a result of cancer of the larynx or serious trauma to the laryngeal area. With adequate speech therapy, they can learn to use the esophageal portion of the vocal tract as the source of speech sound production.

Respiratory Apparatus

Figure 2 shows the general locations of the speech production mechanisms. The human respiratory apparatus acts as the principal agent for providing energy to drive the vocal folds into motion. During the process of inhalation, the thoracic (chest) cavity expands, thereby filling the lungs with air. The air accumulated in the lungs when released on exhalation acts as the driving force necessary for vibrating the vocal folds situated in the larynx. During exhalation, the thoracic cavity resumes its position of rest, thereby forcing the accumulated air past the trachea, larynx, pharynx, and oral and nasal cavities to the outside, as shown in the figure.

Larynx

The larynx is situated in the throat, above the trachea and below the root of the tongue. The part of the larynx situated toward the front is referred to as the anterior part and that situated toward the back of the larynx is referred to as the posterior part. The sides of the larynx are referred to as the lateral parts, and the midline of the larynx extending from the anterior to the posterior part is referred to as the medial part.

The tubular framework of the larynx is composed of cartilages, ligaments, muscles, and mem-

branes. The vocalis muscles of the larynx, together with the vocal ligaments, form the two *vocal folds*, which extend horizontally across the width of the larynx, attaching their anterior and lateral edges along the inner wall of the

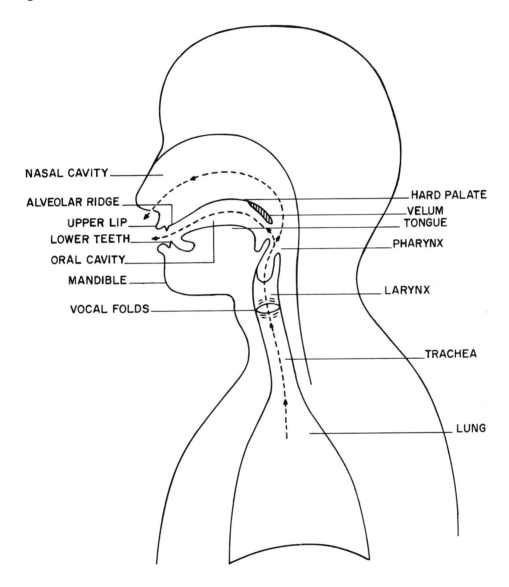

Figure 2.   Diagram showing the various speech-producing organs.

larynx. Their medial edges are unattached and are capable of oscillating (vibrating) toward and away from the midline, guided primarily by the movement of the cartilages to which they are attached posteriorly. The vibration of the vocal folds is responsible for the production of voice. Voiced speech sounds such as vowels /i, ɑ, u, .../ and voiced consonants /b, d, g, .../ are produced with the vibration of the vocal folds. On the other hand, voiceless speech sounds such as /p, t, k, .../ are produced without the participation of the vocal fold vibration.

Pharynx

The pharynx is a tubular, funnel-shaped structure located posterior to the root of the tongue and extending from the base of the skull above to the esophagus or the beginning of the digestive system below. The pharynx may be divided into three parts: the nasopharynx, the oropharynx, and the laryngopharynx. The nasopharynx is a section of the pharynx that lies directly posterior to the nasal cavity and extends from the base of the skull above to the level of the velum below. The oropharynx is the part directly posterior to the oral cavity and extends from the level of the velum above to the level of the root of the tongue below. It is this part of the pharynx that can be viewed easily when the mouth is wide open and the tongue is pulled forth. The laryngopharynx, also known as the hypopharynx, is the lower-most part of the pharynx and lies directly behind the laryngeal structure, extending from the level of the root of the tongue above to the beginning of the esophagus below.

The pharynx has two valves inside it, the velopharyngeal valve and the epiglottis valve. The velopharyngeal valve, situated at the junction of the nasopharynx and the oropharynx, is of great importance in the production of vowels such as /i, ɑ, o, u/ and non-nasal consonants such as /p, t, k, b, d, g/. This valve, when in action, separates the nasopharynx from the oropharynx, thus obstructing the laryngeal air stream from going through the nasopharynx into the nasal cavity, and instead allowing it to enter the oral cavity. The epiglottis valve is situated just below the root of the tongue at the junction of the oropharynx and laryngopharynx. Its primary known function is to act as a cover for the inlet of the larynx during the passage of food from the oral cavity into the laryngopharynx.

Oral Cavity

The oropharynx opens anteriorly into the oral cavity. The oral cavity is bounded anteriorly by the lips and laterally by the cheeks. The tongue rests on the floor of the oral cavity. The hard palate and the velum form the roof of the oral cavity.

Lips

The upper and lower lips are made of muscles that have a great degree of mobility, thereby facilitating the formation of various lip shapes for the production of vowels such as /ɑ, o, æ/ and consonants such as /p, b, m, f, v/.

Teeth

The upper and lower teeth lie posterior to the lips and perform a distinct speech function in the production of consonants such as /f, v, θ, ð/.

Alveolar Ridge

The alveolar ridge houses the upper teeth. It performs the distinct function of acting as the point of contact that the tongue tip approximates in the production of consonant sounds /t, d, n/.

Palate

The anterior two-thirds of the roof of the mouth is arched and comprises the bony hard palate, whereas the posterior one-third is the soft and muscular soft palate or velum. The hard palate serves as the point of contact, or the point of approximation, for the front of the tongue in the production of speech sounds such as /ʃ, ʒ, j/. The velum serves as the point of contact for the back of the tongue in the production of speech sounds such as /k, g, ŋ/.

Velopharyngeal Valve

The velum, aided somewhat by the posterior pharyngeal wall musculature, forms a valve known as the velopharyngeal valve, which closes and opens the port between the nasopharynx and the oropharynx. When the valve is open, the speech sounds produced have a nasal resonance caused by the passage of a portion of the laryngeal air stream through the nasal cavity, as in the production of English consonants /m, n, ŋ/. However, the valve is usually closed during the production of speech sounds that do not necessitate nasal resonance, as in the production of English vowels and non-nasal consonants.

Tongue

The tongue is an exclusively muscular organ that rests on the floor of the oral cavity. It is an extremely mobile organ capable of making innumerable changes in positioning and muscle tension guided by the action of the muscles that attach it to the lower jaw, the base of the skull, and the hyoid bone (which lies between the mandible and the larynx).

Mandible

The lower jaw, or the mandible, helps to move the lower teeth close to or away from the upper teeth. Its movement helps to reduce or enlarge the size of the oral cavity. The maximal downward movement of the mandible is seen during the production of the English vowel /æ/.

Cheeks

The cheeks form the lateral walls of the oral cavity. They are muscular, merging with the lip muscles around the oral orifice. The cheek muscles assist in speech production by helping to build intraoral air pressure, which is necessary for the enunciation of certain consonant sounds like /p, b/.

Nasal Cavity

The nasal cavity and the nasal sinuses lie anterior to the nasopharynx. They provide a unique resonatory effect for the speech sounds that are allowed to pass through both the oral and nasal cavities. When the nasal mucous membrane swells, as happens when one has a common cold, the effect of this resonator on speech production becomes obvious.

PLACE OF ARTICULATION

All consonants can be described in terms of the parts of the oral cavity involved in their production. With the use of these physiological descriptors, they can be described according to their *place* of articulation (where in the oral cavity the sound is formed), *manner* of articulation (how the air stream is passed through the oral cavity), and *voicing* (whether the vocal folds vibrate during sound production).

For the sake of simplification, let us examine the oral cavity along its horizontal and vertical axes. The horizontal axis may be considered to start at the front of the mouth and terminate at its back. The front of the mouth includes the lips, the teeth, and the alveolar ridge. The back of the mouth includes the hard palate, the soft palate, and the pharynx. The vertical axis may be considered to indicate the relative height of the tongue during the production of vowels and the relative opening at the point of contact during the production of consonants. The relative opening in the production of consonants /t, s, l/ is an example. The production of /t/ involves almost no opening at the point of contact, the production of /s/ involves a small degree of opening, and the production of /l/ involves a greater degree of opening. In these ways, the vertical axis of the oral cavity determines the manner in which consonants are produced.

On the other hand, the horizontal axis determines the place of articulation of the consonants. The contact of the tongue with the different points of articulation causes an alteration in the shape of the resonating cavities in front of and behind the point of contact.

Figure 3 shows the changes in the shapes and sizes of the resonating cavities during the production of the various consonant sounds.

Bilabial

Sounds produced at the lips are known as labial sounds. The English phonemes /p, b, m, w/ are produced at the lips and are referred to as labials. In the articulation of these sounds, the resonating cavity size is almost null in front of the point of contact and is large behind it, as shown in Figure 3. The upper and lower lips act as *articulators,* which are movable speech organs involved in the shaping of speech sounds. Specifically, since the production of /p, b, m, w/ involves both lips, these sounds are called bilabial sounds. This classification enables the distinction of these sounds from /f, v/, whose articulation involves the participation of the lower lip only.

Labiodental

The production of /f, v/ involves the contact of the lower lip and the upper teeth. The resonating cavity size is altered a bit, in the sense that there is a slight shortening of the resonation chamber behind the point of contact. In Figure 3 this oral cavity configuration is labeled labiodental. Since there exist only minute differences between bilabial and labiodental phonemes, they are sometimes grouped as labials.

Linguadental

The two sounds called "theta" and "thorne" are represented phonemically by /θ/ and /ð/, respectively. These sounds are produced when the tip of the tongue is between the upper and lower teeth. The cavity size resulting from this contact is further reduced behind the point of constriction and is slightly enlarged in front of the point of constriction. In Figure 3, the oral cavity configuration is labeled linguadental because it uniquely relates to the nature and quality of phonemes /θ/ and /ð/. These two phonemes are described as linguadentals because the tongue and teeth are involved in their production. Some phoneticians refer to them as interdentals because they cannot be produced effectively without the tongue tip being securely placed between the upper and lower teeth. Many languages handle these two sounds in a postdental rather than an interdental position, i.e., with the tongue placed behind the front teeth.

Alveolar

When the tongue contacts the alveolar ridge, the cavity in front of the constriction is the largest of all the cavity configurations described so far. The portion of the cavity behind the constriction, although further reduced, is still slightly larger than that in front. In Figure 3 this configuration is labeled al-

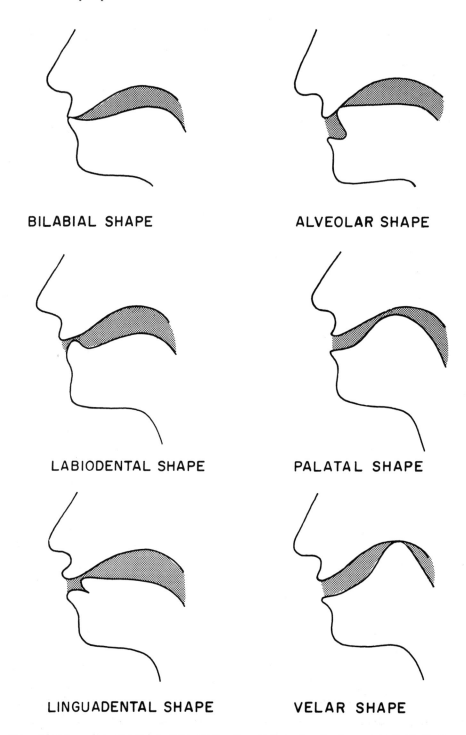

Figure 3. Diagram showing the six different alterations in the oral cavity shape controlled by the lip and tongue contacts at the six different places along the horizontal line of the oral cavity.

veolar. The alveolar ridge is a very prominent point of tongue contact in many languages of the world, including English. Many sounds are produced when the tongue tip touches it, and it seems to be the most natural point of contact for the tongue tip. In order to enunciate the sound /t/, one merely has to lift the tongue tip and touch the alveolar ridge, thus stopping the air flow, and then release it to produce /t/. English sounds such as /t, d, n/ are produced at the alveolar ridge and are called lingua-alveolar sounds. In addition, the consonants /s, z, l, r/ are also produced with the tongue tip contact in the general vicinity of the alveolar ridge.

In the production of the labial, labiodental, linguadental, and alveolar sounds, the size of the resonating cavity is larger behind the point of constriction than in front of it; therefore, these consonants are referred to as *front consonants*.

Palatal

The consonants /ʃ, ʒ, tʃ, dʒ, j/ are produced by the body of the tongue contacting or approximating the hard palate. In Figure 3 this configuration is labeled palatal. The size of the resonating cavity in front of the constriction is enlarged, whereas the size of the cavity behind the constriction is reduced. Because the cavity is now larger in front of the constriction point than behind it, these con-

sonants are referred to as *back consonants*.

Velar

Velar sounds are produced when the point of tongue contact is farthest back in the vocal tract. The back of the tongue touches or approximates the soft palate to form the constriction necessary for the production of the velar sounds /k, g, ŋ, h/.

Summary

We have now mapped in the oral cavity each important location involved in the pronunciation of English consonants: 1) lips, 2) lip and teeth, 3) tip of the tongue and teeth, 4) tip of the tongue and alveolar ridge, 5) body of the tongue and hard palate, and 6) back of the tongue and soft palate (velum). The different sizes of the resonating cavities in front and behind the constriction have been utilized as the criteria for determining the front and back sounds in English. Front sounds are those in which the cavity size is larger behind the point of constriction. Back sounds are those in which the cavity size is larger in front of the point of constriction.

The number of American English consonant sounds associated with the different place categories is as follows: four sounds are bilabial; two are labiodental; two are linguadental; seven are alveolar;

five are palatal, and four are velar.   This is summarized below:

Place of articulation	Consonant	Point of articulation in oral cavity	Resonating cavity (front/back sound)
Bilabial	/p, b, m, w/	Lips	Front
Labiodental	/f, v/	Lower lip and upper teeth	Front
Linguadental	/θ, ð/	Tip of tongue and teeth	Front
Alveolar	/t, d, n, s, z, l, r/	Tip of tongue and alveolar ridge	Front
Palatal	/ʃ, ʒ, tʃ, dʒ, j/	Body of tongue and hard palate	Back
Velar	/k, g, ŋ, h/	Back of tongue and soft palate	Back

Thus, the different points of articulation have an unequal number of consonants associated with them.

We can see in Figure 4 that the consonant system in English is not symmetric. This figure shows the number of consonants for each place of articulation. The abscissa shows the places of articulation, and the ordinate shows the number of consonants. The alveolar place is the first in the rank order because the maximal number of consonants are produced at that place.

So far we have examined the vocal tract subdivisions of an English speaker from the point of view of tongue contact at the various locations of the oral cavity. It must be noted here that the six categorizations or the six places of articulation are specifically related to English speakers. In the analysis of other languages of the world, certain details of this classification system may be altered. For example, Arabic languages include one additional point of contact further beyond the velum to account for consonants /χ, ɣ/. It has been reported by some phoneticians that man is capable of making as many as twenty-six articulatory contact points. Together, they account for the place of articulation in all languages of the world.

MANNER OF ARTICULATION

It is important for students to visualize the very elegant strategy that man utilizes in speech production. Place of articulation subdivides consonants into six discrete categories. Consonants also can be divided by the manner of articulation. Manner means "the way" in which an act is performed. Manner of articulation refers to the way in which speech sounds are produced.

According to the manner of articulation, English consonants may be divided into the sonorant/obstruent classification. The sonorant consonants may be divided into oral and nasal categories, and the obstruent consonants may be divided into stop and fricative categories. In addition, stops and fricatives may be subdivided into sibilant and nonsibilant categories. All obstruent consonants may be classified into voiced and voiceless. (See Figure 5.)

Another convention treats the manner of articulation on a continuum depending on the different degrees of closure involved in the production of consonants. In this convention, the stop category is at one end of the continuum, the sonorant category is at the other end, and the fricative category is in the middle.

The manner category in this text is denoted by two specifications only. This description is not unlike the description of the two sides of a coin, where one side is directly opposite to the other and where each side is considered independent of the other. Such a description is also called a binary function. For example, sonorant is opposite obstruent, stop is opposite

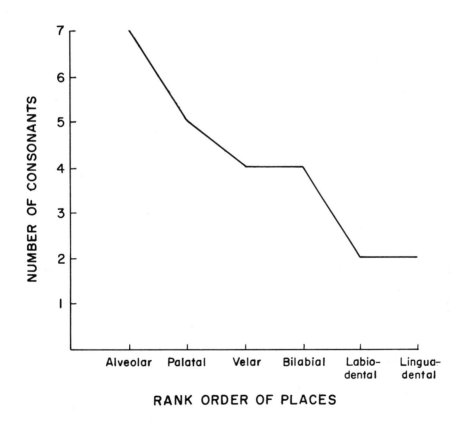

Figure 4. The number of English consonants is shown on the ordinate, and the six different places in the rank order are shown on the abscissa. Alveolar place is listed first because it has the maximal number of consonants in English.

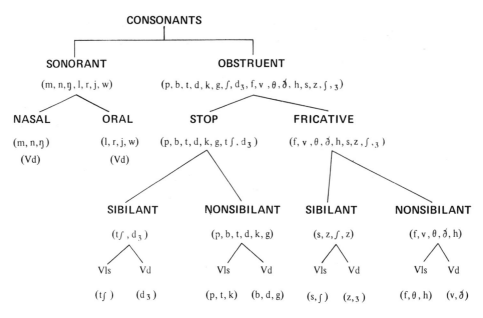

Figure 5. Division of consonants, on binary principles, into sonorant/obstruent, stop/fricative, sibilant/nonsibilant, nasal/oral, and voiceless/voiced groups.

fricative, and nasal is opposite oral. These opposite specifications are important in developing an elegant system for describing the sounds of a language. Although such a binary designation sacrifices a great deal of articulatory detail, it must be understood that a student of phonetics cannot afford to sacrifice the details of phonetic descriptions when pursuing a comprehensive study of speech sounds.

Sonorant/Obstruent

The sonorant/obstruent classification distinguishes all consonants according to the amount of vocal tract obstruction necessary for their production. The obstruent consonants are produced by a considerable amount of obstruction of the laryngeal air stream in the vocal tract. The sonorant consonants, on the other hand, require only a negligible amount of obstruction in the vocal tract.

The phonetic description of sonorants includes a relatively unobstructed flow of air between the articulator and the point of articulation. These consonants contain vowel-like qualities, although their predominant function in English is consonantal. The sonorants in English are /m, n, ŋ, l, r, j, w/. Three of these seven sonorants /m, n, ŋ/ are nasal and four /l, r, j, w/ are oral.

Sonorants are the most open of all the consonant categories. The only sounds greater in openness than sonorants are vowels. Because they are vowel-like, sonorants sometimes serve as the nucleus of a syllable.

It is well known that vowels are usually the nucleus of a syllable. However, if there is no vowel in a syllable, then that syllable invariably contains a sonorant that serves as its nucleus. For example, the second syllabic element in the word 'bottle' /batḷ/ is /ḷ/. The nucleus of the first syllable is /ɑ/ and the nucleus of the second syllable is /ḷ/. The nucleic function is phonetically represented by a stroke (ˌ) under the phoneme. Thus, syllabically, the English sonorants /m, n, ŋ, l/ would be represented as /m̩, n̩, ŋ̩, l̩/. The remaining three phonemes /j, r, w/, when syllabified, completely lose their identity as consonants and become vowels. Thus /j/ becomes /i/ or /ɪ/, /r/ becomes /ɚ/ or /ɝ/, and /w/ becomes /u/ or /ʊ/.

Nasal/Oral

Nasal/oral is also a manner category. It distinguishes speech sounds primarily according to the difference in the resonating cavities. For oral consonants, the resonating cavity is the entire portion of the vocal tract excluding the nasal cavity and the nasopharynx. For nasal consonants, however, the resonating cavity is the entire vocal tracet, i.e., including the nasal cavity and the nasopharynx. Because the air stream is passed through the nose and the point of constriction is in the mouth, there is an added complexity to the nature of the resonator for the nasal consonants. Figure 6 shows the schematic drawing for the production of the nasal consonant /n/. This figure is identical to the "alveolar shape" configuration presented in Figure 3, except that an open nasopharyngeal port (valve) is shown in Figure 6. The mechanism for the nasal consonant /m/ can be shown by depicting an open nasopharyngeal port in the "labial shape" configuration of Figure 3. The mechanism for the nasal consonant /ŋ/ also can be shown by depicting an open nasopharyngeal port in the "velar shape" configuration of Figure 3.

Nasal consonants have been described by some phoneticians as nasal stops and by others as nasal sonorants. We have seen earlier that stops and sonorants are opposite consonant categories, mainly because of amount of closure in the oral cavity. Although the nasal consonants are produced with the stop-like obstruction in the oral cavity, there is an uninterrupted flow of air through the nasal cavity. In addition, the vocal fold vibrations responsible for the voicing aspect of this group of consonants are vowel-like.

Stop/Fricative

The stop/fricative category of obstruents is an important manner category. In English, the stop category includes the consonants

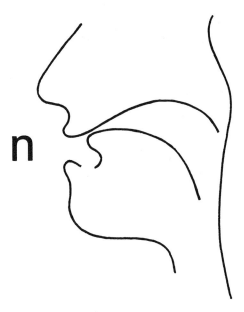

Figure 6. A schematic diagram showing the production of the nasal consonant /n/. Note the open nasopharyngeal port characteristic of the production of nasal consonants.

/p, b, t, d, tʃ, dʒ, k, g/ and the fricative category includes the consonants /f, v, θ, ð, s, z, ʃ, ʒ, h/. Stops are produced with maximal closure at the point of constriction and maximal or total obstruction of the laryngeal air stream. Fricatives are produced with relatively less closure and relatively less air stream obstruction. Because all stops and fricatives require obstruction in the vocal tract, they are called obstruents.

One major difference between stops and their opposite class, fricatives, is the time involved in their production. Stops as a class are relatively shorter in duration than fricatives. In addition, stops involve a complete closure at a given point in the vocal tract while the fricatives do not. This closure is caused by contact of the lips or of the different portions of the tongue with the various points of articulation described above. At the lips, for example, there is a complete closure for the stop consonants /p, b/. There is, however, some opening for the fricative consonants /f, v/. At the alveolar ridge, there is a complete closure for the stops /t, d/. The fricatives /s, z/, however, involve some degree of opening.

Table 1 shows that the manner of articulation helps to make systematic distinctions within the different phoneme groupings at the six places of articulation described earlier. In this table the six discrete places of articulation are on a horizontal axis, and the three manners of articulation (on a continuum: stop, fricative, and sonorant) are on a vertical axis. The elegant distribution of the stop-fricative-sonorant continuum in relation to the six places of articulation can be seen in this table.

Let us first examine the stop/fricative portion of the continuum as it relates to the place of articulation. At any of the six places, the stops and fricatives are not produced exactly at the same place of articulation. The stop category shows a more fronted tendency than its continuant counterpart at the labial, alveolar, palatal, and velar places.

Stops /p, b/ vs. Fricatives /f, v/

While the bilabial place harbors the stops /p, b/, the labiodental place harbors the fricatives /f, v/. The /p, b/ and the /f, v/ pairs are different not only because one pair is stop and the other is fricative, but also because the /p, b/ pair is more fronted than the /f, v/ pair. The relationship between /f, v/ and /θ, ð/, however, is not similar to that between /p, b/ and /f, v/, in that

the /f, v/ pair is only minimally different from the /θ, ð/ pair. Not only are their places of articulation extremely close, but they are both within the same manner category (fricative).

There is ample evidence, therefore, in the fields of articulation disorders, language learning, and teaching English as a foreign language, to show that it is difficult to keep apart /f/ from /θ/ and /v/ from /ð/, both in speech production and speech perception. In some dialects of English /wɪθ/ is pronounced as /wɪf/ and /mʌðɚ/ is pronounced as /mʌvɚ/.

Stops /t, d/ vs. Fricatives /s, z/

The alveolar place, a more stable place of articulation, harbors the /t, d/ pair, which is distinguishable from the /s, z/ pair by the manner of articulation. Using the system we have been describing so far, /s, z/ differs from /t, d/ because the /t, d/ phonemes are stops and the /s, z/ phonemes are fricatives. Fricatives are also sometimes referred to as *continuants* because of the con-

Table 1. Description of English consonants according to the six places of articulation and three manners of articulation*

	Place						
Manner	Bilabial	Labiodental	Linguadental	Alveolar	Palatal	Velar	Oral cavity
Stop	/p, b/			/t, d/	/tʃ, dʒ/	/k, g/	Closed
Fricative		/f, v/	/θ, ð/	/s, z/	/ʃ, ʒ/	/h/	Slight opening
Sonorant	/m, w/			/n, r, l/	/j/	/ŋ/	Greater opening

*Similar to the place of articulation, the manner of articulation has been treated on a continuum: stops are closed, fricatives are slightly open, and sonorants have greater opening in the oral cavity.

tinuous flow of air necessary for their production. Thus, the /s, z/ phonemes are also known as continuants.

There are, however, some researchers who feel that the /s, z/ pair is produced further back on the place continuum than the /t, d/ pair. In addition, we will see in our later discussions that /s, z/, according to some phoneticians, has an added feature, sibilancy, and according to others has an added feature, duration, that further help to distinguish /t, d/ from /s, z/.

Stops /tʃ, dʒ/ vs. Fricatives /ʃ, ʒ/

The phoneme pair /tʃ, dʒ/ may be considered as a stop pair and contrasted with the continuant pair /ʃ, ʒ/ at the palatal place. Although both pairs are shown in Table 1 as being produced at the same place of articulation, it is known that, within the palatal place of articulation, the /tʃ, dʒ/ pair is not produced as far back on the place continuum as is the /ʃ, ʒ/ pair.

Stops /k, g/ vs. Fricative /h/

The phoneme pair /k, g/ is contrasted from /h/, again according to the stop/continuant dichotomy. /k, g/ are stops and /h/ is a continuant.

Summary

In essence, then, we may conclude that the stop/fricative dichotomy is an elegant one, where the system is doubly strengthened by the place distinction to facilitate learning and avoid articulatory and perceptual confusions.

The phonetic category stop is also called *plosive,* mainly because of the phoneticians' differences in viewpoints. Although the term "stop" denotes the complete stoppage of the air flow at the point of constriction in the vocal tract, the term "plosive" implies the release of or explosion of the air flow following that closure. The explosion of stops is mainly realized when the stops are produced at the initial place of a word or syllable. Functionally, then, the term "plosive" is only relevant to initial stop consonants. However, the production of the six consonants /p, t, k, b, d, g/ involves a total stoppage irrespective of their position in a word. Thus, functionally, the term "stop" is more inclusive of the overall function of English stops than the term "plosive."

Stop consonants belong to a universal phonetic inventory implying that all languages of the world include this category of sounds. It appears uniformly at prominent places of articulation with consistent contrast of voicing (in English), voicing and aspiration (in Indic languages), and aspiration and release (in some Southeast Asian languages). The category of fricatives is defined as being in opposition to the category of stops. It must be understood, then, that what is a stop is automatically not a fricative.

Other Aspects

Difference between Phonetic and Phonological Features It may be helpful at this point to clarify the difference between phonetic and phonological categories. A phonetic description implies the description of an articulatory event, whereas a phonological description is the description of the relationship between articulatory events. Before deriving binary phonological specifications of consonants, an independent phonetic inquiry must be made regarding the presence of a given description or feature. The presence of a given feature in one set of phonemes, and the presence of the opposite feature in another set of phonemes, play a crucial role in the origination of a phonological feature. Phonetic observation therefore forms the basis of phonological description.

(+) and (−) Fricatives Phonetically, while stops and fricatives are descriptions of independent articulatory gestures, phonologically they can be defined by utilizing a unitary set of features. The term *frication* may be used to describe the complete stop/fricative dichotomy in the phonology of a language where all fricatives are labeled as *plus* fricative and all stops are labeled as *minus* fricative. In this kind of a notation system, those sounds that are neither stops nor fricatives are not considered for either the plus or the minus specification. For example, the /l/ consonant is neither a stop nor a fricative, and therefore /l/ will not be marked by either the plus (+) or minus (−) specification of the feature frication.

Fricatives as Continuants Fricatives are sometimes described as *continuants*. In such cases, the opposite of stop is continuant. A continuant category is defined as being opposite to the stop category, i.e., not requiring stoppage in the oral cavity. Continuants by definition may be considered a broader category than the fricatives, since fricative implies the continuation of the air stream necessarily created by frication at the point of constriction in the vocal tract. On the other hand, continuant only requires the continuation or uninterruption of the air stream, thus including both fricatives and sonorants.

Slit and Groove Fricatives Fricatives may be created by molding the opening of the vocal tract so as to form either a slit or a groove. In both instances, the air stream is allowed to pass through the opening in the vocal tract. Slit implies a small, flat opening, whereas groove refers to a large and curled opening, both of which create some friction during the passage of the air stream through the constriction in the vocal tract. The slit fricatives include /f, v, θ, ð/ and the groove fricatives include /s, z, ʃ, ʒ/. The phoneme /h/ is neither a slit nor a groove fricative because it does not require closure in the vocal tract.

Complexity of Fricatives The fricative category contains one of the largest number of sounds in English and has many diversities. It contains the most frequently used English consonant /s/ as well as the least frequently used consonant /ʒ/. The fricative category has a very complex relationship with the other manners of articulation. In English, the stops appear at the lips, the alveolar ridge, and the velum, and the fricatives appear at all the other places of articulation. The stop category bears a relationship with the two manners of articulation, i.e., nasality and sonorancy, but the fricative category is unrelated to both of them. Because of its distributional and phonetic complexities, the fricative is a constant source of problem to speech and hearing pathologists, teachers of English as a foreign language, and teachers of dialectal English.

Sibilant/Nonsibilant

Besides being classified as stop/fricative, obstruent consonants also may be divided into sibilant/nonsibilant. In the English system of sounds the sibilant category includes four fricative consonants and two stop consonants. The four fricatives are /s, z, ʃ, ʒ/ and the two stops, which traditionally are called *affricates*, are /tʃ, dʒ/. The phonological feature sibilancy is marked by the prominence of a hissing sound. The division of the obstruent consonants can be seen in Figure 5. These consonants are first divided by the stop/fricative dichotomy. All stops and all fricatives further branch into sibilants/nonsibilants. This figure also shows how the feature

voicing subdivides all obstruents into voiced and voiceless consonants.

Voiced/Voiceless

The phonological feature voicing relates to the presence or the absence of vibration of the vocal folds in the production of consonants. Therefore, it applies to all place and manner categories of consonants. In English, however, voicing is used to distinguish only among the obstruent group of consonants. The sonorants are all voiced, and thus, like vowels, the voicing feature is not necessary for their phonological description.

Parallel Pairs

Voicing, in English, distinguishes eight pairs of consonants. Consider the two pairs /p, b/ and /t, d/. The members of the first pair (/p/ and /b/) differ by the same feature (voicing) as the members of the second pair (/t/ and /d/). Therefore, these two pairs are referred to as parallel pairs.

Cognates

The voiceless/voiced consonants of each pair also may be called cognates because the first consonant is identical to the second in all respects except for the feature voicing. For example, /p/ is identical to /b/ in terms of its place (bilabial) and manner (oral stop) of articulation. The single difference between them is voicing. Thus, /p/ is the voiceless cognate of the /b/ phoneme, and /b/ is the voiced cognate of the /p/ phoneme. Identical statements may be made regarding the phoneme pairs /t, d/, /k, g/ /f, v/, /θ, ð/, /s, z/, /ʃ, ʒ/, and /tʃ, dʒ/.

Voiced and Voiceless Consonants

The articulatory description of the feature voicing and the associated definition and nomenclature differ. The traditional and most widely used term, voicing, relates directly to the function of the vocal folds. Voiced consonants are produced with the vibration of the vocal folds while voiceless consonants are produced without such vibration. Thus, in English, the production of the consonants /p, t, k, f, θ, s, ʃ, tʃ, h/ does not involve the vibration of the vocal folds. All other consonants are produced with vocal fold vibrations and, therefore, are called voiced.

Difference between Voiced Consonants and Vowels

In describing voiced consonants on the basis of the vibratory function of the vocal folds, a distinction must be made between vowels and voiced consonants. Vowel production involves a smooth vibration of the vocal folds, whereas voiced consonants involve some interruption in the vibration of the vocal folds. In addition, consonant production requires a closure in the oral cavity, but vowel production does not.

Fortis/Lenis

The fortis/lenis dichotomy also describes the voiceless/voiced differentiation. The term "fortis" suggests a greater amount of force and the term "lenis" suggests a smaller amount of force employed in the production of consonants. This description is especially relevant to the voiceless and voiced stops. The difference in the amount of physiological force can be demonstrated by holding a lighted match close to the lips. For producing voiceless consonants, an unusual amount of force is exerted, thus causing the extinction of the lighted match. The lack of such force involved in producing the voiced consonants will not cause the extinction of the match.

Tense/Lax

The voiceless consonants also have been called tense consonants, and the voiced consonants have been called lax consonants by phonetic scientists who believe that it is the muscle tension of the articulators that distinguishes the voiceless from the voiced consonants. There is a greater amount of tension involved in the production of voiceless consonants than is involved in the production of their voiced cognates. It may be observed that the tense/lax aspect of the consonants is very much related to the fortis/lenis distinction. The greater the physiological force behind the point of closure, the greater the muscle tension.

Aspiration Noise

It has been argued by some phoneticians that the real distinction, in English, between the voiced and voiceless stops lies in the amount of aspiration noise present or absent during their production. Aspiration noise accompanies the production of voiceless stops, whereas the lack of aspiration noise causes the stop to be heard as voiced.

Summary

Voicing is a prominent articulatory feature in most languages of the world. In English, the feature voicing helps to distinguish within the stop/fricative (obstruent) manner category. All sonorant consonants in English are naturally voiced and, therefore, in strict phonological terms, do not require distinction based on the feature voicing. However, phonetically, the sonorants are voiced, and they may be described as being produced with vocal fold vibration, without force, and with relaxed muscles.

All consonants that have been described as produced with vocal fold vibration are marked by the plus (+) voicing notation, and those described as produced without the vocal fold vibration are marked by the minus (−) voicing notation.

EXERCISES

Fill in the Blanks

1. The source for the production of vowels is the _____.
2. Consonants produced without vocal fold vibration are known as _____ consonants.
3. The sound-producing apparatus is situated in the _____.
4. The _____ is situated above the trachea and below the root of the tongue.
5. The vocal folds are formed by the _____ muscle and the _____ ligament.
6. The pharynx may be divided into three parts, namely, _____, _____, and _____.
7. The velopharyngeal valve separates the _____ from the _____.
8. During swallowing, the inlet of the larynx is covered by the _____ valve.
9. The oral cavity is bounded anteriorly by the _____ and laterally by the _____; its roof is formed by the _____ and _____ palate, and on its floor rests the _____.

10. Sounds produced by contact of the upper and lower lips are known as _____ sounds.

11. Velar sounds are produced when the _____ touches the _____.

12. The way in which speech sounds are produced is referred to as the _____ of articulation.

13. A complete closure at given points in the vocal tract is characteristic of _____ consonants.

14. At the alveolar place of articulation, the stop pair _____ is contrasted with the continuant pair _____.

15. The consonants /f, v/ are produced by air passing through a small, flat opening; hence they are known as _____ fricatives.

16. Sonorants contain vowel-like qualities although their predominant function in English is _____.

17. The class of sounds greater in openness than sonorants is _____.

18. Because of their vowel-like quality, sonorants sometimes serve as the _____ of a syllable.

19. The prominence of a hissing sound in a consonant is indicative of the feature _____.

20. Two pairs of sounds in which the members of the first pair differ by the same feature as the members of the second pair are known as _____ pairs.

21. The single feature differentiating /ʃ/ and /ʒ/ phonemes is _____.

True or False

____ 1. Consonant production does not necessarily involve vocal fold vibration.

____ 2. The source for the vowel production for laryngectomees is other than the vocal folds.

____ 3. The vocal folds are composed of cartilages, muscles, and membrane.

____ 4. The nasopharynx extends from the root of the tongue to the esophagus.

____ 5. The tongue is an exclusively muscular organ.

____ 6. Labiodental sounds are produced when the upper lip touches the lower teeth.

____ 7. Linguadental sounds are produced when tongue tip is between the upper and lower teeth.

____ 8. Front consonants are those in which the resonating cavity size is large in front of the point of constriction in the oral cavity.

_____ 9. Different points of articulation have an unequal number of phonemes associated with them.

_____ 10. The term "plosive" is functionally more inclusive than the term "stop" for English consonants.

_____ 11. The fricatives are also described as continuants.

_____ 12. The production of /n/ includes a closed nasopharyngeal port.

_____ 13. Sonorant consonants may be voiced or voiceless.

Multiple Choice

_____ 1. The vocal tract serves as a resonator for:
    a. vowels
    b. consonants
    c. vowels and consonants

_____ 2. The nasal cavity is an added resonator in the production of:
    a. /p, t, k/
    b. /b, d, g/
    c. /m, n, ŋ/

_____ 3. The vibration of the vocal folds is possible because of the driving force of the:
    a. inhaled air
    b. exhaled air
    c. nasal air

_____ 4. Thoracic cavity means:
    a. chest cavity
    b. laryngeal cavity
    c. oral cavity

_____ 5. The larynx is situated _____ the trachea.
    a. above
    b. below
    c. beside

_____ 6. The open velopharyngeal valve is of great importance in the production of:
    a. nasal consonants
    b. nasal vowels
    c. non-nasal consonants

_____ 7. The alveolar ridge serves as the point of contact in the production of English consonants:
    a. /k/ and /ʃ/
    b. /dʒ/ and /g/
    c. /m/ and /ŋ/
    d. /t/ and /n/

_____ 8. The upper teeth serve as the point of contact in the production of:
        a. /l/
        b. /f/
        c. /j/
        d. /b/

_____ 9. The phonemes /θ/ and /ð/ are produced by:
        a. upper teeth contacting lower lip
        b. upper teeth contacting lower teeth
        c. upper and lower teeth contacting tongue

_____ 10. /t, d, n/ are _____ sounds.
        a. linguadental
        b. lingua-alveolar
        c. labiodental

_____ 11. Two examples of palatal sounds are:
        a. /θ/ and /ð/
        b. /f/ and /b/
        c. /t/ and /n/
        d. /ʃ/ and /j/

_____ 12. Stops as a class are relatively _____ in duration than fricatives.
        a. longer
        b. shorter
        c. the same

_____ 13. /l, r, j/ are _____ consonants.
        a. fricative
        b. obstruent
        c. sonorant

_____ 14. The obstruent category includes:
        a. fricatives and sonorants
        b. stops and fricatives
        c. nasals and fricatives

_____ 15. The feature voicing is used in English to distinguish only between:
        a. fricatives
        b. obstruents
        c. sonorants
        d. stops

_____ 16. The /p, b/ and /t, d/ pairs are referred to as:
        a. parallel pairs
        b. similar pairs
        c. unique pairs

_____ 17. Voiceless consonants also have been referred to as:
      a. tense consonants
      b. lax consonants
_____ 18. Voiced consonants also have been referred to as:
      a. fortis consonants
      b. lenis consonants

Phonemic Transcription: Place

Transcribe phonemically using place of articulation as the criterion.

Bilabials /p, b, m, w/

1. pencil _____
2. sheep _____
3. ape _____
4. people _____
5. apple _____
6. pig _____

7. bed _____
8. about _____
9. cab _____
10. boat _____
11. rabbit _____
12. knob _____

13. milk _____
14. command _____
15. them _____
16. snowman _____
17. lime _____
18. monkey _____

19. watch _____
20. walk _____
21. Hawaii _____
22. tower _____
23. wood _____

Labiodentals /f, v/

24. fork _____
25. elephant _____
26. giraffe _____
27. fool _____
28. rifle _____
29. life _____

30. valentine _____
31. river _____
32. live _____
33. native _____
34. violin _____
35. event _____

Linguadentals /θ, ð/

36. three _____
37. thin _____
38. healthy _____
39. path _____
40. bathroom _____
41. both _____

42. mother _____
43. that _____
44. wreath _____
45. smooth _____
46. father _____
47. those _____

Alveolars /t, d, n, s, z, r, l/

48.	toes _____	72.	zipper _____
49.	tape _____	73.	zoo _____
50.	detect _____	74.	roses _____
51.	turtle _____	75.	razor _____
52.	it _____	76.	scissors _____
53.	pet _____	77.	eyes _____
54.	dime _____	78.	rare _____
55.	bird _____	79.	rose _____
56.	doodle _____	80.	carrot _____
57.	duck _____	81.	barometer _____
58.	head _____	82.	fair _____
59.	bidding _____	83.	car _____
60.	nickel _____	84.	lily _____
61.	oxen _____	85.	lake _____
62.	porcupine _____	86.	alligator _____
63.	banana _____	87.	sailboat _____
64.	nose _____	88.	doll _____
65.	bonanza _____	89.	cool _____
66.	Santa _____		
67.	salad _____		
68.	sister _____		
69.	passing _____		
70.	horse _____		
71.	walrus _____		

Palatals /tʃ, dʒ, ʃ, ʒ, j/

90.	chair _____	102.	shoes _____
91.	church _____	103.	share _____
92.	catch _____	104.	nation _____
93.	marching _____	105.	milkshake _____
94.	matches _____	106.	dish _____
95.	notch _____	107.	fish _____
96.	jail _____	108.	measure _____
97.	judge _____	109.	vision _____
98.	July _____	110.	beige _____
99.	orange _____	111.	decoupage _____
100.	dodging _____		
101.	judgment _____		

112. yes _____
113. universe _____
114. yellow _____
115. yo-yo _____

Velars /k, g, ŋ, h/

116. candy-cane _____
117. cup _____
118. stocking _____
119. tackle _____
120. clock _____
121. back _____

122. gun _____
123. gift _____
124. again _____
125. tiger _____
126. dog _____
127. pig _____

128. donkey _____
129. sing _____
130. ceiling _____
131. thank you _____

132. he _____
133. hit _____
134. ham _____
135. behave _____
136. inherent _____

Phonemic Transcription: Manner

Transcribe phonemically using manner of articulation as the criterion.

Stops /p, b, t, d, k, g/

1. Pennsylvania _____
2. open _____
3. up _____

4. boy _____
5. lobster _____
6. rob _____

7. Texas _____
8. Kentucky _____
9. bat _____

10. Delaware _____
11. Indiana _____
12. bird _____

13. California _____
14. picking _____
15. sack _____

16. get _____
17. buggy _____
18. log _____

Fricatives /f, v, θ, ð, s, z, ʃ, ʒ, h/

19. Florida _____
20. telephone _____
21. scarf _____

22. Virginia _____
23. survey _____
24. carve _____

25. thread _____
26. nothing _____
27. math _____

28. the _____
29. brethren _____
30. bathe _____

31. celery _____
32. Kansas _____
33. caps _____
34. zoom _____
35. bizarre _____
36. buzz _____
37. shine _____
38. crucial _____
39. leash _____

40. treasure _____
41. decision _____
42. garage _____
43. house _____
44. inherit _____
45. New Hampshire _____
46. Ohio _____

Sonorants /j, r, l, w, m, n, ŋ/

47. Utah _____
48. youth _____
49. New York _____

50. raise _____
51. Missouri _____
52. tar _____

53. lap _____
54. Alabama _____
55. camel _____

56. Wisconsin _____
57. Iowa _____
58. stoneware _____

59. Michigan _____
60. lemon _____
61. come _____

62. North Carolina _____
63. onion _____
64. clown _____

65. ringing _____
66. song _____

Sibilants /s, z, ʃ, ʒ, tʃ, dʒ/

67. see _____
68. Mississippi _____
69. bus _____

70. zero _____
71. Arizona _____
72. snooze _____

73. shore _____
74. Washington _____
75. push _____

76. precision _____
77. leisure _____

78. chase _____
79. catcher _____
80. hatch _____

81. Georgia _____
82. judging _____
83. baggage _____

Nasals /m, n, ŋ/

84. Maryland _____
85. bumper _____
86. name _____

87. Nevada _____
88. Illinois _____
89. Maine _____

90. hungry _____
91. long _____

Orthographic Counterparts:
Voicing

Write the orthographic counterparts of the following phonemically transcribed words using voicing as the criterion.

Voiceless /p, t, k, f, θ, s, ʃ, tʃ/ | **Voiced** /b, d, g, v, ð, z, ʒ, dʒ/

1. /pʌpɪ/ _____
2. /peɪpɚ/ _____
3. /tætu/ _____
4. /pəteɪto/ _____
5. /keɪk/ _____
6. /klɔk/ _____
7. /fʌnɪ/ _____
8. /sʌfɚ/ _____
9. /θɚstɪ/ _____
10. /bæθtʌb/ _____
11. /sɛsəmɪ/ _____
12. /strit/ _____
13. /slʌʃ/ _____
14. /ʃʊgɚ/ _____
15. /tʃɔɪs/ _____
16. /mʌntʃ/ _____

17. /beɪbɪ/ _____
18. /bʌbl̩/ _____
19. /dædɪ/ _____
20. /dor/ _____
21. /gæmbl̩/ _____
22. /dʒaɪgæntɪk/ _____
23. /vɛrɪ/ _____
24. /vɔɪs/ _____
25. /ðeɪ/ _____
26. /læðɚ/ _____
27. /zibrə/ _____
28. /zuɑlədʒɪ/ _____
29. /liʒʌn/ _____
30. /ruʒ/ _____
31. /dʒʌmp/ _____
32. /porɪdʒ/ _____

Phonemic Transcription:
Consonant Clusters

Transcribe phonemically using consonant clusters as the criterion.

1. sixth _____
2. explode _____
3. consist _____
4. thinks _____
5. screw _____
6. strong _____
7. misspell _____
8. distract _____
9. spin _____
10. crack _____

11. someone _____
12. frosty _____
13. snow _____
14. spider _____
15. skates _____
16. strawberries _____
17. clown _____
18. train _____
19. glass _____
20. flowers _____

Chapter 4 ARTICULATORY ASPECTS OF PHONETICS: VOWELS AND DIPHTHONGS

There are inherent differences in the overall principles underlying consonant and vowel production. One important difference is that consonant production involves discrete articulatory contacts in the vocal tract but vowel production does not.

VOWELS

Prominent Articulatory Positions

Advancement: Front/Central/Back

English vowel production is accomplished by the positioning of the tongue in three general locations along the horizontal axis of the oral cavity. The tongue body either protrudes toward the front of the mouth to produce the front vowels, remains relatively neutral or centrally located for the production of the central vowels, or retracts toward the back of the mouth for the production of the back vowels (see Modules 41, 49, and 50 in Chapter 7). The movement of the tongue along the horizontal axis is also referred to as tongue *advancement*.

Chapter 3 presented the influence of the oral cavity shape on the quality and nature of consonant sounds. This notion also applies to vowels. Front vowels have most of the resonating cavity in the back of the mouth; central vowels have half of the resonating cavity in the front and half in the back of the mouth; and back vowels have most of the resonating cavity in the front of the mouth.

Height: High/Mid/Low

Besides the positioning of the tongue along the horizontal dimension of the oral cavity, the tongue also moves simultaneously along the vertical axis. The tongue is either at its highest position to produce high vowels, at its mid position to produce mid vowels, or at its lowest position to produce low vowels (see Modules 41, 45, and 47 in Chapter 7). The movement of the tongue along the vertical axis is also referred to as tongue *height*.

Total Positions

Because the tongue is capable of assuming three positions along the horizontal axis and three positions along the vertical axis, a simultaneous movement along these two axes allows the tongue to assume a total of nine positions. As a result, the tongue can be (1) front-high, (2) front-mid, (3) front-low, (4) central-high, (5) central-mid, (6) central-low, (7) back-high, (8) back-mid, and (9) back-low.

In Figure 7, an articulatory vowel diagram is presented to plot the general location of these nine tongue positions to represent eight English vowels /i, e, æ, ə, ʌ, u, o, ɑ/. The American English vowel system does not have a vowel represented in the central-high position. Thus, like the American

English consonant system, which is asymmetric (shown in Figure 4), the American English vowel system is also without complete symmetry.

If the English language had only eight vowels, a complete phonological distinction could be made between each one of them based on the tongue advancement and tongue height criteria. However, there are six additional vowels that have not yet been represented on the above vowel diagram.

Tenseness

Vowels such as /ɪ, ɛ, ɚ, ɝ, ʊ, ɔ/ remain to be described in a manner so that they are different from each other, as well as from the preceding eight vowels. An appropriate placement of these six vowels on the vowel diagram shown in Figure 7 would be as follows: /ɪ/ front-high, /ɛ/ front-mid, /ɚ/ central-mid, /ɝ/ central-mid, /ʊ/ back-high, and /ɔ/ back-mid.

However, this placement would create a serious phonological problem because two vowels would have identical specifications; e.g., both /i/ and /ɪ/ would be front-high and /u/ and /ʊ/ would be back-high. Since the English language requires a distinction between the word 'Pete' /pit/, which utilizes the vowel /i/, and the word 'pit' /pɪt/, which distinctly utilizes the vowel /ɪ/, the vowels /i/ and /ɪ/ must be distinguished from each other. Similar distinctions must be maintained between the vowel pair /u/ and /ʊ/ to distinguish

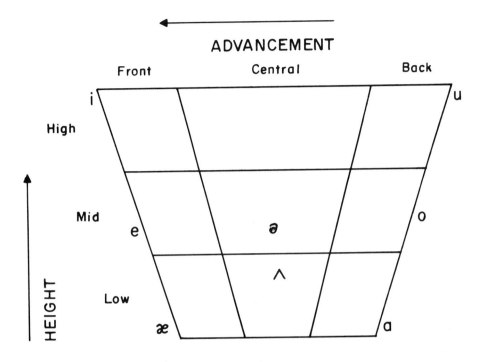

Figure 7. A vowel diagram showing eight English vowels covering the prominent articulatory positions.

the word 'wooed' /wud/ from the word 'would' /wʊd/. This distinction is possible by the inclusion of an additional articulatory feature, tenseness.

Difference between Tense and Lax

It may be recalled that the feature tenseness was defined earlier in the context of English consonants. The definition of this feature as it pertains to vowels essentially remains the same. The tense vowels are produced with added muscle tension while the lax vowels are produced without such tension. Some English vowels are tense, others are lax, and still others are neutral for the feature tenseness.

The phonologically tense vowels are /i, e, ə, ɚ, u, o/ and their lax counterparts are /ɪ, ɛ, (ɜ), ɝ, ʊ, ɔ/, respectively, as shown in Figure 8. The vowels /æ, ʌ, ɑ/ are neutral for the feature tenseness. In Figure 8 the vowel /ɜ/ is in parentheses because of its rare use in American English. With the introduction of the feature tenseness, all fourteen vowels are now phonologically distinct. For example, /i/ is front, high, and tense; /ɪ/ is front, high, and lax; /u/ is back, high, and tense; /ʊ/ is back, high, and lax, etc.

Function of Tenseness Feature

In the English language the feature tenseness is functional in the

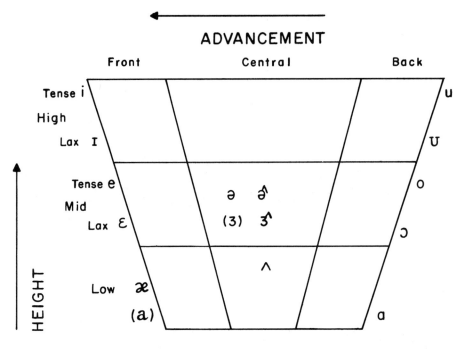

Figure 8.   A vowel diagram showing all English vowels on the advancement, height, and tenseness continua.

formation of open and closed syllables. An open syllable always terminates in a vowel. On the other hand, a closed syllable ends with a consonant. The tense vowels /i/, /u/, and /o/ appear in both open and closed syllables, and their respective lax counterparts generally appear in closed syllables only. The tense vowels /i/, /u/, and /o/ occur not only in closed syllables like 'beat' /bit/, 'boot' /but/, and 'boat' /bot/, respectively, but also in open syllables such as 'bee' /bi/, 'boo' /bu/, and 'bo' /bo/. Their lax counterparts /ɪ/, /ʊ/, and /ɔ/, however, appear only in closed syllables like 'pit' /pɪt/, 'put' /pʊt/, and 'caught' /kɔt/.

Retroflex/Nonretroflex

In English, the two vowels /ɚ/ and /ɝ/ are retroflex because they are produced with an added tongue tip curling, producing the retroflexion quality. All other vowels are nonretroflex.

Round/Unround

Of the fourteen English vowels (shown in Figure 8), some vowels are accompanied by lip rounding, others are not, and still others are neutral for the feature rounding. The round vowels are produced with added lip rounding, and the unround vowels are produced without lip rounding.

In English, the round vowels are, in order of degree of roundedness, /u, ʊ, o, ɔ, ɑ/, and the unround vowels are /i, ɪ, e, ɛ, æ/. The vowels /ə, ɚ, ɝ ʌ/ are neutral for the feature rounding. All round vowels are back and all unround vowels are front.

Vowel Transcription

Because of the nondiscrete nature of vowel articulation, compared with the very discrete nature of consonant articulation, students may find it more difficult to learn the phonetic representations of the vowels when transcribing ongoing speech. Consonant production always involves a direct contact between the articulators, thus providing the transcriber with a more direct kinesthetic reference. In vowel production such reference is vague. After much practice, vowel transcription may be perfected by systematically moving on the vowel diagram from one vowel to another utilizing "key words" (sample words, like the ones in Chapter 2, for demonstrating the use of a letter or symbol) that contain each vowel.

DIPHTHONGS

Definition

A diphthong may be defined as the single or unisyllabic utilization of two otherwise different vowels of a language. In articulatory terms, a diphthong begins by approximating the articulatory position of one vowel and ends by approximating the articulatory position of another vowel. For example, the two independent vowel phonemes /a/, and /ɪ/, appearing in words like 'not' /nat/ and 'knit' /nɪt/, join together and formulate the diphthong /aɪ/, as in the words 'I' /aɪ/, 'bye' /baɪ/, and 'tie' /taɪ/. The vowel /a/ used in the diphthong /aɪ/ does not often occur as an independent vowel in American English. The remaining four diphthongs are /eɪ/, /aʊ/, /ɔɪ/, and /oʊ/.

The articulatory complexity of these diphthongs may be revealed by the fact that, at the beginning of their production, they contain the articulatory dimensions of the first vowel, but their target is the articulatory dimension of the second vowel. Thus, /eɪ/ is the summation of /e/ and /ɪ/, /aɪ/ is the summation of /a/ and /ɪ/, and so on. In the production of diphthongs, the articulators move very rapidly from one articulatory position to another, sometimes involving totally opposing tongue movements.

The classification system of vowels, in terms of the articulatory features of tongue advancement, tongue height, and tenseness, cannot be directly applied to diphthongs because of the complexities involved in their production. When approached from the unitary point of view, i.e., from the view that diphthongs are independent phonemic units rather than a combination of two different units (vowels), they require a more complex phonetic classification because the initiating target is one vowel but the terminating target is another vowel.

Tongue Movements

The following tongue movements are necessary for the realization of the five American English diphthongs:

Diphthong	Tongue movement	
/eɪ/	(a)	from front to front
	(b)	from tense to lax
	(c)	from mid to high
/aɪ/	(a)	from front to front
	(b)	from low to high
/aʊ/	(a)	from front to back
	(b)	from low to high
/ɔɪ/	(a)	from mid to high
	(b)	from lax to lax
	(c)	from back to front
/oʊ/	(a)	from tense to lax
	(b)	from mid to high
	(c)	from back to back

The direction of the change in tongue movement is somewhat predictable. For example, in terms of the feature tenseness, all five diphthongs show a tendency for moving from tense to lax (as in /eɪ/) or lax to lax (as in /ɔɪ/), but not from lax to tense. In terms of tongue advancement, diphthongs are capable of movement from front to front (as in /eɪ/), back to back (as in /oʊ/), back to front (as in /ɔɪ/), and front to back (as in /aʊ/). Finally, in terms of tongue height, although the diphthongs start at either the mid or low tongue positions, they all terminate in the high tongue position. English diphthongs do not terminate in any tongue position other than high. For examination, it may be seen that /eɪ/, /oʊ/, and /ɔɪ/ go from mid to high, and /aɪ/ and /aʊ/ go from low to high.

Thus, we can establish two general principles regarding the utilization of diphthongs:

1. Diphthongs involve an appreciable amount of tongue body movement within the perimeter of one syllable.
2. The direction of the movement of the tongue in terms of its advancement, height, and tension is determined by rules.

EXERCISES

Fill in the Blanks

1. The feature advancement divides vowels into _____.
2. The feature height divides vowels into _____.

3. The feature tenseness divides some English vowels into
    _____.
4. /i/ is a _____, _____ English vowel.
5. /ə/ is a _____ English vowel.
6. A unisyllabic utilization of two independent vowels is known as a
    _____.
7. In the production of /ɔɪ/ the initiating target is _____ and the
    terminating target is _____.

True or False

_____ 1. /o/ is a back-central voiceless vowel.
_____ 2. /ɪ/ is a lax back-high vowel.
_____ 3. /ɔ/ is a lax back-mid vowel.
_____ 4. The American English vowel diagram does not have a vowel in the
         high-mid position.
_____ 5. There are nine diphthongs in American English.

Multiple Choice

_____ 1. The vowel /u/ is:
          a. front-high
          b. back-low
          c. back-high
_____ 2. The vowel /æ/ is:
          a. front-high
          b. front-low
          c. back-low
_____ 3. The lax counterpart of /e/ is:
          a. /ɔ/
          b. /æ/
          c. /ɛ/
_____ 4. Tense vowels appear in the following types of syllables:
          a. open
          b. closed
          c. open and closed
_____ 5. The tongue movements and tension in the production of diph-
         thongs are:
          a. determined by rules
          b. not rule-oriented
          c. unpredictable

Phonemic Transcription: Advancement

Transcribe phonemically using advancement of vowels as the criterion.

Front /i, ɪ, e, ɛ, æ/

1. each _____
2. eat _____
3. meat _____
4. lean _____
5. he _____
6. key _____

7. it _____
8. inside _____
9. big _____
10. rigid _____

11. age _____
12. acre _____
13. beige _____
14. gaze _____
15. lay _____
16. they _____

17. egg _____
18. end _____
19. pet _____
20. head _____

21. at _____
22. apple _____
23. bat _____
24. that _____

Mid /ə, ʌ, ɚ, ɝ/

25. again _____
26. about _____
27. telephone _____
28. potato _____
29. transitive _____

30. up _____
31. us _____
32. but _____
33. cup _____

34. urbane _____
35. earthly _____
36. curse _____
37. nurse _____
38. butter _____
39. tiger _____
40. irk _____
41. burr _____
42. fur _____
43. bird _____
44. shirt _____

Back /u, ʊ, o, ɔ, ɑ/

45. ooze _____
46. oops _____
47. cool _____
48. fruit _____
49. blue _____
50. shoe _____

51. foot _____
52. put _____

53. oasis _____
54. open _____
55. motor _____
56. rotate _____
57. toe _____
58. go _____

59. awful _____
60. all _____
61. caught _____
62. ball _____
63. straw _____
64. law _____

65. are _____
66. argue _____
67. hot _____
68. cot _____
69. spa _____
70. mama _____

Phonemic Transcription: Height

Transcribe phonemically using height of vowels as the criterion.

High /i, ɪ, u, ʊ/

1. eat _____
2. Easter _____
3. seem _____
4. beat _____
5. see _____
6. free _____

7. injure _____
8. impossible _____
9. sister _____
10. fist _____

11. umlaut _____
12. oolong _____
13. fool _____
14. room _____
15. flew _____
16. true _____

17. book _____
18. shook _____

Mid /e, ɛ, ə, ð, ɝ, o, ɔ/

19. angel _____
20. ancient _____
21. sale _____
22. trail _____
23. say _____
24. may _____

25. engine _____
26. envy _____
27. bed _____
28. set _____

29. announce _____
30. another _____
31. gelatin _____
32. tomato _____

33. urgent _____
34. urge _____
35. curry _____
36. servant _____
37. father _____
38. sister _____

39. earth _____

40. heard _____

41. occurred _____

42. ozone _____

43. omit _____

44. dope _____

45. rope _____

46. no _____

47. show _____

48. orange _____

49. organ _____

50. fought _____

51. thought _____

52. paw _____

53. claw _____

Low /æ, ʌ, ɑ/

54. ant _____

55. add _____

56. back _____

57. pack _____

58. untied _____

59. unwanted _____

60. cut _____

61. shut _____

62. onset _____

63. olive _____

64. not _____

65. hearth _____

Orthographic Counterparts: Tenseness

Write the orthographic counterparts of the following phonemically transcribed words using tenseness of vowels as the criterion.

Tense /i, e, ə, ɚ, u, o/

1. /ikɑnəmi/
2. /hit/
3. /ni/
4. /ek/ or /eɪk/
5. /nel/ or /neɪl/
6. /bæle/
7. /əʃemd/ or /əʃeɪmd/
8. /əbaʊt/
9. /ɚnɪŋ/
10. /sɚdʒɪn/
11. /mʌðɚ/
12. /udəlz/
13. /but/
14. /gru/
15. /oke/ or /oʊkeɪ/
16. /kop/ or /koʊp/
17. /flo/ or /floʊ/

Lax /ɪ, ɛ, ɝ, ʊ, ɔ/

18. /ɪgnaɪt/
19. /kɪs/

20. /ɛdʒ/
21. /bɛt/
22. /ɝn/
23. /klɝk/

24. /lʊk/
25. /ɔsəm/
26. /tɔl/
27. /sɔ/

Orthographic Counterparts: Retroflexion

Write the orthographic counterparts of the following phonemically transcribed words using retroflexion as the criterion.

Nonretroflex /ə/

1. /ɔgəst/
2. /nɛsəsɛrɪ/
3. /ɔfən/
4. /frikwənt/
5. /əsoʃiet/ or /əsosiet/
6. /kɑləm/
7. /səfaɪs/
8. /ətɝnɪ/

9. /ədvɝs/
10. /əlɛdʒ/
11. /əlaɪd/ or /ælaɪd/
12. /əluf/
13. /həvænə/
14. /aɪowə/
15. /dɪfθɪriə/

Retroflex /ɚ/

16. /tugɛðɚ/
17. /ɪŋkjubetɚ/
18. /ʌðɚ/

19. /ræðɚ/
20. /dɔtɚ/

Phonemic Transcription: Diphthongs

Transcribe phonemically using diphthongs as the criterion.

/aɪ/

1. ice _____
2. eyes _____
3. I _____
4. isle _____
5. dime _____
6. time _____
7. dice _____
8. bite _____
9. kite _____
10. tie _____
11. sigh _____
12. lie _____
13. pie _____

/aʊ/

14. ounce _____
15. ouch! _____
16. outside _____
17. owl _____
18. about _____
19. house _____
20. mouse _____
21. prowl _____
22. cloud _____
23. cow _____
24. how _____
25. now _____
26. plough _____

/eɪ/

27. ace _____
28. aid _____
29. ache _____
30. aim _____
31. ate _____
32. tape _____
33. safe _____
34. bait _____
35. late _____
36. pray _____
37. day _____
38. bay _____
39. stray _____

/ou/

40. oak _____
41. oar _____
42. oat _____
43. toes _____
44. boat _____
45. coat _____
46. throat _____
47. goal _____
48. slow _____
49. blow _____
50. mow _____

/ɔɪ/

51. oyster _____
52. ointment _____
53. oil _____
54. avoid _____

55. choice _____
56. hoist _____
57. poise _____

58. boy _____
59. toy _____
60. decoy _____

Chapter ACOUSTIC
5 PHONETICS

The study of certain limited aspects of the acoustics of speech will enhance our understanding of some of the principal components of speech sounds. Recent work in speech science research shows that certain articulatory properties of speech sounds (e.g., voicing) have corresponding specific and unique acoustic correlates. In order to determine the important articulatory aspects of speech production, it is crucial to determine the acoustic elements associated with them. For example, the fact that labial stops /p, b/ are articulated differently from alveolar stops /t, d/, and that alveolar stops /t, d/ are articulated differently from velar stops /k, g/, can be verified by examining the acoustic representations of these three pairs of consonants. In addition, the fact that the first consonant in each pair is voiceless and the second consonant is voiced also can be acoustically verified. If, by

examining acoustic details, we learn that labial stops have prominent low frequency components, then we can measure these components accurately and obtain an exact acoustic measure of the labiality feature. The acoustic correlates of all other articulatory features can be similarly determined. Such measurements can be obtained from the normal speech patterns of individuals of varying ages and can be utilized as norms for comparing similar measures obtained from persons with defective speech.

ACOUSTIC PROPERTIES:
Frequency, Time, and Amplitude

Definition

Speech sounds are comprised of different proportions of the frequency, time, and amplitude components. The *frequency* of a speech sound refers to the rate of vibration of the vocal folds during the production of that sound. Speech sounds are either primarily high frequency, primarily low frequency, or a combination of both. *Time*, as it relates to the acoustics of a speech sound, refers to the number of milliseconds necessary for the speech sound to be produced. Some speech sounds are known to take twice as much time as others to complete their production. *Amplitude* refers to the energy with which the vocal folds vibrate during the production of a speech sound. Certain speech sounds are produced with a minimal amount of energy vibrating the vocal folds and consequently are referred to as sounds of low amplitude. Other sounds are produced only when a great deal of energy is used to vibrate the vocal folds and are referred to as high amplitude sounds.

Measurement

The three acoustic properties of speech sounds—frequency, time, and amplitude—can be visually examined with the help of electronic equipment known as a *sound spectrograph*. This equipment is able to display the acoustic properties of speech sounds on a graph known as a *sound spectrogram* or sonogram. Figure 9 shows a sample sound spectrogram on which has been superimposed a grid for measuring the frequency, time, and amplitude of speech. The

abscissa in this figure represents time, the ordinate represents frequency, and the relative darkness of the bands represents amplitude.

In the production of speech sounds, the low, mid, and high frequency regions are amplified and attenuated (dampened) differently. The frequency region that is significantly amplified for a continuous period of time is known as a *formant frequency*. A sound spectrogram shows several of these formants arranged from the low to the high frequency ends. The formant at the lowest end having a continuous stretch of darkness (in Figure 9, the area closest to the abscissa) is called the first formant and is denoted by F_1. The next higher bandwidth with a noticeable stretch of darkness is the second formant, denoted by F_2; the third higher bandwidth is the third formant, denoted by F_3; and so on.

ANALYSIS OF VOWELS

Differences between the vowels of English can be explained in terms of the different locations and widths of the formant frequencies. For example, observation of the sound spectrogram of the vowel /ɑ/ (see Chapter 7, Module 45) shows that the distance between F_1 and F_2 is negligible but the distance between F_2 and F_3 is relatively large. The formant frequencies of the vowel /ɑ/ are unique; i.e., no

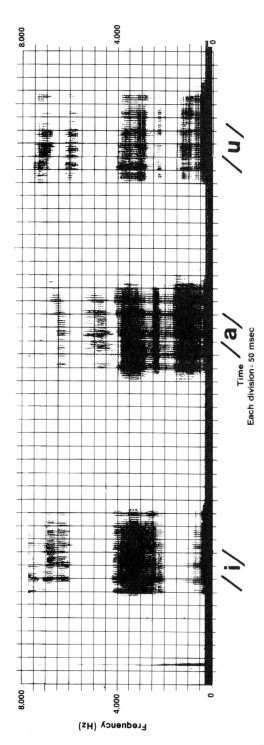

Figure 9. A sample sound spectrogram for vowels /i, a, u/. A measuring scale for frequency and time has been superimposed for instant determination of frequency and duration components of the speech sounds.

other English vowel will have formant frequencies identical to it.

An examination of the formant frequencies of the vowel /i/ in Figure 9 (also see Chapter 7, Module 41) shows that its first formant (F_1) is around 250 Hz and its second formant (F_2) is around 2,250 Hz. These values are obtained by determining the center of the width of each formant, also known as the *center* or *mid-formant frequency*. Thus, a gap of 2,000 Hz exists between the centers of formants F_1 and F_2. To the contrary, an examination of the formant frequencies of the vowel /ɑ/ reveals substantially differing values. The first formant of /ɑ/ is around 750 Hz and the second formant is around 1,250 Hz. The gap between the centers of the first and second formants is thus only 500 Hz. It is known that the vowels /ɑ/ and /i/ are at the two extremes of the articulatory vowel diagram (see Figure 7). The production of the vowel /ɑ/ is accomplished by the maximal opening of the vocal tract, whereas the production of the vowel /i/ is accomplished by minimal opening. The distance between F_1 and F_2 is large for the vowel /i/ but small for the vowel /ɑ/. Therefore, the greater the opening of the vocal tract, the less the distance between F_1 and F_2, and vice versa.

The center frequencies of the first and second formants of ten selected English vowels have been plotted in Figure 10 to show if a relationship exists between these mid-formant frequencies and the articulatory dimensions of tongue height and advancement. The results demonstrate a resemblance between the plotting and the shape of the articulatory vowel diagram, with F_1 showing a relationship with tongue height and F_2 showing a relationship with tongue advancement.

For students of speech and hearing, such information regarding the formant frequencies and their relationships is valuable. Sound spectrograms of defective speech patterns can be made and the exact gap between F_1 and F_2 can be measured. This measurement can then be compared with that of a normal speaker, and the amount of deviancy can be determined.

The acoustic interpretations of frequency, time, and amplitude become increasingly complex when vowels are produced in the context of words rather than in isolation.

ANALYSIS OF CONSONANTS

Just as there is a correlation between the formant frequencies of vowels and the articulatory dimensions of tongue height and tongue advancement, it may be hypothesized that a similar relationship exists between the formant frequencies of consonants and their articulatory dimensions. Because of the large number of English consonants and their great

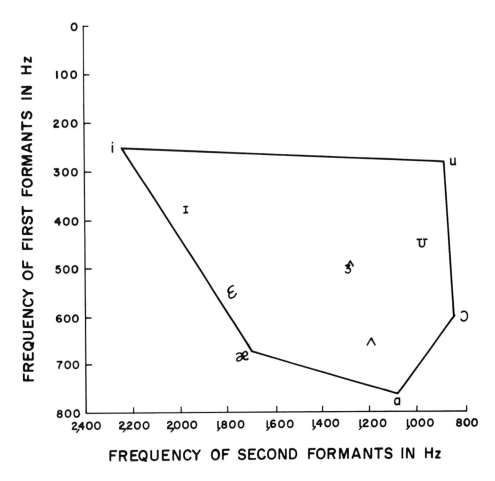

Figure 10. An acoustic vowel diagram showing the plotting of F_1 and F_2 frequencies of ten selected English vowels in the word-medial position.

variety and complexity, the articulatory features necessary for their distinction are greater than those required for vowels. The acoustic characteristics that correspond with the articulatory features of voicing, place, and manner are outlined below.

Voicing Feature

In the articulatory description of voicing, it has been stated several

times that the vocal folds do not vibrate in the production of voiceless consonants and do vibrate in the production of voiced consonants. The feature voicing in English helps to distinguish the voiceless phonemes /p, t, k, f, θ, s, ʃ, tʃ, h/ from the voiced phonemes /b, d, g, v, ð, z, ʒ, dʒ, m, n, ŋ, j, r, l, w/. Spectrographic analysis shows that the vocal fold vibrations in the production of the consonant sounds are acoustically represented. The /t/ phoneme, for example, is voiceless, and the sound spectrogram shows a short burst of energy with no evidence of any definable glottal wave characteristics (see Chapter 7, Module 3). On the other hand, the sound spectrogram of the /d/ phoneme, which is voiced, shows a glottal wave tracing before the release of the plosive burst (see Chapter 7, Module 7). Thus, it may be stated that the voiced consonants show traces of vocal fold vibrations whereas the voiceless consonants only show evidence of a burst of air.

Place Features (Front and Back)

For simplicity's sake, the place of articulation is divided only into front and back to denote the corresponding portions of the oral cavity. In English the front consonants /p, b, m, w, f, v, θ, ð, t, d, n, s, z, r, l/are distinguished from the back consonants /j, tʃ, dʒ, ʃ, ʒ, k, g, ŋ, h/. Observation of sonograms of all consonants shows that front consonants have energy concentration areas that are clearly definable either in the low frequency region or in the high frequency region. On the other hand, back consonants generally have energy concentration areas in both low and high frequency regions. Thus, if a sound spectrogram evidences a clearly low or a clearly high frequency energy concentration, we may conclude that the consonants have been produced in the front of the mouth.

However, when the energy is found simultaneously in the low and high frequencies, we may conclude that the consonants have been produced in the back of the mouth.

Manner Features

There are several aspects of the manner of articulation category. In this text we have chosen four manner categories for describing English consonants: sonorancy, continuancy, sibilancy, and nasality.

Sonorancy

The feature sonorancy in English helps to distinguish the sonorants /j, r, l, w, m, n, ŋ/ from the non-sonorants /p, b, f, v, θ, ð, s, z, t, d, tʃ, dʒ, ʃ, ʒ, k, g, h/. The sonorant consonants have vowel-like qualities. The formant structure of sonorants is therefore similar to that of vowels. Also, sonorants show marked acoustic duration, low frequency resonance, and glottal wave representation similar to that of vowels. The sonorant /w/ is similar in its acoustic representation to the vowel /u/ except that /w/ has a lower first formant. The sonorant /j/ is similar to the vowel /i/ except again that /j/ has a lower first formant. It is for this reason perhaps that sonorants are also referred to as semivowels.

Continuancy

The feature continuancy distinguishes the continuants /f, v, θ, ð, s, z, ʃ, ʒ, h/ from the stops /p, b, t, d, tʃ, dʒ, k, g/. The term "continuancy" implies relatively longer duration than stops. Besides being longer in duration than stops, continuants also have energy components in higher frequencies than stops do. Because of the complex acoustic and articulatory characteristics of the feature continuancy, continuant phonemes are some of the most frequently misarticulated phonemes and also some of the last to be acquired when children develop language.

Sibilancy

The feature sibilancy distinguishes the sibilant phonemes /s, z, ʃ, ʒ, tʃ, dʒ/ from the nonsibilant phonemes /p, b, t, d, k, g, f, v, θ, ð, j, r, l, w, m, n, ŋ, h/. Sibilants have energy components in the high frequencies and also have longer duration than any other consonant category. Within the sibilant category, phones /s, z/ have energy concentration in one broad high frequency bandwidth with their center frequency around 4,000 Hz. The sibilants /ʃ, ʒ, tʃ, dʒ/ have energy concentration divided into two bandwidths, both in the high frequency region, one bandwidth with a center frequency at 3,500 Hz

and the other with a center frequency at 6,500 Hz.

Nasality

The feature nasality helps to distinguish the nasals /m, n, ŋ/ from the non-nasals /p, b, f, v, θ, ð, t, d, s, z, ʃ, ʒ, tʃ, dʒ, k, g, j, r, l, w, h/. In the production of nasal consonants, the nasal cavity resonates in conjunction with the oral cavity. The effect of the coupling of these two cavities has a certain acoustic trait that is found in all nasal consonants. This property is called *antiresonance*. Antiresonance is an appreciable loss of amplitude in certain well defined frequency regions. For example, the antiresonance or appreciable energy loss for /m/ is found at 750 Hz and 1,250 Hz, for /n/ at 1,450 Hz and 2,200 Hz, and for /ŋ/ above 3,000 Hz.

The foregoing discussion enables us to verify the speech production parameters by using measurements in the acoustic domains. What we have seen so far is that each articulatory class has its own unique acoustic representation. In the following chapter the perceptual aspects of speech sounds are discussed with an effort to find a relationship between the articulatory and perceptual aspects.

EXERCISES

Fill in the Blanks

1. The articulatory fact that labial stops /p, b/ are different from alveolar stops /t, d/ can be verified by observing their _____ representations.

2. The acoustic properties of speech sounds can be visually examined with the help of electronic equipment known as a _____.

3. The sonogram presents the acoustic analysis of speech in the three dimensions _____, _____, and _____.

4. The frequency region that is significantly amplified for a continuous period of time is known as _____.

5. The feature voicing in English helps to distinguish the voiceless phonemes /f, θ, s/ from their voiced counterparts _____.

6. The formant structure of sonorants is similar to that of _____.

7. A sibilant consonant has energy concentration in the _____ frequency range.

8. In the production of nasal consonants, the nasal cavity resonates in conjunction with the _____.

9. An appreciable loss of amplitude in certain well defined frequency regions is known as _____.

True or False

_____ 1. The abscissa on the sound spectrogram represents frequency.

_____ 2. The relative darkness of the bands on the sound spectrogram represents amplitude.

_____ 3. In English the front consonants /p, b, m/ are distinguished from the back consonants /t, d, n/.

_____ 4. The sonorant /w/ is similar in its acoustic representation to the vowel /i/.

_____ 5. Continuants are longer in duration than stops.

Multiple Choice

_____ 1. The formant at the lowest end of the sound spectrogram having a continuous stretch of darkness is called the:
   a. third formant
   b. second formant
   c. first formant

_____ 2. A comparison of the F_1/F_2 gaps for the vowels /i/ and /ɑ/ shows that the gap is:
   a. large for /i/ and small for /ɑ/
   b. large for /ɑ/ and small for /i/
   c. the same for both /i/ and /ɑ/

_____ 3. Consonants having energy concentration areas that are clearly in the low or high frequency regions are:
   a. front consonants
   b. back consonants
   c. voiced consonants

Chapter 6 PERCEPTUAL PHONETICS

In speech production, the speaker establishes a continuous synchrony between the *cortical* (from the brain) commands and the articulatory tools. A normal speaker of a language demonstrates a perfect concordance between his cortical commands and their execution, but a person with speech problems may not. In studying speech perception, we may ask whether the brain utilizes one set of commands for the articulatory mechanisms and another set of commands for the perception of speech sounds, or whether it has overlapping sets of controls for both the articulatory and speech perception mechanisms. It may be hypothesized that an economical system would prefer the latter to the former model.

PROPOSED MODEL FOR CORTICAL INTERPRETATION OF SPEECH SIGNALS: MINI-INTERPRETERS

An examination of the articulatory and acoustic features of the phoneme has given us adequate insight into the property of the stimulus reaching the human ear. When the speech signal reaches the ear, it is conveyed to the brain via a transportation system referred to as the *auditory pathway*. The brain then makes certain decisions about the incoming speech signals, enabling it to identify them.

Figure 11 attempts to explain the process of this cortical decision making. It is a simplified model showing the mapping of the speech signal produced by the speaker,

Speech
interpreter
device

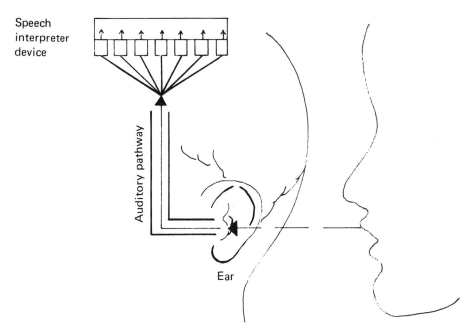

Auditory pathway

Ear

Figure 11. A schematic diagram showing the flow of acoustic energy from the speaker's mouth to the listener's brain and being understood by the listener via the seven mini-interpreters or distinctive features.

received by the ear, and transmitted to the brain. The brain is considered to be equipped with a "speech interpreter" device. The function of this device is to make an instant decision regarding the identity of the speech signal. This speech interpreter device can be thought of as a group of "mini-interpreters" which make decisions about the different properties of the signal and collectively interpret it. In Figure 11, we have proposed seven mini-interpreters that the listener utilizes to perceive consonants. We also may propose a group of mini-interpreters utilized in vowel perception.

For example, when the speech sound /p/ produced by the speaker reaches the listener's brain, the

mini-interpreters set to work in somewhat the following fashion:

Mini-interpreter 1: decides if the incoming signal is voiced or voiceless depending on the vocal fold function and interprets the signal as being *voiceless.*

Mini-interpreter 2: decides if the signal is front or back depending on whether it has been produced in the front or the back of the oral cavity and interprets the signal as being *front.*

Mini-interpreter 3: decides if the signal is labial or nonlabial depending on lip involvement and interprets the signal as being *labial.*

Mini-interpreter 4: decides if the

signal is sonorant or obstruent depending on the amount of obstruction in the oral cavity and interprets the signal as being *obstruent*.

Mini-interpreter 5: decides if the signal is stop or continuant depending on its duration and interprets the signal as being *stop*.

Mini-interpreter 6: decides if the signal is sibilant or nonsibilant depending on the prolonged hissing and interprets the signal as being *nonsibilant*.

Mini-interpreter 7: decides if the signal is nasal or oral depending on the participation of the nasal resonance and interprets the signal as being *non-nasal*.

These mini-interpreters work simultaneously and collectively to assign the phonemic label /p/ to the speech signal just processed. In explaining these mini-interpreters we have necessarily entered their decisions in a sequence. However, these decisions register in the brain at the same instant. Because these mini-interpreters are essential elements that help to distinguish one phoneme from another, they are called *distinctive features*.

FACTORS IMPEDING THE CORTICAL PROCESS

The decision-making ability of the mini-interpreters is impeded when: a) the signal becomes distorted before it reaches the ear; b) the listener's hearing is impaired or brain is damaged; or c) the listener is not a native listener of the language.

Signal Distortion

Signal distortion generally implies that the speech signal has been distorted by electronic or other means. Three different signal distortion procedures are described below to show their effect on the distinctive features.

1. Environmental noise of varying loudness influences most drastically the distinctive features front/back and stop/continuant. In severe noise conditions the listener's ability to maintain the distinctions of the front from the back consonant and the stop from the continuant consonant deteriorates.

2. A speech signal consisting of the low, mid, and high frequencies can be electronically manipulated such that the mid and high frequencies are eliminated and only the low frequency is allowed to reach the ear. In such an instance the distinctive features influenced maximally are stop/continuant and sibilant/nonsibilant.

3. Similar elimination of the low and mid frequencies allows only the high frequencies to reach the ear. The features significantly influenced are voiced/voiceless, sonorant/obstruent, and nasal/non-nasal. Change in the duration

of the speech signal influences the distinctive features stop/continuant, sibilant/nonsibilant, and voiced/voiceless.

Hearing Impairment and Brain Damage

Hearing problems can be in the low frequency domain, in the mid frequency domain, in the high frequency domain, or in any and all combinations of these. Persons with high frequency hearing loss are unable to maintain the distinctions of front/back place, stop/continuant, and sibilant/nonsibilant. On the other hand, persons with low frequency hearing loss are unable to maintain the distinctions between the features voiced/voiceless, sonorant/obstruent, and nasal/non-nasal.

When speech perception ability is affected because of brain damage, some of the mini-interpreters may cease to carry out their function of interpreting incoming speech signals. This malfunction leads to the person's inability to perceive the otherwise greatly familiar speech sounds. Speech therapy with persons having speech perception difficulty (aphasics) may result in the mini-interpreter regaining some of its usage.

Non-native Listeners

Listeners of any two languages may share a number of distinctive features and may differ by others.

For example, Figure 12 shows that the listeners of Hindi and English have a number of mini-interpreters in common. The figure also shows that both the English and the Hindi listeners also have some additional mini-interpreters that are special to their language: e.g., the mini-interpreter that decides if the speech signal is aspirated/unaspirated is specific to the Hindi listener. Because the English listener does not possess this mini-interpreter, he perceives no difference between the two Hindi phonemes /pʰ/ and /p/. The Hindi listener, however, is able to decide that the former phoneme is aspirated and the latter unaspirated.

CHILDREN'S PERCEPTION OF PHONEMES

When children learn to speak and comprehend speech, they utilize the mini-interpreters differently from adults. The younger the child, the smaller the number of mini-interpreters that are activated. As the child grows, more mini-interpreters are added to his perceptual competency. Therefore, a one-year-old child may be unable to distinguish between /s/ and /t/, thus implying that he does not possess the mini-interpreter stop/continuancy that enables the brain to distinguish the continuant /s/ from the stop /t/.

It is very interesting to see young children slowly acquire the use of these mini-interpreters. Until the

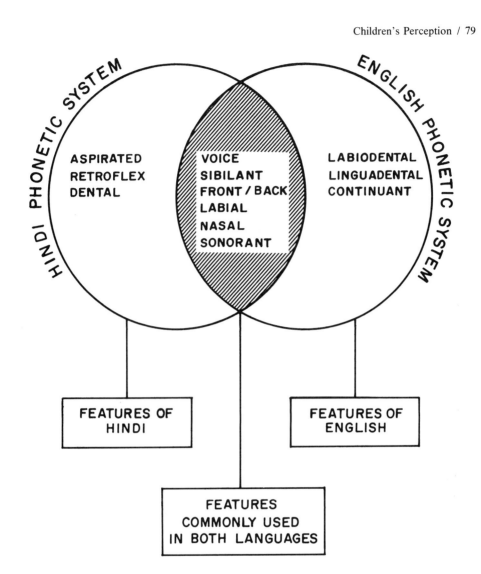

Figure 12. A comparison of phonetic features in two different languages (English and Hindi), showing the features common to these languages by the shaded area of the overlapping circles and the phonetic features unique to these languages by the unshaded areas of these two circles.

age of eighteen months, our daughter said "mice" for "nice." We tried to determine through various means whether the /m-n/ confusion was only in her productive repertoire or whether she perceived "mice" for the auditory stimulus "nice." Our conclusion was that at that age her confusion extended to both the productive and perceptual levels. When we said, "Kalpa, mice" and "Kalpa, nice," her reactions were not different. Presently she is twenty-two months old and still says "mice" for "nice." However, we believe that she has perceptually acquired the difference between

/m/ and /n/ because when we say, "Kalpa, mice," she gives us a look indicating that something strange was said. To the contrary, when we say, "Kalpa, nice," she smiles.

These reactions imply that initially at age eighteen months she was unable to distinguish between labial/nonlabial for the nasal group of consonants. However, at some point between the ages of eighteen and twenty-two months, she acquired the use of the mini-interpreter that made such a distinction possible. Literature pertaining to the development of children's phonology has shown in very general terms the chronology of the acquisition of these mini-interpreters by children. The features learned first are labial/nonlabial, nasal/oral, and voiced/voiceless, and the features learned last are stop/continuant and sibilant/nonsibilant.

VERIFICATION OF MINI-INTERPRETERS VIA PSYCHOLOGICAL TESTS

What job the mini-interpreters do and how well they do it has been determined by a number of psychological tests. In one such test, two phonemes in a pair are compared with each other by a group of listeners, and the similarity between them is assessed. The results of such tests show that the judgments made by listeners are directly based on the number of mini-interpreters shared by the pair of phonemes. The greater the number of features shared by the two phonemes, the more similar are the phonemes. Also, the fewer the features shared, the less similar are the phonemes. For example, the phonemes in the pair /p, b/ have in common the mini-interpreters labial, front, obstruent, stop, nonsibilant, and non-nasal. The only feature distinguishing these two phonemes is voicing. The mini-interpreter voiced/voiceless decides that /p/ is voiceless and /b/ is voiced. However, the phoneme pair /p, ŋ/ shares only two mini-interpreters: stop and nonsibilant. Consequently, the first pair /p, b/ is invariably rated by the listeners as a more similar pair than the second one /p, ŋ/. The results of a number of psychological tests show that these mini-interpreters are activated when people make any judgments regarding the comparison of phonemes.

EXERCISES

Fill in the Blanks

1. Signal distortion generally implies that the speech signal has been distorted by _____ means.

2. The features learned last by young children developing language are
_____ and _____.

3. Of the two phoneme pairs /p, b/ and /p, ŋ/, the phonemes in the
_____ pair are rated by listeners as being more similar.

True or False

_____ 1. The decisions made by the mini-interpreters register in the brain in
an orderly sequence.

_____ 2. In the presence of environmental noise, the listener's ability to
maintain the distinction of the front from the back consonant
deteriorates.

_____ 3. Two independent languages do not have distinctive features in
common.

_____ 4. Environmental noise affects man's communication process by
distorting the speech signal.

Multiple Choice

_____ 1. The feature sibilancy would be affected if the following frequencies were not permitted to reach the ear:
a. low
b. mid
c. high

_____ 2. When the components of a phoneme pair differ by one distinctive
feature they are perceived as being:
a. most similar
b. most dissimilar
c. the same

Chapter 7 DYNAMIC ASPECTS OF SPEECH PRODUCTION

This chapter is designed to depict speech sounds while they are being produced naturally. The purpose is to make available the direct viewing of the phenomenon of speech production in order to facilitate the thorough understanding of the differences and similarities in the articulation of consonants and vowels produced under varying contextual influences.

With a few exceptions, each English consonant is presented at the initial, medial, and final positions of meaningful words. Each of the vowels and diphthongs is presented at the medial position of meaningful words such that it is preceded and followed by different consonants.

The presentation of the "total" picture of phoneme production in context is called a *module*. With certain limitations, these modules are the self-contained complete story of a sound of speech as it is being produced. A total of fifty-six

modules are in this chapter, forty depicting the consonants and sixteen depicting the vowels and diphthongs. The readers (viewers) are advised to examine them in detail, first one at a time and then comparatively.

For example, Module 1 depicts the English phoneme /p/ at the word-initial and word-final positions, and Module 2 depicts /p/ at the word-initial and word-medial positions. A perusal of these two modules independently and simultaneously provides a better understanding of the phoneme /p/.

Analytic comments are presented for seventeen selected modules: twelve modules involving consonants, three involving vowels, and two involving diphthongs. These comments focus on certain dimensions of speech production and speech acoustics that the authors consider important. The remaining thirty-nine modules can be studied by following the patterns established in the analyses of the seventeen modules. Readers are requested to utilize the remaining modules for practice in analyzing and describing the dynamic aspects of speech production. Additional practice is provided by the phoneme identification exercises at the end of the chapter.

Before we present the analytic comments, some information regarding the formation of these modules needs to be explained. Each module contains three different representations of a given speech sound: 1) the strips of picture films, 2) the schematic drawing of the tongue movements, and 3) the sound spectrogram.

STRIPS OF PICTURE FILMS

First, it must be noted that these strips of picture films are in absolute continuation. The only reason that some are presented in two or sometimes three different strips is the limitation of space. One uninterrupted strip for the word /pɑp/ would have been too long for any reasonable symmetric presentation. The bottom of the first strip continues at the top of the second strip.

Second, it must be noted that these strips have been edited for presentation. The editing has been done only at the beginning and at the end of a word. Because of the long duration of prephonatory articulatory gestures, the part of the film strip between the neutral stage of the articulators and the first trace of acoustic energy is not included in a compact module. However, in each module, certain amounts of prephonatory and postphonatory articulatory gestures are included to show that the articulators activate long before the sound is emitted. An examination of Module 13 shows that the first trace of acoustic energy (denoted by the arrow) does not appear until the upper portion of the second strip; the first full strip is devoted to showing the lip movement from the neutral position to the onset of the production of /t/.

Third, it must be noted that on their lefthand margin these picture film strips show the acoustic tracings (sound track) associated with each moment of speech sound production. The arrows point to the general location of the beginning of the sound tracking of each phoneme in a word. It must be understood that these arrows point only to the area of transition, not to the discrete phoneme boundary. A keen student of phonetics will enjoy observing these locations with the help of a magnifying glass.

Finally, it is important to note that, during filming, the words were spoken in isolation, and very naturally, in order to avoid articulatory exaggerations. The picture film strips were made from picture negatives of 35mm high speed motion picture film accompanied by sound track.

SCHEMATIC DIAGRAMS
SHOWING TONGUE MOVEMENTS

Although the high speed motion picture presentations provide a great deal of information regarding the articulatory gestures involved in the production of speech sounds, these pictures primarily emphasize the frontal portion of the mouth. In addition, because these pictures possess an overwhelming amount of detail regarding the movement of the lips, teeth, and tongue, it may not be very easy to visualize the overall function of the tongue—its elasticity, its flexibility, and its limits, all of which contribute to its systematic movements in the oral cavity.

Therefore, a schematic line drawing accompanies each module so as to emphasize the movement of the tongue from one position to another during the production of consonants and vowels. These schematic diagrams are extremely simplified and, therefore, may not be absolutely accurate when examined against cineradiographic data.

It is important to note that in these schematic drawings the tongue position for the vowels is marked by a heavy line and that for the consonants is marked by a thin line.

The arrows create an animation-type impression, showing the starting point and the target for the tongue movements. The position of these arrows, from left to right, indicates the sequencing of the tongue movements. For example,

in Module 1, the first arrow at the extreme left shows the movement of the tongue from the position for consonant /p/ (neutral position) to the position for vowel /ɑ/, and the second arrow shows the movement of the tongue from the position for vowel /ɑ/ to the position for consonant /p/.

A relatively more complex involvement of the tongue movements can be seen in Module 2. In this module the arrow at the extreme left shows the movement of the tongue from the position for /p/ (the neutral position) to the position for /ʌ/, the following arrow shows the tongue movement from /ʌ/ to /p/, and the arrow to the extreme right shows the movement of tongue from /p/ to /ɪ/. Because there are two different vowels in the word /pʌpɪ/, there are two heavy lines.

Schematic diagrams are omitted on modules that have numerous consonant-to-vowel and vowel-to-consonant changes, making a diagram cumbersome and difficult to interpret. Students are encouraged to use the diagrams that are presented as a basis for determining the others.

SOUND SPECTROGRAMS

The third item in these modules is a sound spectrogram of the speech sounds (see Chapter 5). When the speech sound under investigation is a consonant (Modules 1 through 40), the sound spectrogram presented is for the entire word containing that criterion consonant phoneme. However, when the criterion phoneme is a vowel (Modules 41 through 56) the sound spectrogram is only for the vowel in isolation, even though the picture film strips and the schematic diagrams depict the entire key word that contains the criterion vowel phoneme. Although it is possible to obtain sound spectrograms of some consonants in isolation, it is more practical to present them in the context of vowels. For readers of this text, only an introductory idea of formant locations of vowels and energy concentrations of consonants is considered adequate. The sound spectrograms may be examined for gaining this knowledge. On the sound spectrograms, the first arrow at the abscissa shows the beginning of the acoustic places for a phoneme, and the following arrows show the boundaries of the successive phonemes.

MODULES

Consonants

Module 1 /pɑp/

Film Strip The criterion phoneme /p/ is at the initial and final positions of the word /pɑp/. The complete closure of the lips can be seen in the first frame, a slight opening in the second frame, and a full opening pertaining to the target vowel /ɑ/ is seen in the sixth frame. The subsequent nine frames (7 through 15) sustain the lip position exclusively attributable to the vowel /ɑ/. The next seven frames

(16 through 22) gradually show the accomplishment of the final target /p/. Because final stops in English are sometimes unexploded, as in this case, no lip opening can be seen in the final frame.

The three arrows along the side of these strips indicate the general location of the beginning of the sounds. The first arrow indicates the beginning of /p/, the second arrow marks the beginning of /ɑ/, and the third arrow indicates the beginning of /p/. The vowel /ɑ/ is clearly marked in the sound track by waveforms characterized by high amplitude and a repetitive pattern.

Schematic Diagram In the schematic diagram the thin line represents the neutral tongue position for the consonant /p/ (the dotted line represents lip closure); the downward movement of the tongue as it goes from the /p/ position to the /ɑ/ position is represented by the arrow on the left; and the upward movement of the tongue as it travels from the /ɑ/ position back to the /p/ position is represented by the arrow on the right.

Sound Spectrogram The acoustic representation of the word /pɑp/ is shown by the sound spectrogram. The low frequency energy for the phoneme /p/ is followed by almost indistinguishable F_1 and F_2 formant frequencies for the vowel /ɑ/. The F_2 and F_3 frequencies are far apart for this vowel. The final /p/ also shows the presence of low frequency energy.

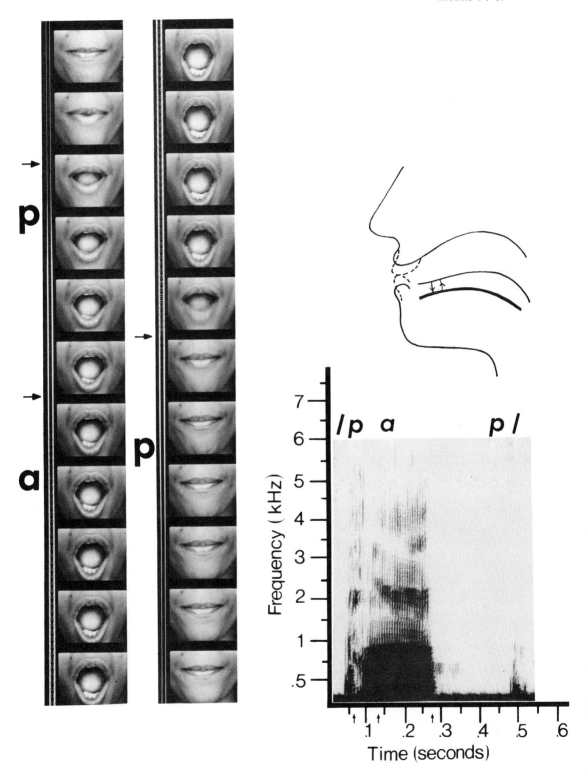

Module 2 /pʌpɪ/

Film Strip The criterion phoneme /p/ is at the initial and medial positions of the word /pʌpɪ/. The first three frames show the complete lip closure for the initial /p/, and the middle four frames (11 through 14) show the complete lip closure for the medial /p/. Because the vowel /ʌ/ following the initial /p/ is more open than the vowel /ɪ/ following the medial /p/, the lip opening following the initial /p/ is relatively greater and more round (see frame 4) than the flat and small lip opening following the medial /p/ (see frame 15). At both the initial and medial positions, the acoustic tracing of /p/ starts after the lips have opened into the vowel.

Schematic Diagram In the schematic drawing of the tongue positions, the first arrow on the left points downward and shows the movement of the tongue from /p/ to /ʌ/. The second arrow shows the movement of the tongue from /ʌ/ to /p/, and the third arrow shows the movement of the tongue from /p/ to /ɪ/. In moving from the consonant to the first vowel, the tongue moves to a central-low position; however, in moving from the consonant to the second vowel, it moves to a front-high position.

Sound Spectrogram The acoustic representation of the word /pʌpɪ/ shows low frequency energy concentration and short duration for both the initial and medial /p/. Before explosion, the stop /p/ is marked by a period of silence in the middle of the sound spectrogram. While F_1, F_2, and F_3 of /ʌ/ are approximately equidistant from each other, /ɪ/ is marked by a low F_1, a high F_2, and a narrow gap between the F_2 and F_3 frequencies.

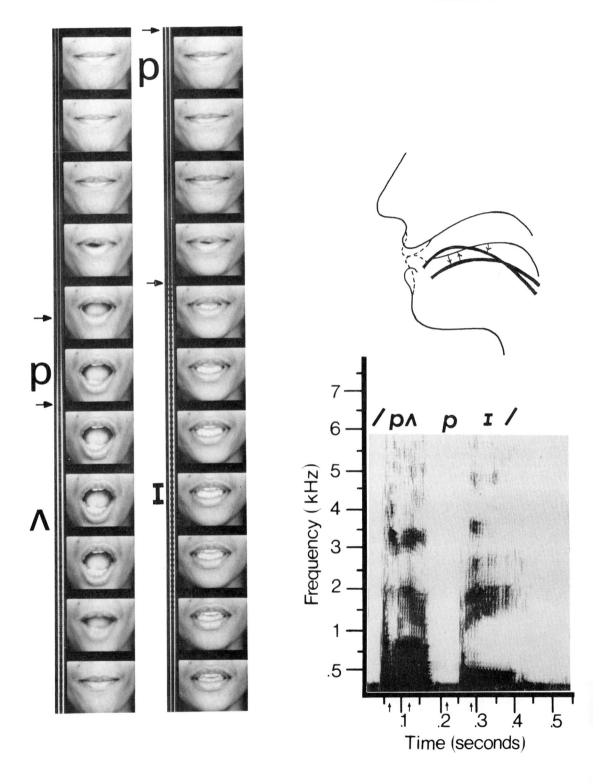

Module 3 /tæt/

Film Strip The criterion phoneme /t/ is at the initial and final positions of the word /tæt/. The wide lip opening starts at the first frame. In the third frame the tongue is seen touching the alveolar ridge. The following vowel /æ/ shows a front-low tongue position with wide and open lips accompanied by considerable excursion of the mandible. The vowel /æ/ is a long vowel used in the stressed position and hence can be seen sustained from frames 7 through 13. Starting with frame 14, the tip of the tongue begins to rise and continues to do so until complete contact is made with the alveolar ridge in frame 16.

Schematic Diagram The schematic drawing of the tongue positions shows that the tongue moves from the alveolar ridge to a front-low vowel, represented by the arrow on the left, and from a front-low vowel to the alveolar ridge, represented by the arrow on the right.

Sound Spectrogram The acoustic representation of the initial /t/ shows a high frequency en-energy concentration with noise-like spectrum followed by a period of silence. The following vowel /æ/ shows the F_1 and F_2 close together. The final consonant /t/ is not clearly seen in this spectrogram because the acoustic energy for the final /t/ remained unexploded.

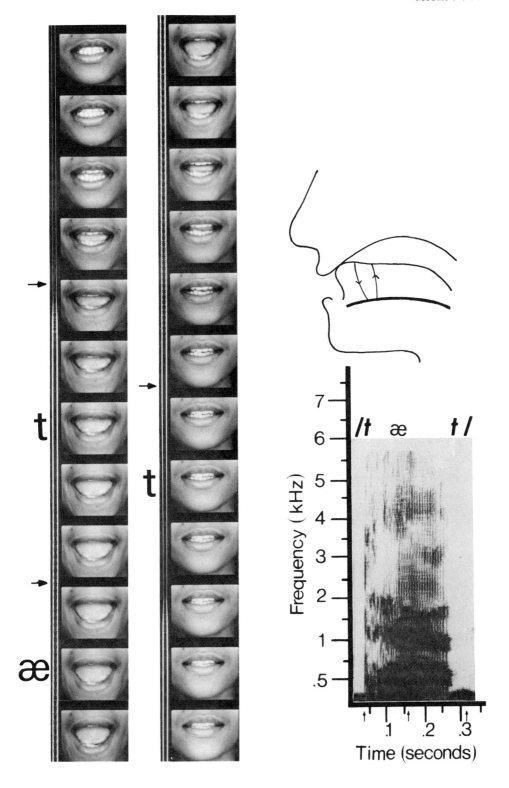

Module 4 /kɪtɪ/

Film Strip The criterion phonemes are /k/ and /t/ at the initial and medial positions, respectively, of the word /kɪtɪ/.
Although it was not possible to
photograph the velar contact of the
tongue, the lip formation for the /k/
phoneme seems to be governed by
the vowel that follows it. Because
the medial vowel and the final
vowel are both /ɪ/, the lips have
assumed a wide and narrow shape.

Schematic Diagram The schematic drawing of the tongue positions shows that the tongue moves:
1) from the velum to the front-
high vowel position indicated
by the arrow on the left, 2) from the
front-high vowel position to the
alveolar ridge consonant position
indicated by the arrow in the
middle, and 3) from the alveolar
ridge position to the front-high
vowel position. At the time the
dorsal portion of the tongue makes
the velar contact for /k/, its front
portion accomplishes the height
and fronting for the following
vowel /ɪ/.

Sound Spectrogram The spectrogram shows the two areas of
energy concentration of the /k/
phoneme, a very high frequency
region and a low frequency region.
The nature of the acoustic spectrum of the /k/ phoneme is noise-
like; i.e., the acoustic spectrum is
without any formant structure. The
duration of the spectrum for /k/ is
longer than that for the voiceless
stops /p/ and /t/. Because of its
duration and its high frequency
energy concentration, consonants
/s/ and /t/ are sometimes mis-
pronounced as /k/.

The vowel /ɪ/ in this utterance has
a short duration. The prominence of
higher formant frequencies of this
vowel is partly a result of the presence of high frequency energy in the
preceding consonant.

The consonant /t/ at the medial
position shows a stoppage of the air
stream, with absence of aspiration
noise, thus confirming that /t/ in the
medial position is unaspirated.

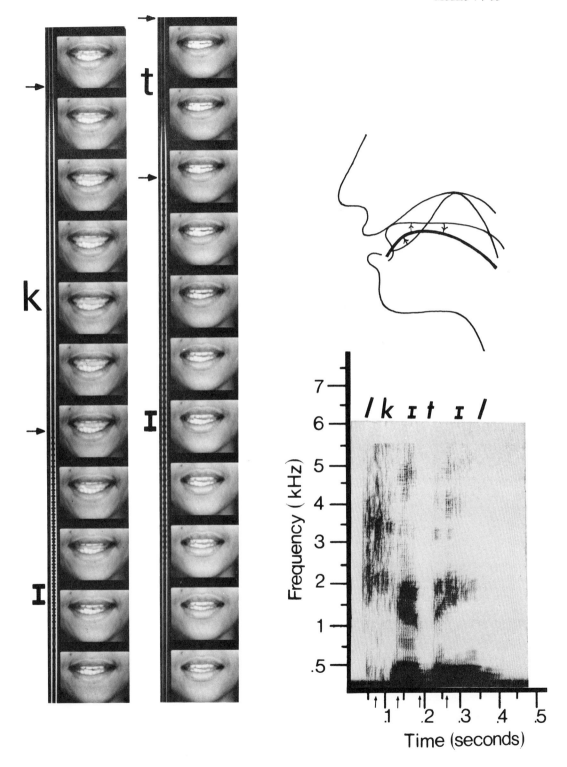

Module 5 /bɪb/

Film Strip The criterion phoneme /b/ is at the initial and final positions of the word /bɪb/.
The first nine frames show the lips
closed. A slight trace of acoustic
energy begins at frame 4, indicating
that, unlike voiceless stops, voiced
stops emit acoustic energy before
the opening at the point of contact.

Frame 10 shows the lip opening,
and, at that point, the nature of the
acoustic tracing changes from a
low frequency, low amplitude /b/ to
a high frequency, high ampltiude
/ɪ/. The maximal opening of the
vowel /ɪ/ can be seen sustained in
frames 12, 13, and 14. Then the lips
gradually close for production of
the final target /b/.

Schematic Diagram The arrows in the schematic diagram
point in the direction of the tongue
from a relatively neutral position
for /b/ to a front-high position for /ɪ/
and back to the position for /b/.

Sound Spectrogram Because
of the low frequency energy of the
initial and final /b/ phonemes, the
acoustic indication of their presence can be traced only in the
second formant transition of /ɪ/.
Because of the high frequency
nature of /ɪ/, its F_2 shows considerable downward movement,
thus signaling the presence of a low
frequency consonant.

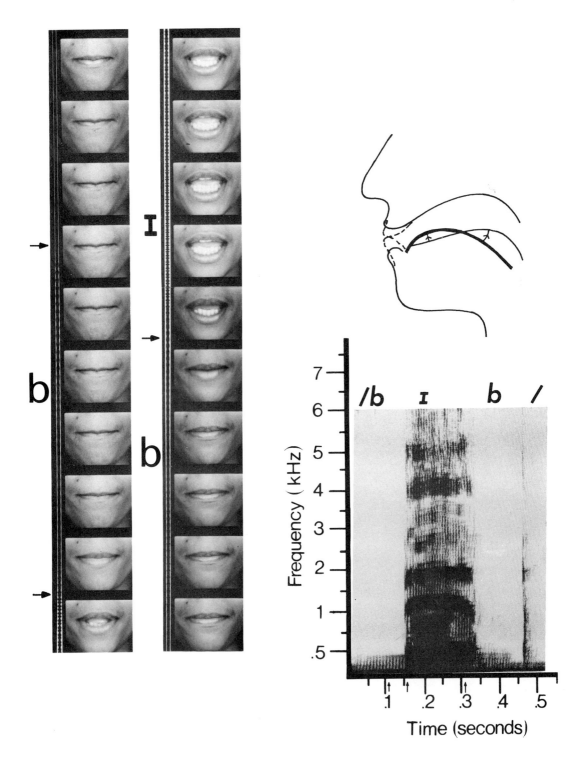

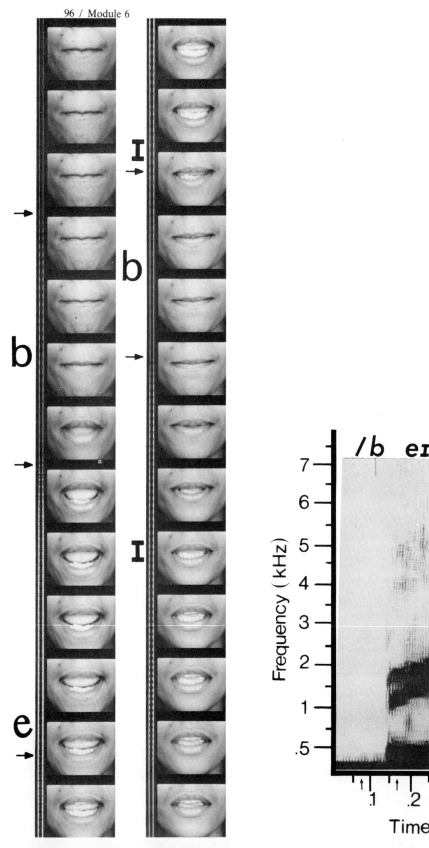

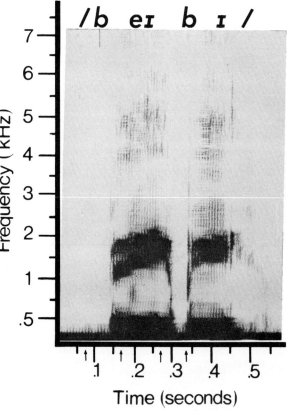

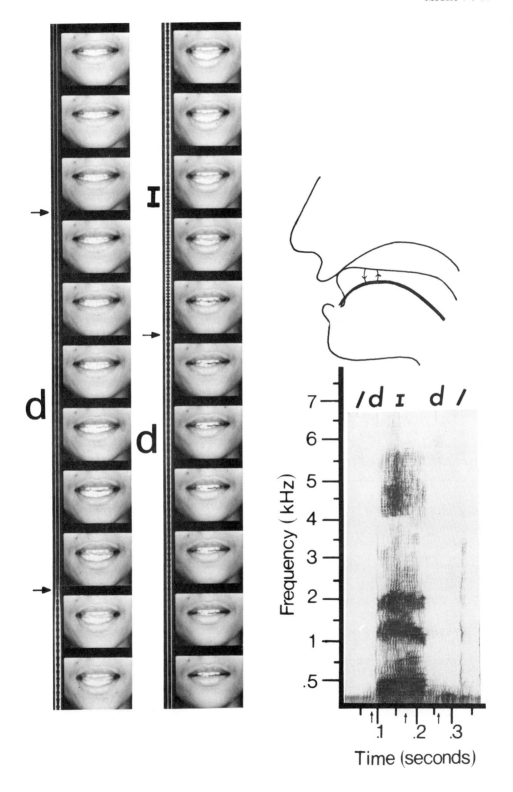

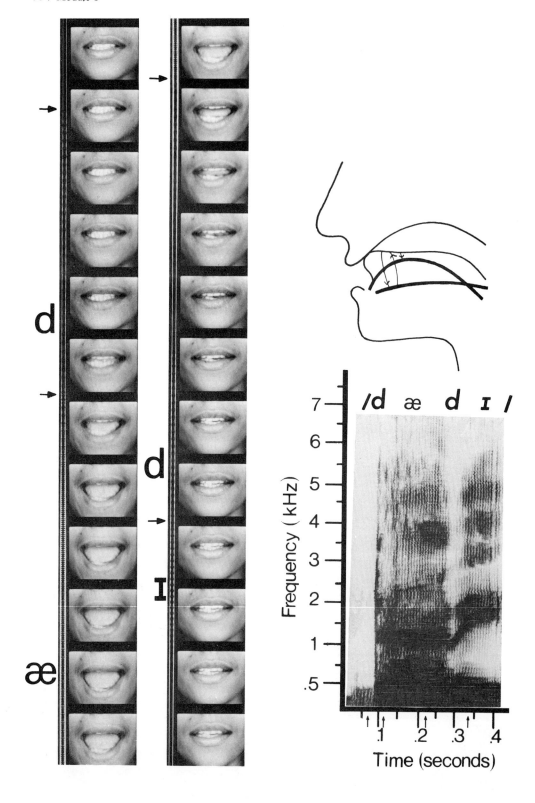

/d æ d ɪ /

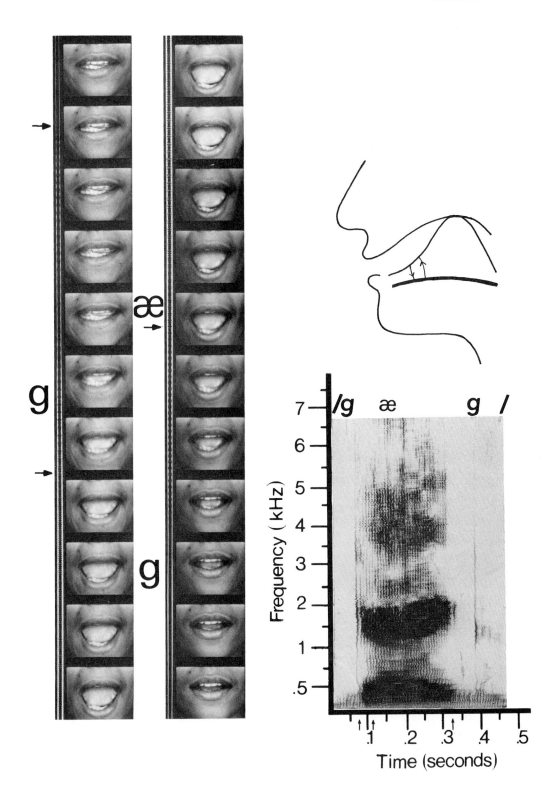

æ

g

g

g

/g   æ   g /

7

6

5

4

Frequency (kHz)

3

2

1

.5

.1   .2   .3   .4   .5
Time (seconds)

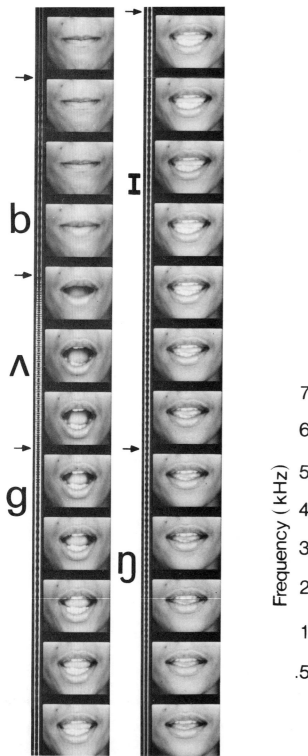

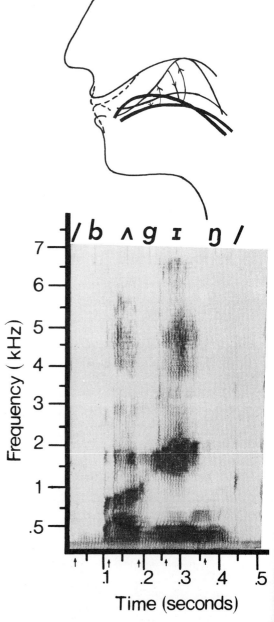

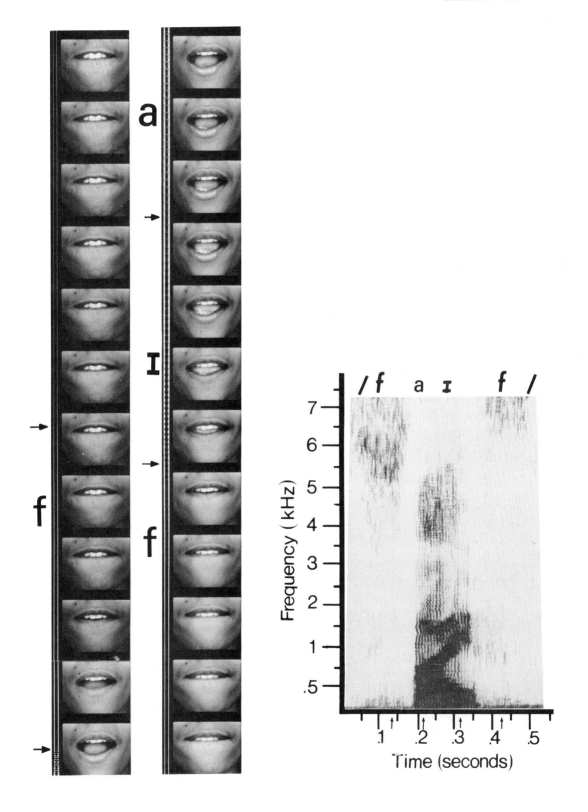

Module 12 /θɪn/

Film Strip The criterion phoneme /θ/ is at the initial position of the word /θɪn/. In the first frame, the tongue tip can be seen securely placed between the lower and upper teeth. In frame 4 the grip of the teeth is beginning to relax. Frame 5 shows a complete release of the tongue tip, and frame 7 shows the tongue's approximation for the vowel /ɪ/.

The acoustic energy tracings for the vowel begin at this point. Frames 7, 8, and 9 show the almost steady-state waveforms in the sound track for the vowel /ɪ/. Frame 10 shows the movement of the tongue away from the position for vowel /ɪ/, and frame 11 shows the alveolar contact of the tongue tip for the final consonant /n/. This contact can be seen throughout the following strip. Because of insufficient space, the final release of the tongue from the alveolar contact is not shown.

Schematic Diagram The schematic diagram shows the tongue movement from the interdental position to the front-high vowel position, and from the front-high vowel position to the alveolar ridge position. The direction of the movement is shown by the arrows.

Sound Spectrogram The spectrogram of the word /θɪn/ shows very low (almost invisible) amplitude energy in the mid to the high frequency domain. After the vowel /ɪ/, the spectrogram shows small traces of acoustic energy at the first and third formants. The acoustic energy is conspicuously missing at the second formant. The overall resonation of the consonant /n/ is weak, as indicated by the very low amplitude of the formants. However, the energy present is all invested in the formation of formants, indicating that this consonant is vowel-like.

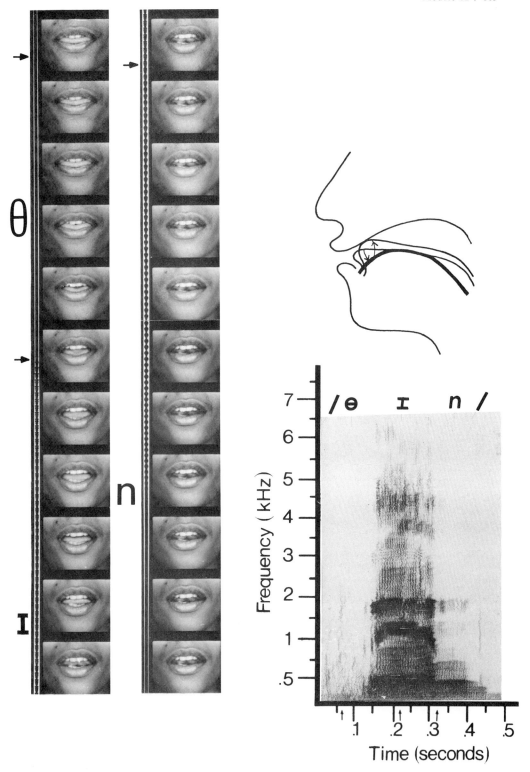

Module 13 /tuθ/

Film Strip The criterion phoneme /θ/ is at the final position of the word /tuθ/. Because of rounding nature of the medial vowel, some signs of lip rounding seem to have begun in the first frame during the production of /t/. The lip rounding persists until the last frame in the third strip, which is involved in the production of /θ/.

A comparison of the shape of the lips in Modules 12 and 13 shows that when /θ/ is followed by vowel /ɪ/, the lips are spread and less open (consistent with vowel /ɪ/); however, when /θ/ is preceded by the vowel /u/ the lips are round and more open (consistent with vowel /u/).

Schematic Diagram The schematic diagram of the tongue movements shows that the tongue moves from the alveolar ridge to the back-high vowel and from the back-high vowel to the interdental tongue position.

Sound Spectrogram The initial consonant /t/ in the sound spectrogram shows mid and high frequency noise of high amplitude followed by the vowel /u/. The final consonant /θ/ also shows the spread of noise-like energy from the mid to high frequencies. The phoneme /θ/ is marked by long duration and very low amplitude characteristics. Also, there is no energy present below 2,500 Hz, and the energy present in the high frequency region is very weak.

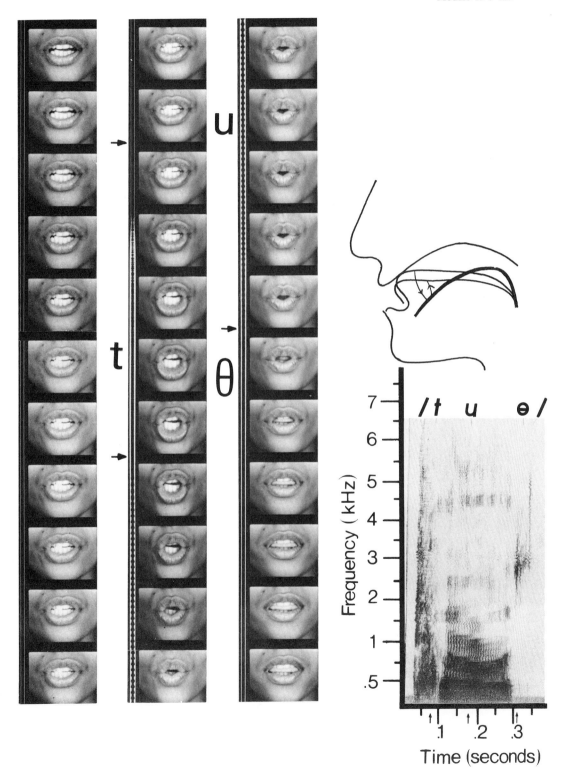

Module 14 /sɔs/

Film Strip The criterion phonemes are initial and final /s/ in the word /sɔs/. The first four frames show the alveolar contact of the tongue. Frame 5 shows the release of the tongue tip from the alveolar contact and the beginning of lip rounding for the vowel /ɔ/. A sustained state of the vowel /ɔ/ persists between frames 8 and 15. Beyond frame 15, the lips begin to approximate the final /s/, and by frame 19, the tip of the tongue has again made a contact in the vicinity of the alveolar ridge. Frames 19 through 24 show the steady state of the consonant /s/.

Schematic Diagram The schematic diagram shows the tongue movement from the alveolar ridge to the back-low vowel and from the back-low vowel to the alveolar ridge.

Sound Spectrogram The long duration, noise-like characteristics, and high amplitude in the high frequency area mark the /s/ phoneme at both the initial and final positions. The spectrogram shows that, contrary to /s/, the vowel /ɔ/ has prominent low frequency components. Because of the inherent low frequency nature of the vowel /ɔ/, the high frequency components of the phoneme /s/ do not influence this vowel.

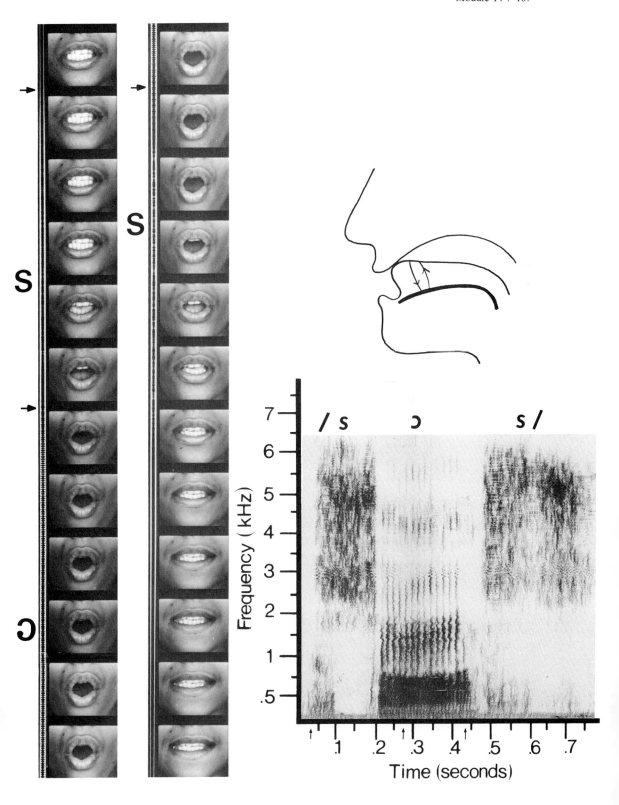

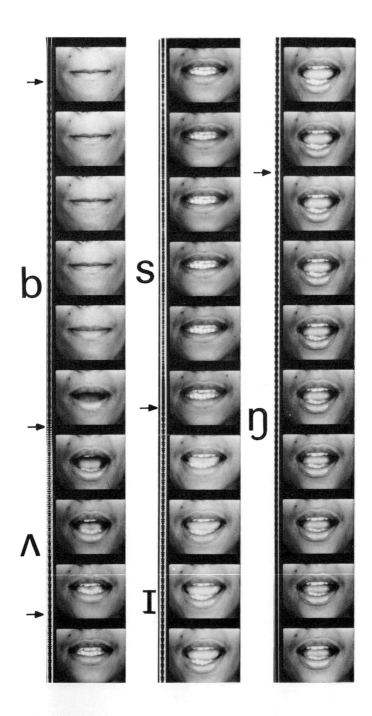

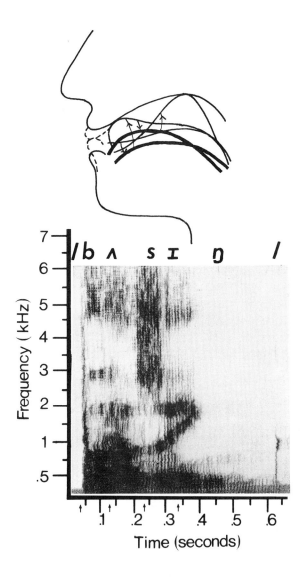

Module 16 /ʃʌʃ/

Film Strip The criterion phoneme /ʃ/ is at the initial and final positions of the word /ʃʌʃ/. The consonant /ʃ/ exhibits a significant amount of lip rounding at both the initial and final positions. Although the vowel /ʌ/ is neutral for lip rounding, the consonant /ʃ/ influences it to become rounded. The lip rounding gesture begins at frame 1 and considerable rounding is accomplished at frame 4, but the audible acoustic energy does not start until frame 8 or 9. The long duration of the phoneme /ʃ/ results in the persistence of the lip rounding until frame 13.

At frame 14 an opening is seen between the upper and lower teeth. This opening enlarges to accomplish the target vowel /ʌ/. The duration of this vowel is considerably short, ranging from frame 14 to frame 18. The beginning of lip rounding is seen at frame 19. This frame also marks the beginning of the acoustic energy for the final /ʃ/. Frames 20 through 36 show the steady-state lip rounding for the phoneme /ʃ/.

Schematic Diagram The schematic drawing indicates that the tongue moves from the palatal position to the central-low vowel position, and from the central-low vowel position back to the palatal position.

Sound Spectrogram The sound spectrogram shows that both initial and final /ʃ/ have ample energy in the high frequency domain. More specifically, there is a strong concentration of energy in the mid to high frequency areas, and no energy in the low frequency area (below 2,000 Hz). Because of the neutral nature of the vowel /ʌ/, F_1, F_2, and F_3 each show equal distances from the other. The F_2 shows an arched shape, a result of its efforts to make a transition with the high frequency energy of the /ʃ/ phoneme at both ends.

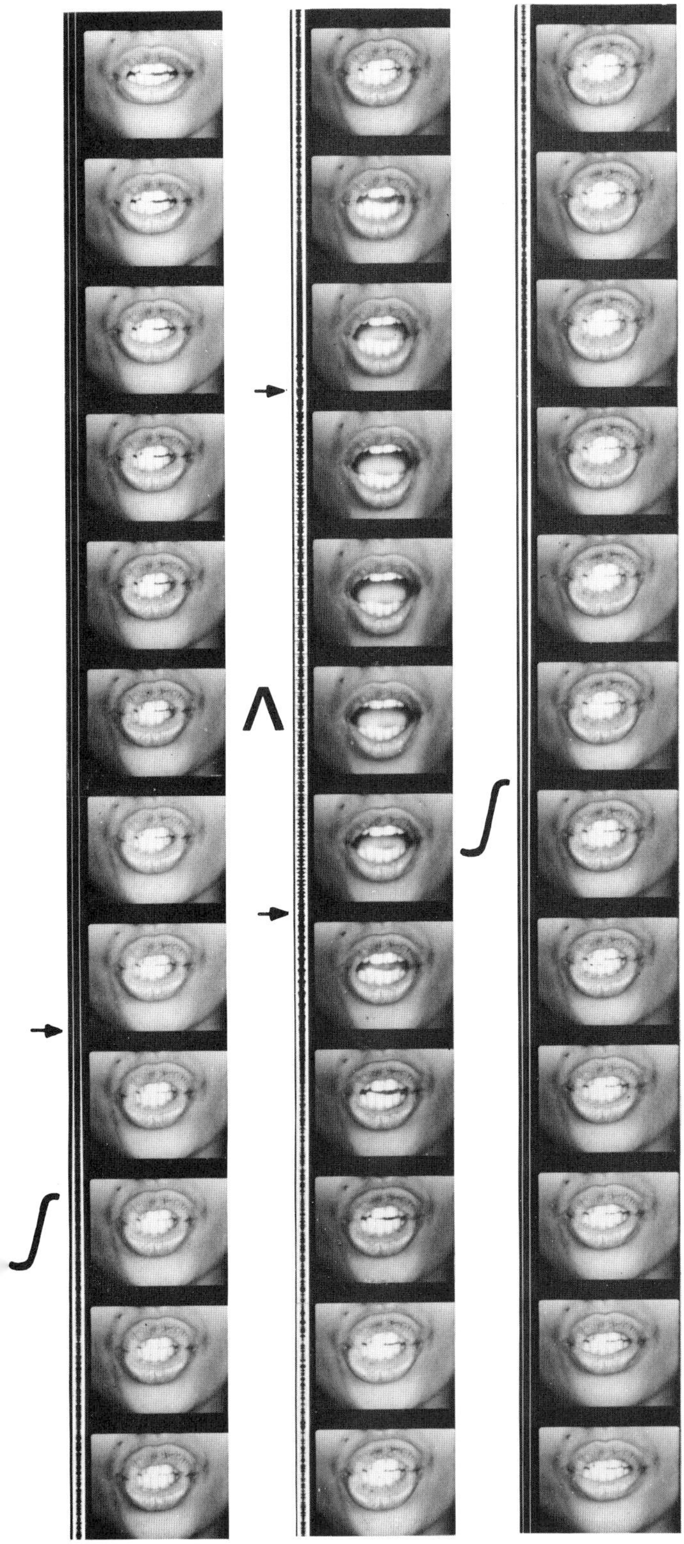
ʃ
ʌ
ʃ

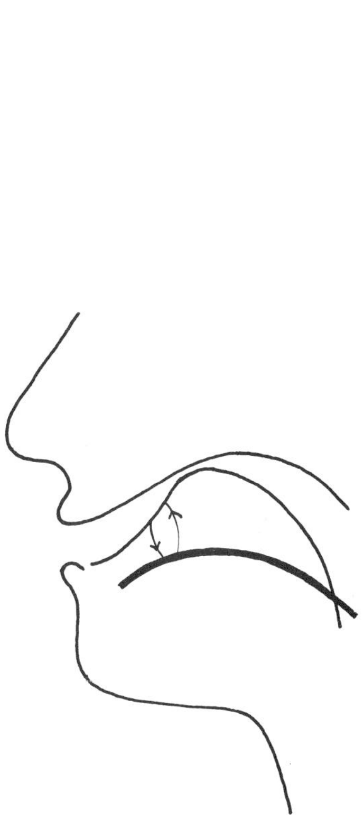

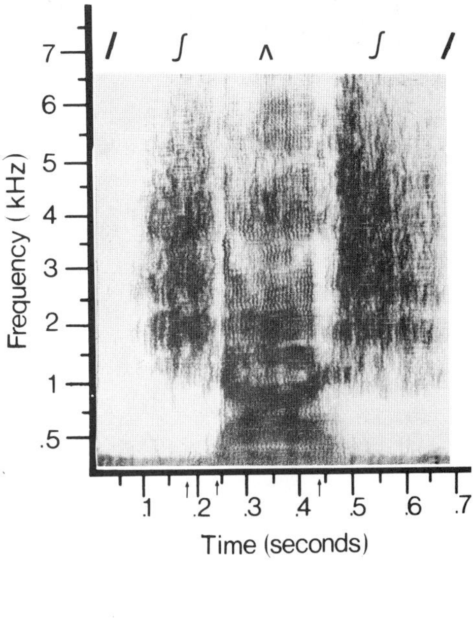
/ ʃ ʌ ʃ /
Frequency (kHz)
7
6
5
4
3
2
1
.5
.1 .2 .3 .4 .5 .6 .7
Time (seconds)

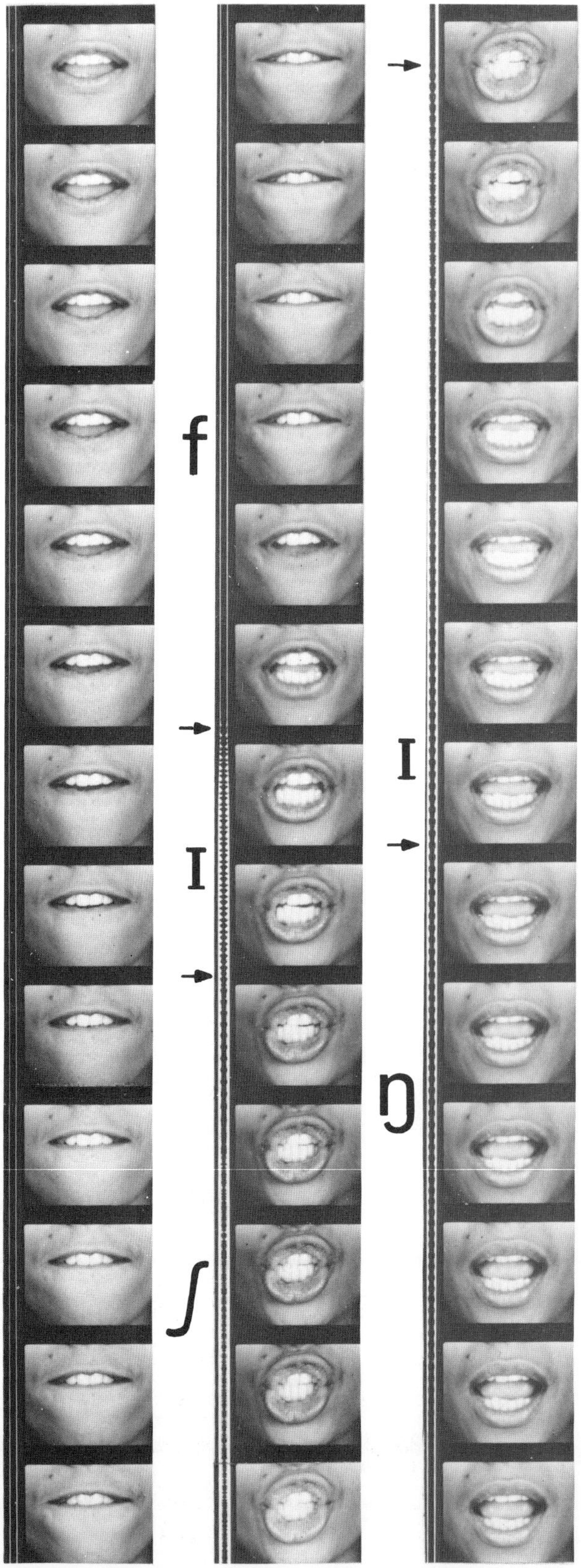

f

I

∫

I

ŋ

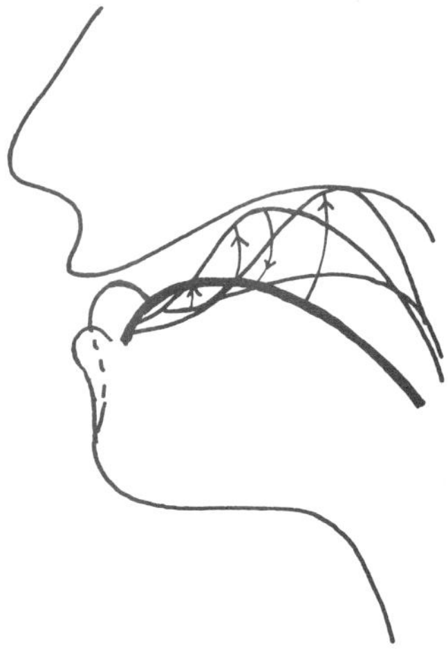

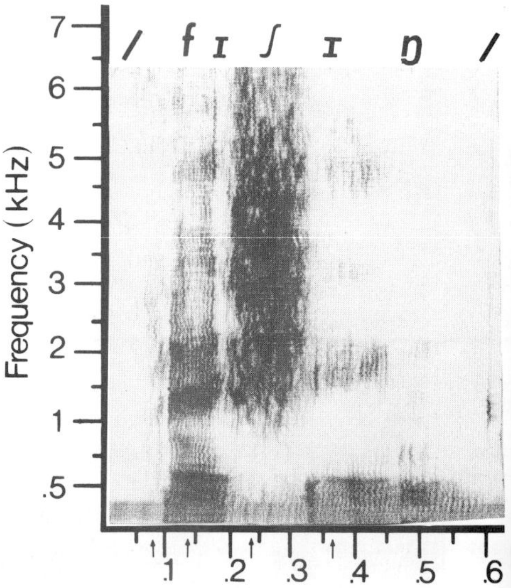

/ f ɪ ∫ ɪ ŋ /

Frequency (kHz)

7
6
5
4
3
2
1
.5

.1 .2 .3 .4 .5 .6
Time (seconds)

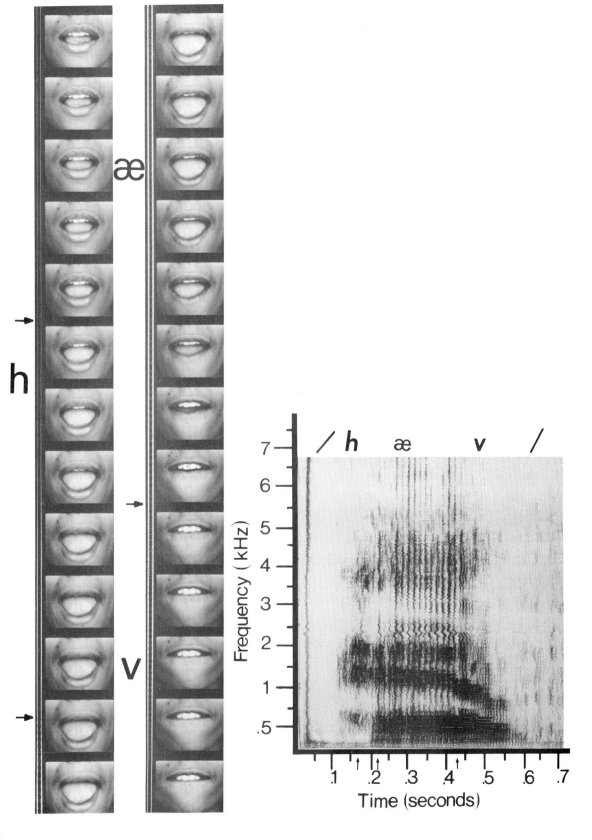

/ h   æ   v   /

Frequency (kHz)

7
6
5
4
3
2
1
.5

.1   .2   .3   .4   .5   .6   .7

Time (seconds)

Module 19 /vil/

Film Strip The criterion phoneme /v/ is at the initial position of the word /vil/. The first six frames show the lips before the labiodental closure. Frames 7 through 15 show the state of labiodental contact necessary for the production of English consonants /f/ and /v/. Frame 16 shows the beginning sign of lip opening for the vowel /i/. Frames 17 through 23 show the tongue at the front-high position for the production of the vowel /i/. Frame 24 shows the upward movement of the tongue tip for the production of the final consonant /l/. The last two frames show the tongue touching the alveolar ridge area.

Schematic Diagram The schematic drawing shows the movement of the tongue from a somewhat neutral position to the front-high vowel position, and from the front-high vowel position to the alveolar position.

Sound Spectrogram The sound spectrogram of both the /v/ and /l/ phonemes shows some low frequency energy tracing. The three formants of vowel /i/ exhibit a downward trend toward the low frequency energies in the preceding and following consonants.

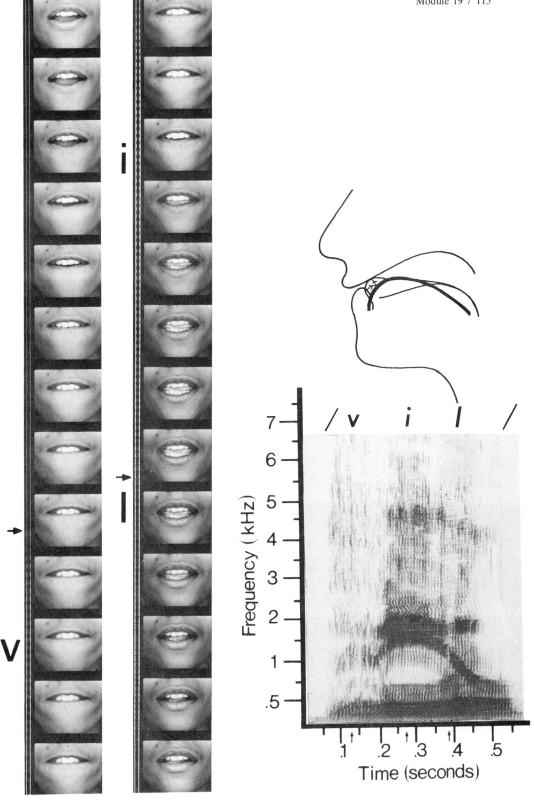

Frequency (kHz)

/ v   i   l   /

Time (seconds)

/ h æ v ɪ ŋ /

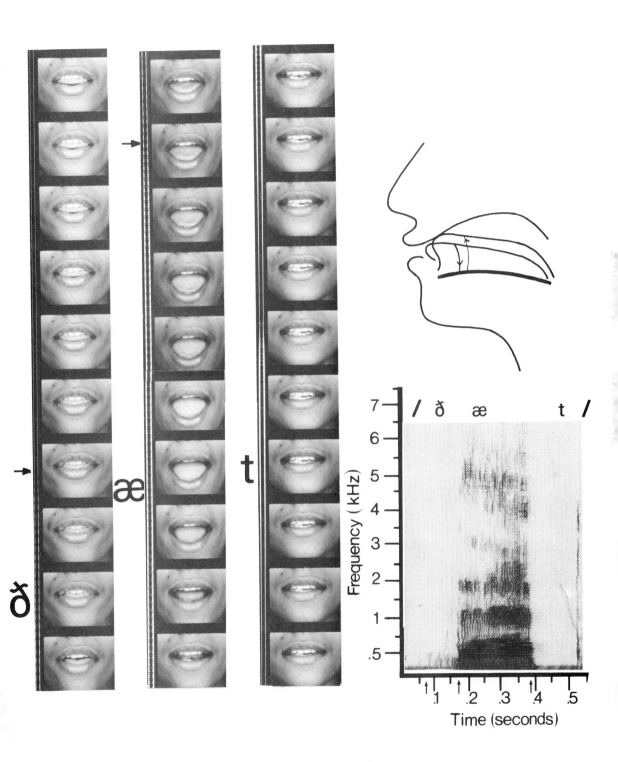

/ ð æ t /

/ b e ɪ   ð /

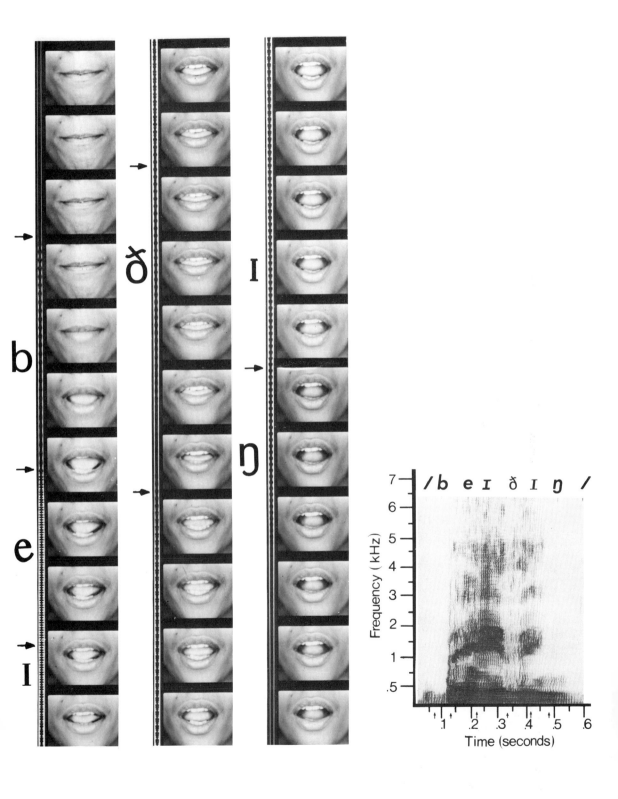

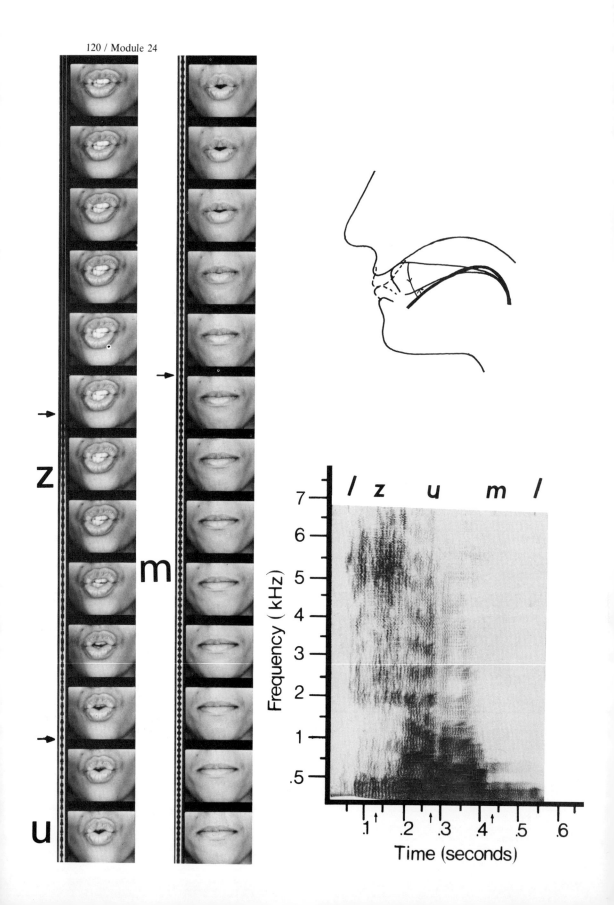

/ z u m /

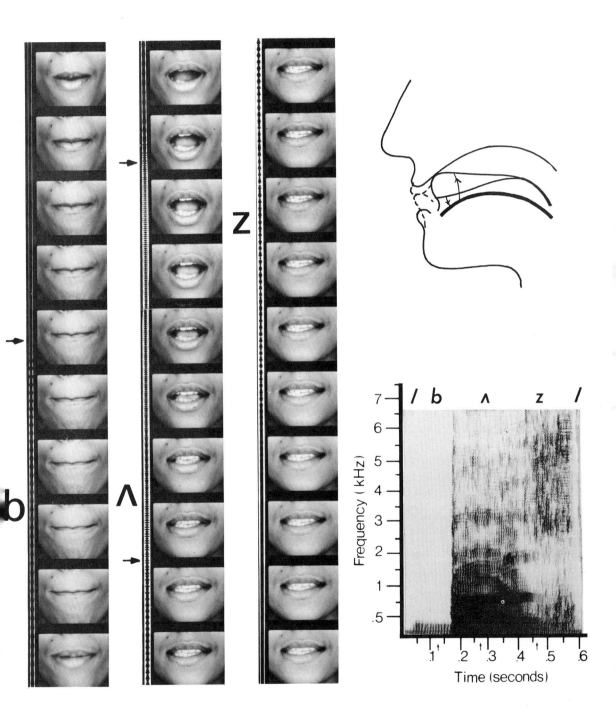

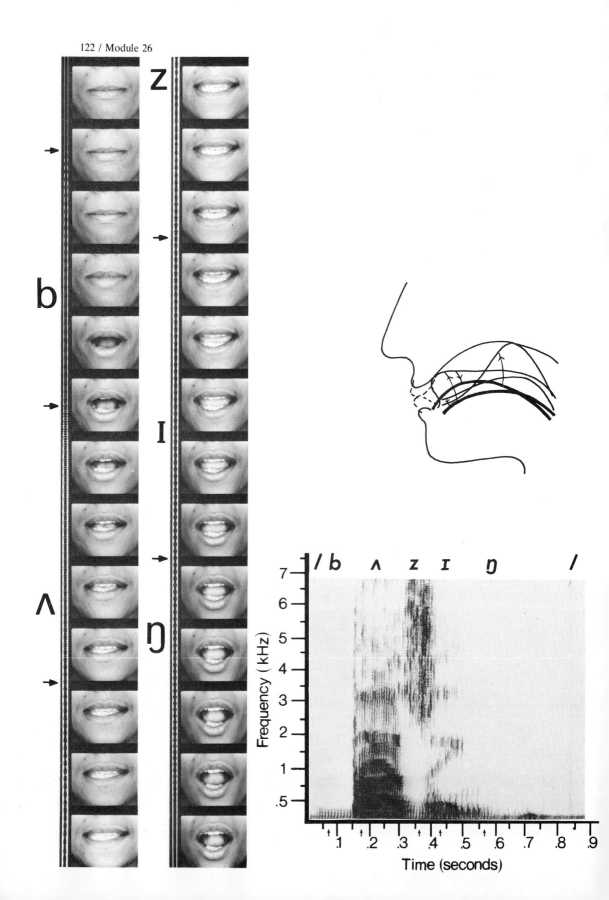

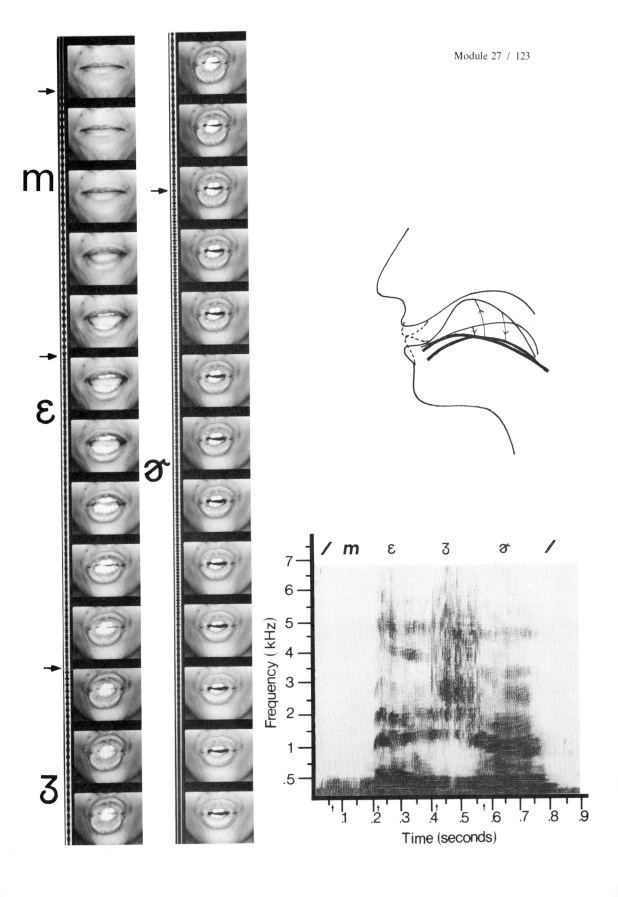

Module 28 /tʃɝ·tʃ/

Film Strip The criterion phoneme /tʃ/ is at the initial and final positions of the word /tʃɝ·tʃ/. The phoneme /tʃ/ is marked by considerable lip rounding. The first thirteen frames show the lip rounding that occurs before the emission of the acoustic energy. Because the following vowel is /ɝ·/, the rounding persists through the vowel. The boundary between the rounded /tʃ/ and the rounded /ɝ·/ is exhibited by the mouth opening for the /ɝ·/ phoneme, as seen in frames 17 through 26. After frame 27, the mouth opening closes, the lips remain rounded, and the final consonant /tʃ/ is produced.

Schematic Diagram The schematic diagram shows the tongue movement from the palatal position to the central-mid vowel position, and from the central-mid vowel position to the palatal position.

Sound Spectrogram The sound spectrogram of the word /tʃɝ·tʃ/ clearly shows the high frequency, noise-like acoustic spectrum for the initial and final /tʃ/ sounds. In addition, the stoppage of the air flow during the production of this phoneme is indicated by a gap (silent interval) preceding and following the vowel. This gap clearly supports the contention of some phoneticians that /tʃ/ and /dʒ/ are stop phonemes.

The vowel /ɝ·/ at the medial position shows low F_1 and F_2 frequencies.

tʃ

ɝ

tʃ

ɝ

ɪ

ŋ

s

tʃ

/ s ɝ tʃ ɪ ŋ /

Frequency (kHz)

7
6
5
4
3
2
1
.5

.1 .2 .3 .4 .5 .6 .7 .8 .9 1.0

Time (seconds)

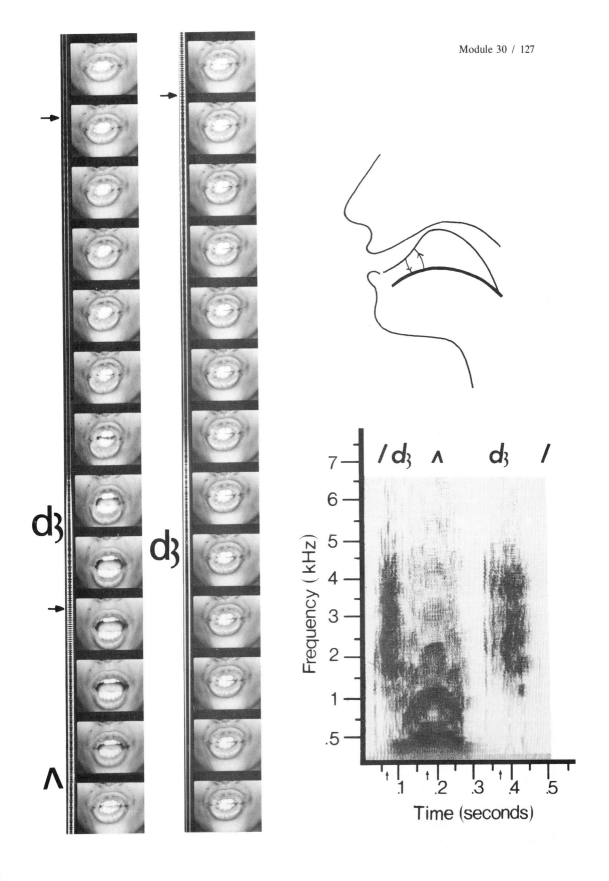

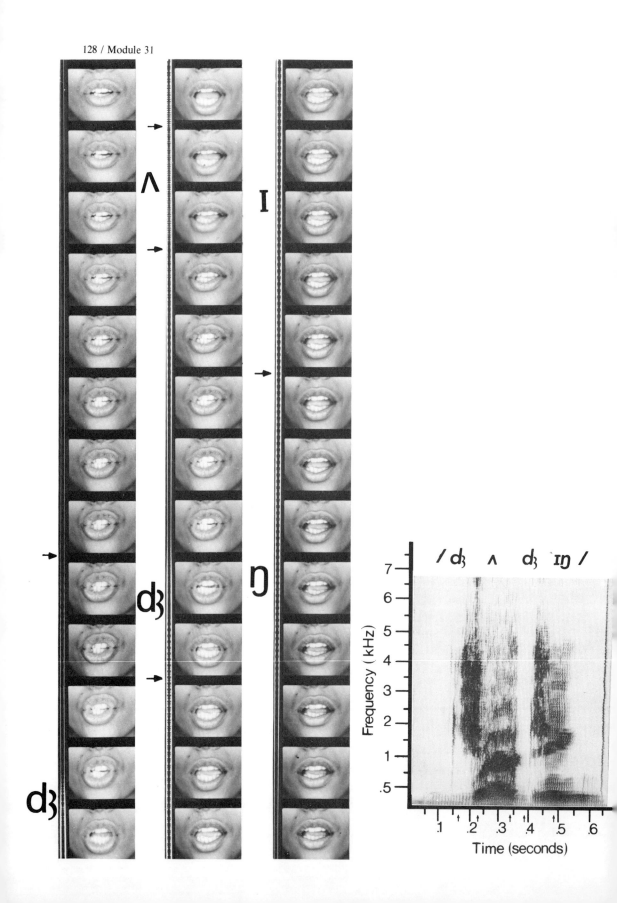

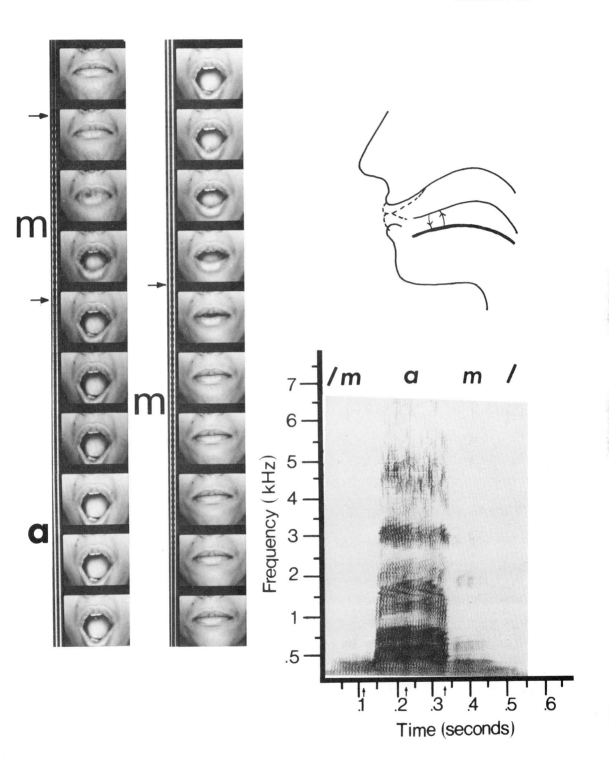

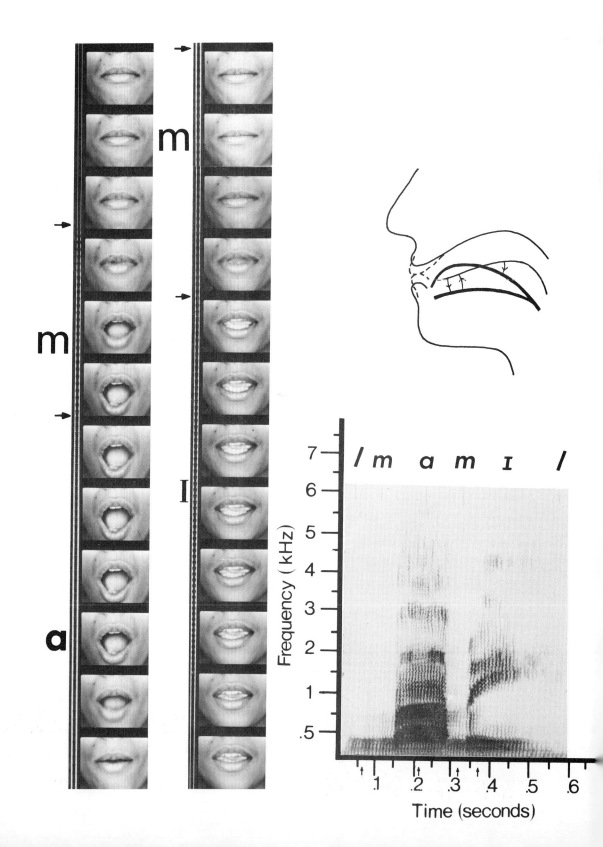

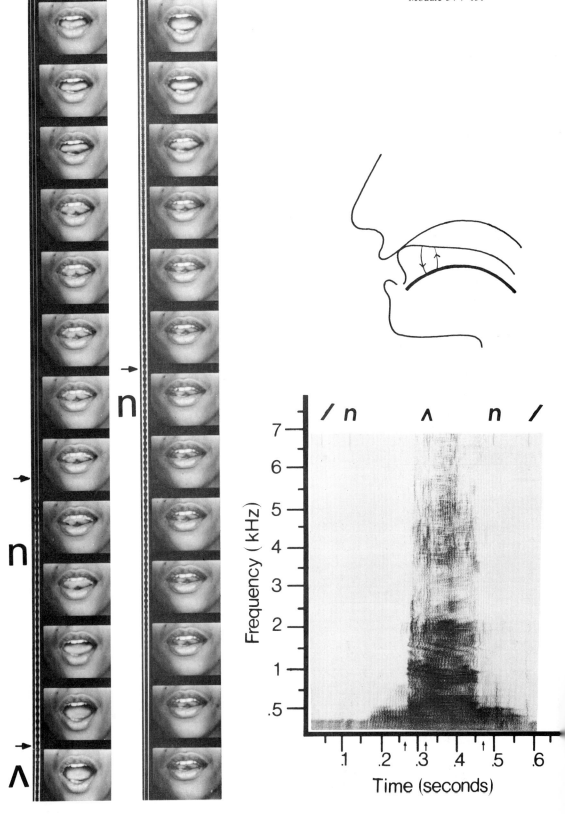

/ n ʌ n /

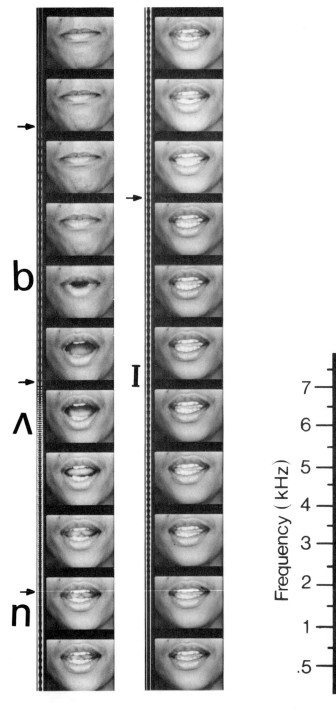

b

∧

n

I

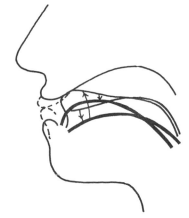

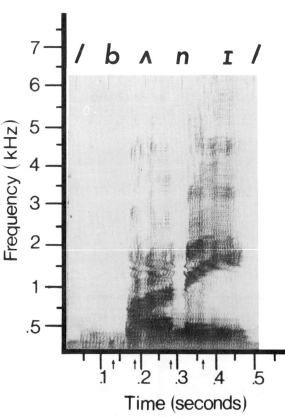

/ b ∧ n I /

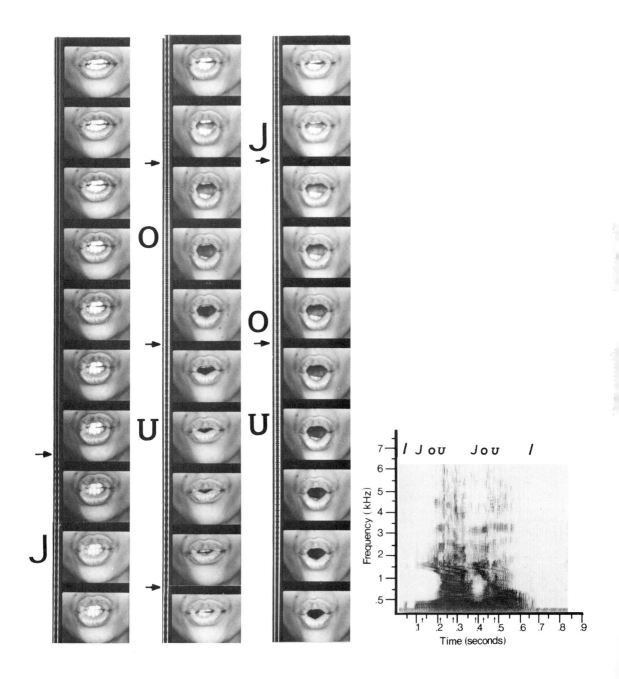

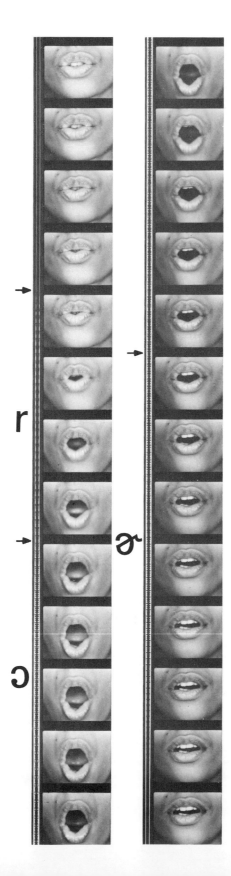

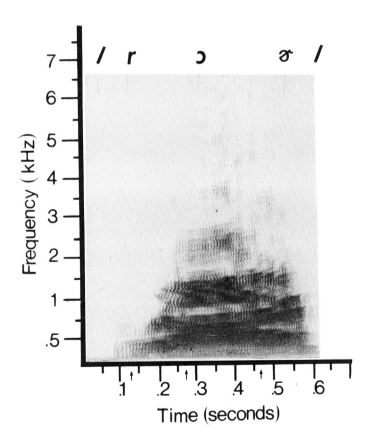

Module 38 /lʌl/

Film Strip The criterion phoneme /l/ is at the initial and final positions of the word /lʌl/. The first frame shows the neutral lip and tongue positions. In the third frame, the tongue is touching the alveolar ridge with an opening laterally for the passage of the air stream. The next twelve frames show the steady state of the alveolar contact for the /l/ phoneme.

In frame 16 (at the middle of the second strip of film), the tongue contact is released and the mouth is opened for the production of the vowel /ʌ/. In frame 17, the tongue and lips have assumed the position for the vowel /ʌ/. Beginning with frame 19 (toward the bottom of the second strip of film), the tongue begins to rise so as to accomplish the alveolar position for the final /l/. In frame 22 the tongue tip touches the alveolar ridge.

A comparison of the production of the /l/ phoneme in this module and in Module 39 strikingly reveals that the lip rounding and opening for the /l/ phoneme are considerably different. These differences are attributed to the open and slightly rounded nature of the vowel /ʌ/, compared to the flat and unopen nature of the vowel /ɪ/, as in Module 39. When /l/ is followed and preceded by /ʌ/, the lips are more open and rounded. However, when /l/ is followed and preceded by the vowel /ɪ/, the lips are flat and less open.

Schematic Diagram The schematic diagram shows the tongue movement from the alveolar ridge to the central-low vowel position and from the central-low vowel position to the alveolar ridge position.

Sound Spectrogram The sound spectrogram shows the presence of energy in the low and mid frequency domains for the /l/ consonant. The very close approximation of F_1 and F_2 for the vowel /ʌ/ clearly indicates that, in this instance, the phoneme /ʌ/ is a low vowel.

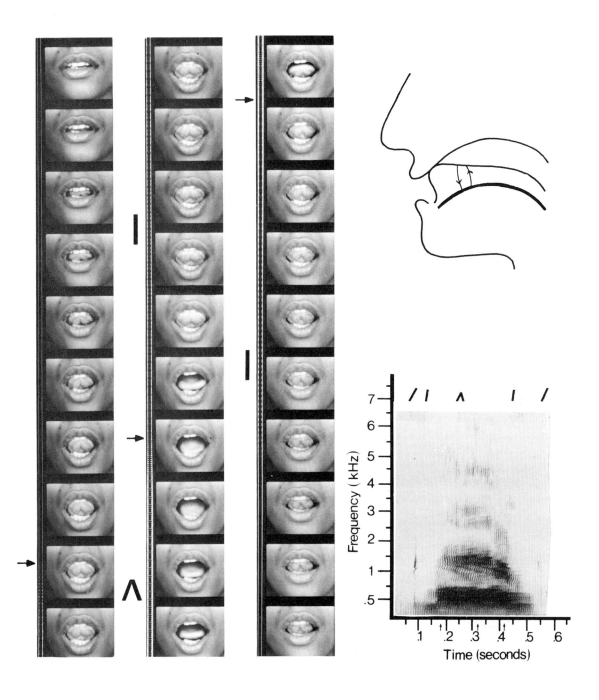

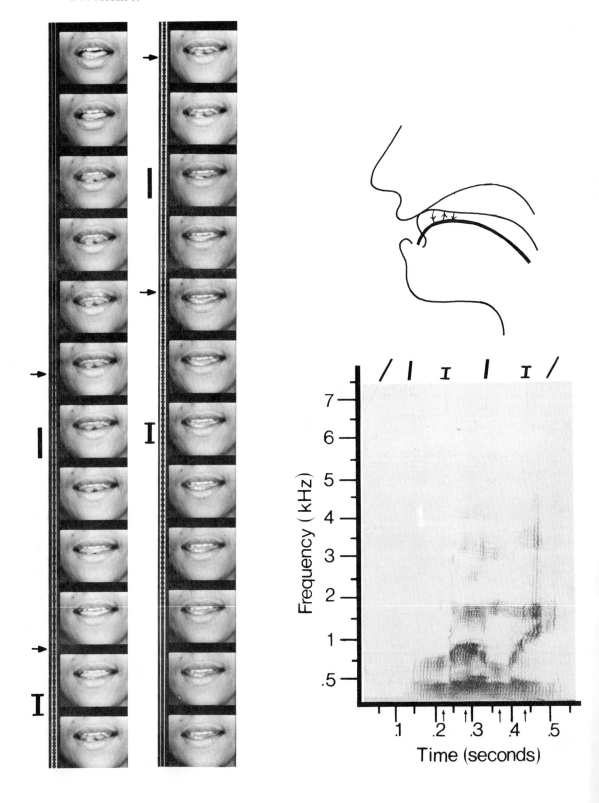

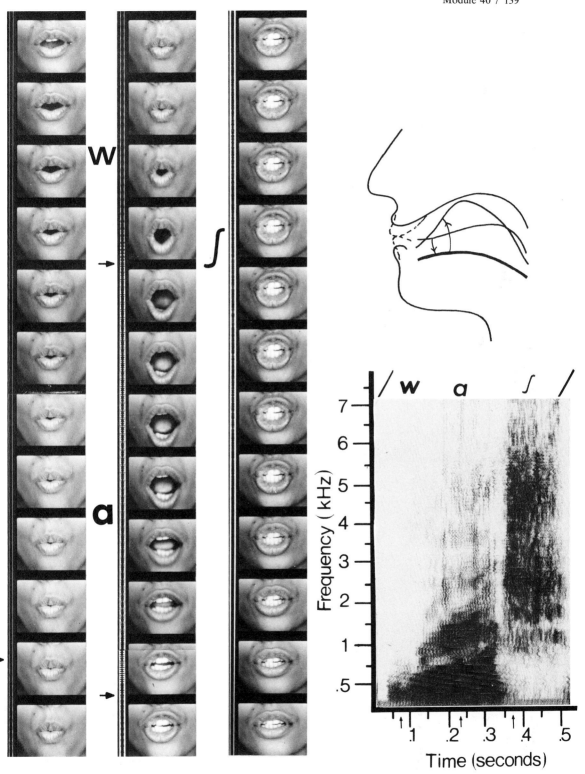

Vowels

Module 41 /bit/

Film Strip The criterion vowel phoneme /i/ is at the medial position of the word /bit/. The lip closing for the initial /b/ can be seen in the first five frames. In frame 6 the lips relax for the opening. In frame 7 they open into the vowel /i/. The lip position of the vowel /i/ is least open, most wide, and unrounded. The fact that /i/ is a tense vowel is well represented in the production of the preceding consonant /b/. A comparison of Modules 41 and 42 reveals that the lip closure for /b/ in the context of a tense vowel /i/ is much more intense than the lip closure for /b/ in the context of a lax vowel /ɪ/.

One frame has been taken from the continuous enunciation of the sustained vowel /i/ and presented enlarged to show the most open state of this vowel.

Schematic Diagram The schematic drawing of the vowel tongue position is shown without any co-articulation with the consonants. The skeleton of the vowel diagram is superimposed with arrows terminating at the points of height and advancement. The vowel /i/ is shown by the horizontal arrow as being most advanced and by the vertical arrow as being most high.

Sound Spectrogram The sound spectrogram shows the formant frequencies of the vowel /i/ in isolation; F_1 is low, F_2 is high, and the distance between F_2 and F_3 is small.

/ b i t /

Frequency (kHz)

Time (seconds)

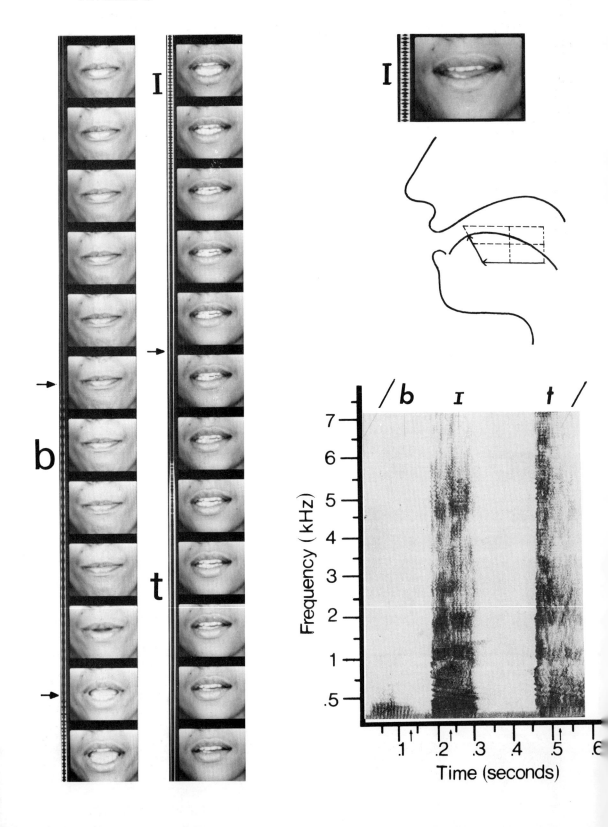

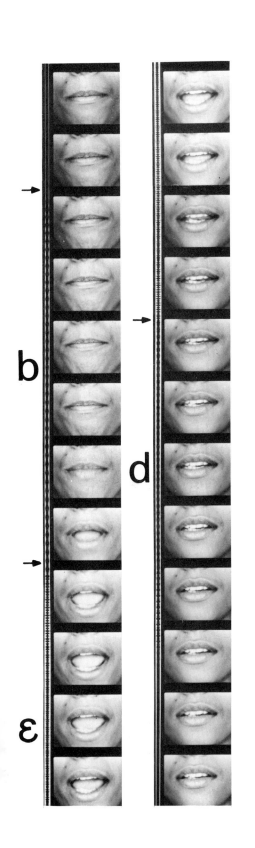

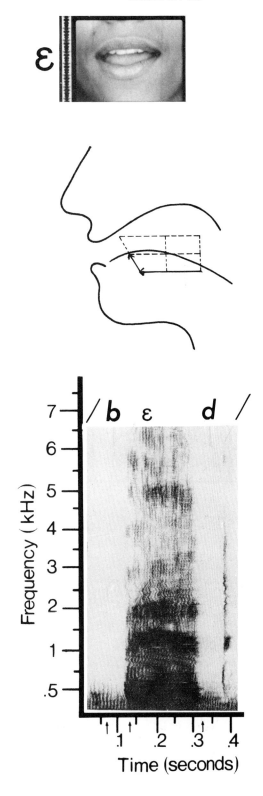

Module 44 /kæt/

Film Strip The criterion phoneme /æ/ is at the medial position of the word /kæt/. In the first frame the influence of the vowel on the initial consonant /k/ can be clearly seen. Although the audible sound tracing for /k/ cannot be seen until frame 4 or 5, the production of the vowel /æ/ already has been initiated in the beginning frames. The tongue has started making a downward movement, and the mandible has begun to lower.

In frame 9, a complete vowel /æ/ position has been assumed by the lips, tongue, and the mandible. The mouth is wide open, the tongue is low, and there is a lack of noticeable rounding.

The one frame presented separately has been taken from the sustained isolated production of the vowel /æ/. This frame represents the most open lip position for this vowel.

Schematic Diagram The schematic diagram representing the tongue position for this vowel shows a front-low tongue position. The horizontal arrow showing tongue advancement has gone to its limit, but there is no arrow shown on the vertical dimension, indicating a complete lack of tongue height.

Sound Spectrogram The sound spectrogram shows a high F_1 and a closer approximation between F_2 and F_3 than between F_1 and F_2.

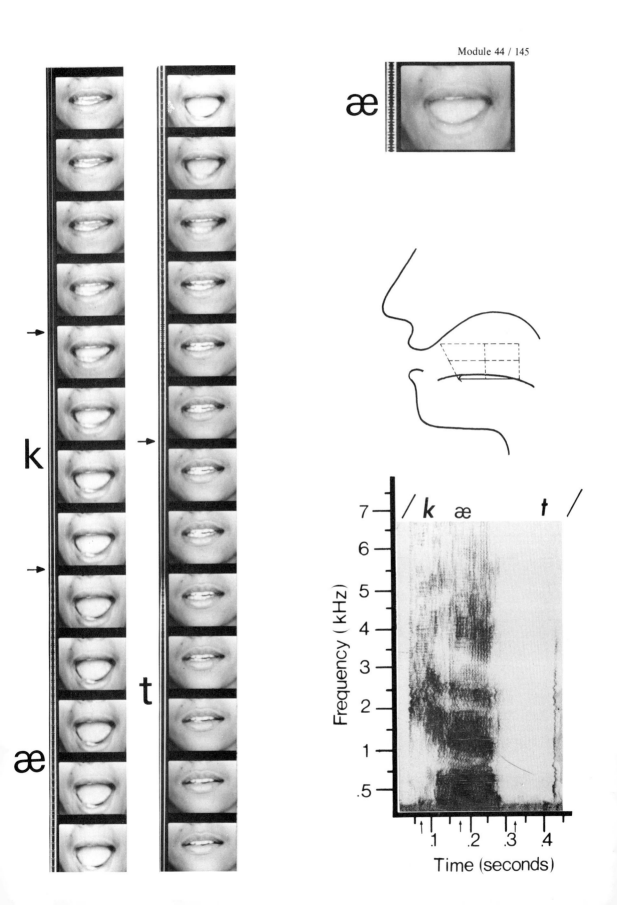

æ

k

æ

t

/ k æ t /

Frequency (kHz)

7
6
5
4
3
2
1
.5

.1 .2 .3 .4

Time (seconds)

Module 45 /faðɚ/

Film Strip The criterion vowel /ɑ/ is at the medial position of the word /faðɚ/. In addition, the vowel /ɚ/ can be viewed at the final position of this word. The vowel /ɑ/ following the consonant /f/ begins at the first frame of the second strip of film. The two frames preceding this full opening show the state of the articulatory transition between the consonant /f/ and the vowel /ɑ/. The vowel is maintained through the first six frames of the second strip of film.

The final eight frames of the third strip of film show the lip position for the vowel /ɚ/. For the vowel /ɑ/ the lips are fairly open and the tongue is low and somewhat in the central region. For the vowel /ɚ/ the lips are less open. The degree of lip roundedness for both of these vowels is approximately the same.

The one frame presented separately has been taken from the sustained isolated production of the vowel /ɑ/. This frame represents the most open lip position for this vowel.

Schematic Diagram The schematic diagram shows a central-low tongue position for the vowel /ɑ/.

Sound Spectrogram The sound spectrogram shows high F_1 and low F_2 to the extent that F_1 and F_2 are interlocked. The distance between F_2 and F_3 is relatively wide.

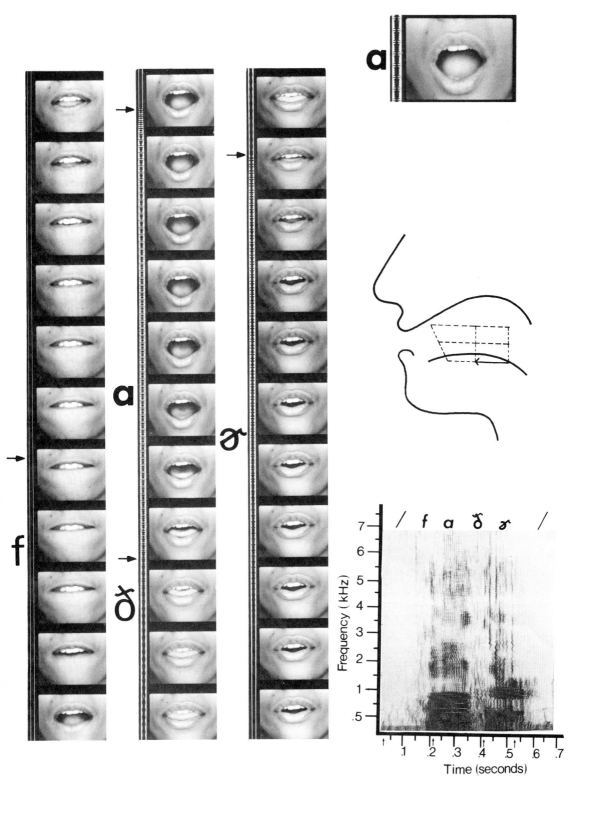

Frequency (kHz)

/ f a ð ɚ /

Time (seconds)

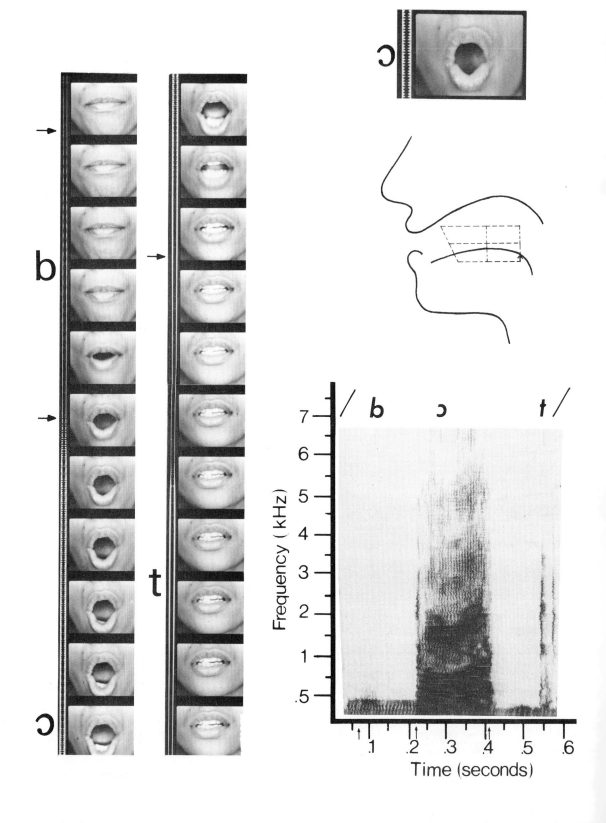

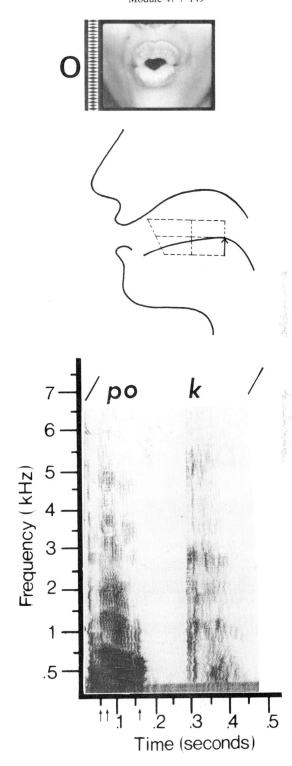

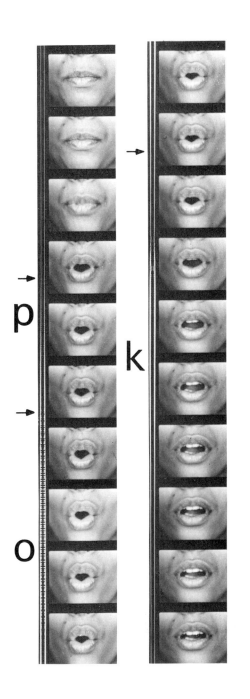

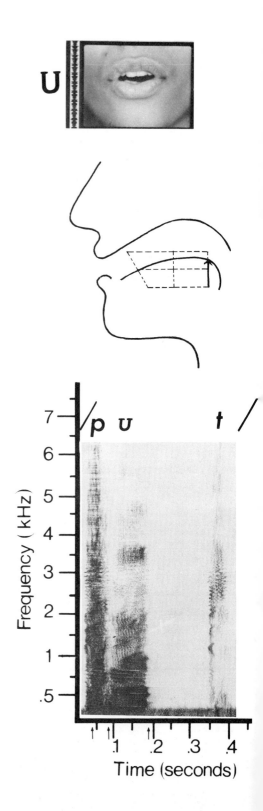

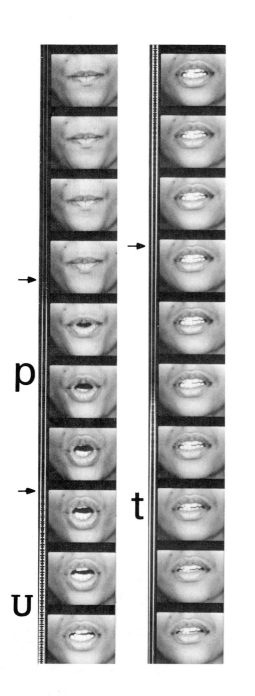

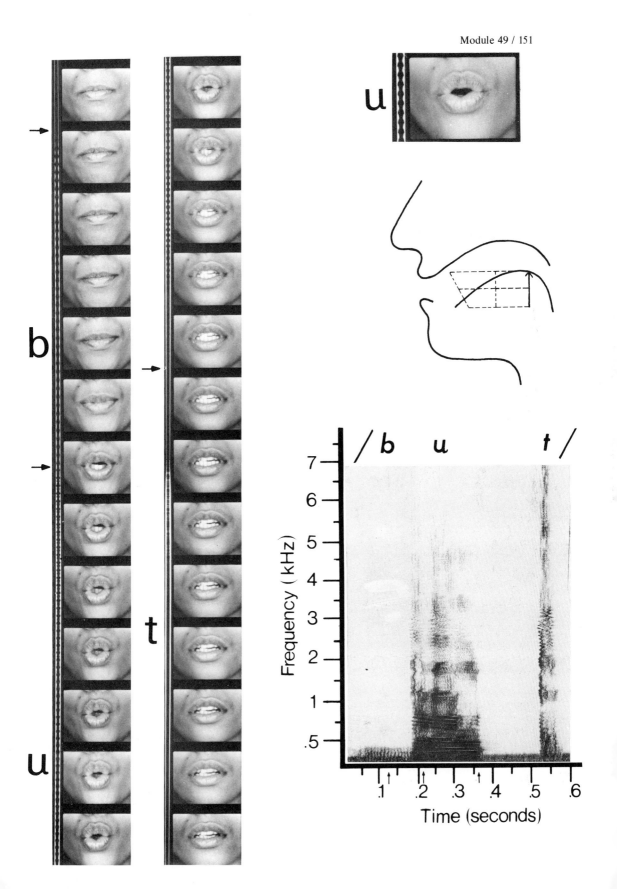

/ b   u   t /

u

b

t

u

Frequency (kHz)

7
6
5
4
3
2
1
.5

.1   .2 .3   .4   .5   .6
Time (seconds)

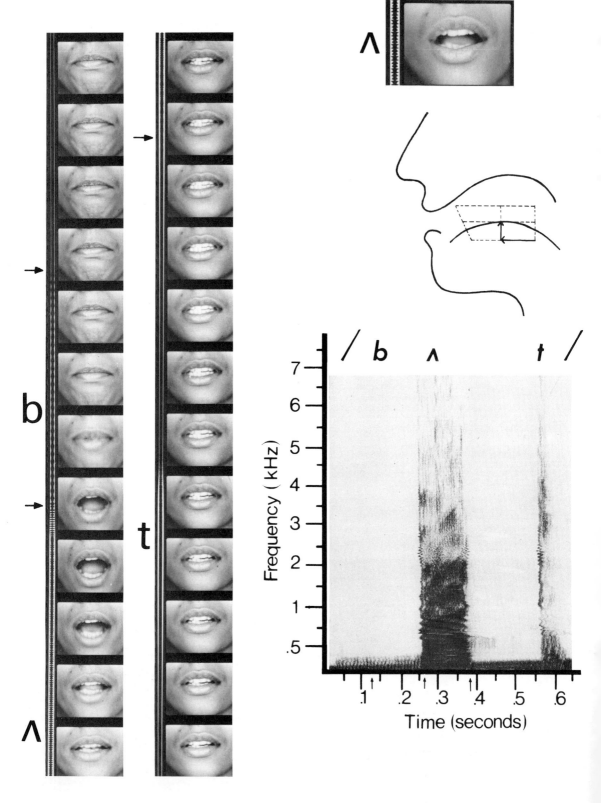

/ b ʌ t /

Frequency (kHz)

7
6
5
4
3
2
1
.5

.1 .2 .3 .4 .5 .6

Time (seconds)

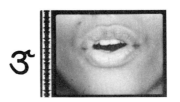

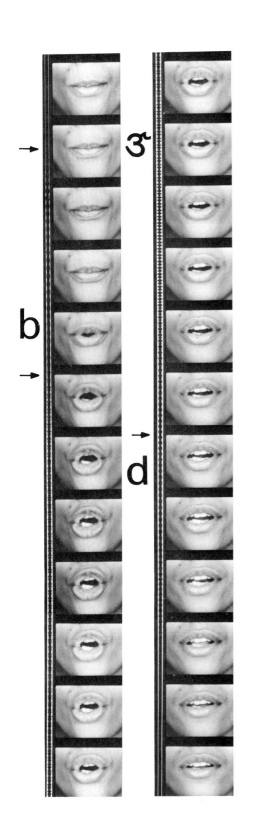

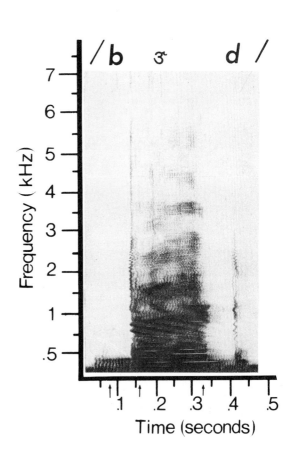

Diphthongs

Module 52 /beɪk/

Film Strip It is most interesting to observe the formation of the diphthongs. Actually, the two vowel elements involved in the formation of a diphthong are influenced by each other, like the coarticulatory influence of any two neighboring phonemes. In addition, each of the two vowels involved maintains its independent identity.

In this module, the criterion diphthong /eɪ/ is at the medial position of the word /beɪk/. It can be seen that, although there is an influence of vowel /e/ on /ɪ/ and vice versa, these vowels also maintain their uniquenesses for several frames. The vowel /e/, without any influence from the vowel /ɪ/, can be seen in frames 8 through 11. The gliding of the tongue and lip positions continues in frames 12 and 13. The vowel /ɪ/ can be seen in its "pure" state in frames 14, 15, and 16.

Two separate frames have been taken, one from the /e/ portion and another from the /ɪ/ portion of the diphthong /eɪ/ when pronounced in isolation. These two portions further support the hypothesis that /e/ and /ɪ/ may have independent phonemic status in the formation of the diphthong /eɪ/.

Schematic Diagram The schematic drawing shows the movement of the tongue from the front-mid position to the front-high position.

Sound Spectrogram The sound spectrogram shows the steady state of the formants for the vowel /e/ followed by the falling F_1 and rising F_2 for the vowel /ɪ/.

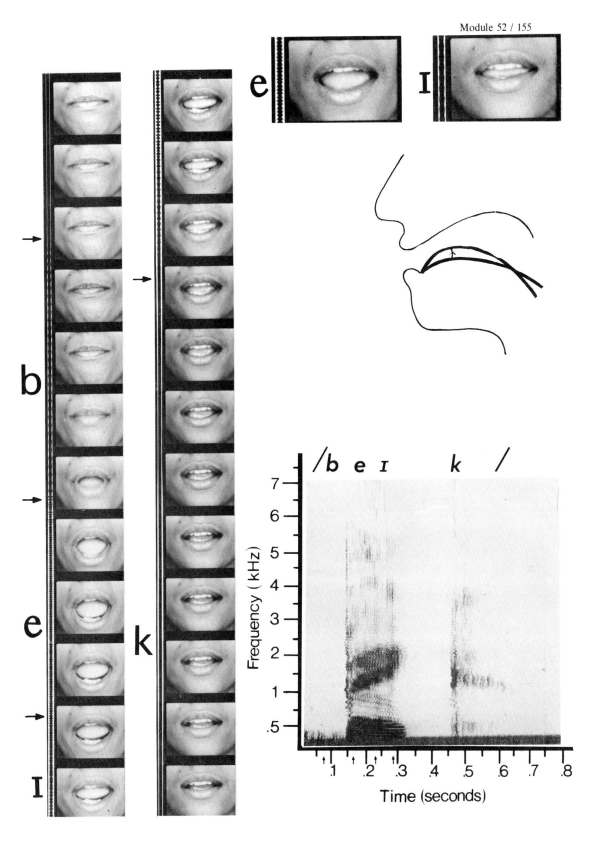

/b eɪ   k /

Module 53 /baɪk/

Film Strip The criterion diphthong is /aɪ/ in the word /baɪk/. After the lip closure for the /b/ consonant in the first four frames, the first sign of opening for the vowel /a/ is seen in frame 5. The next four frames (6 through 9) show the production of the vowel /a/. These four frames involved in the production of the /a/ portion of diphthong /aɪ/ may be compared with frames 13 through 18 of Module 45 involved in the production of vowel /ɑ/; their similarities may be noted.

Frames 10 and 11 of this module show the gliding from the vowel /a/ to the vowel /ɪ/. Frames 12 through 15 show the vowel /ɪ/ independently. Again, these four frames can be compared with frames 11 through 16 of Module 42, and the similarities in the production of /ɪ/ may be noted.

Two separate frames have been taken, one from the /a/ portion and another from the /ɪ/ portion of the diphthong /aɪ/ when produced in isolation. These two portions further support the hypothesis that /a/ and /ɪ/ may have independent phonemic status in the formation of the diphthong /aɪ/.

Schematic Diagram The schematic diagram shows the tongue movement from the central-low to the front-high vowel.

Sound Spectrogram The sound spectrogram shows the steady state formant frequency of the /a/ vowel followed by the falling F_1 and rising F_2 for the vowel /ɪ/.

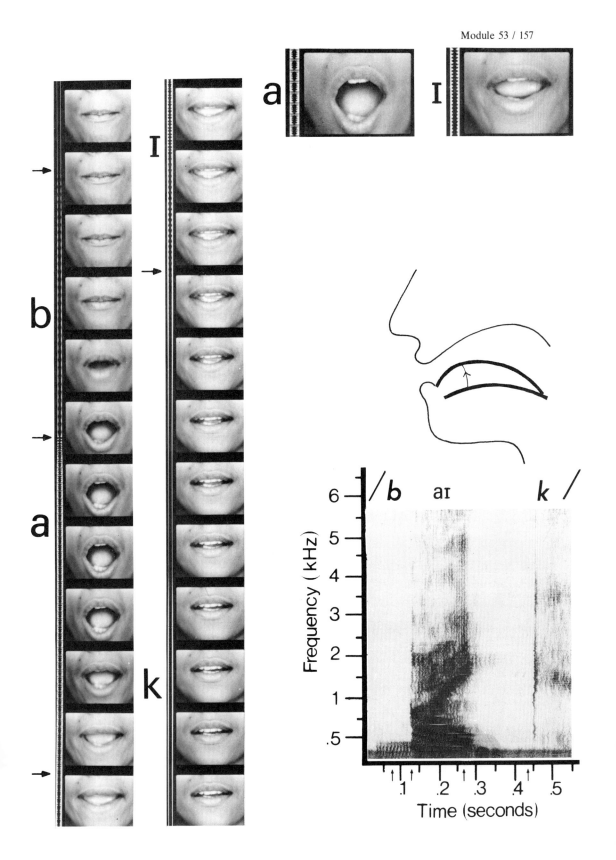

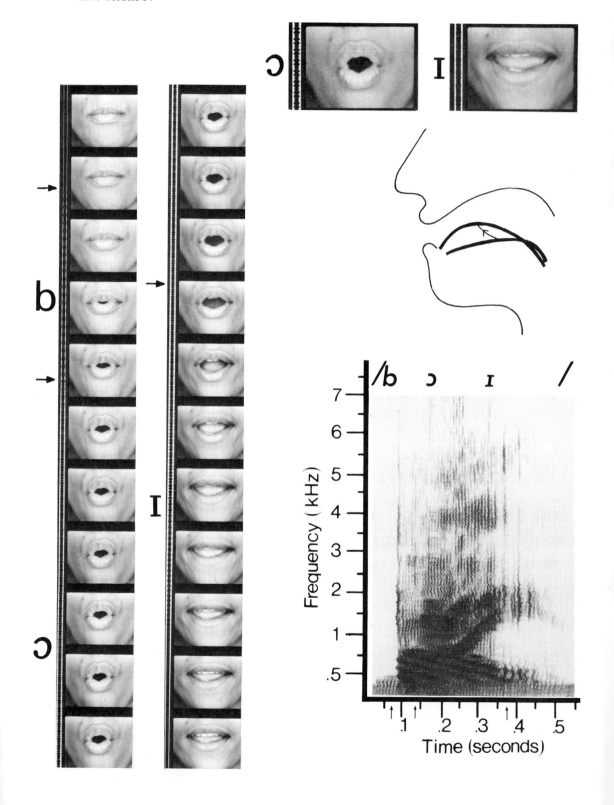

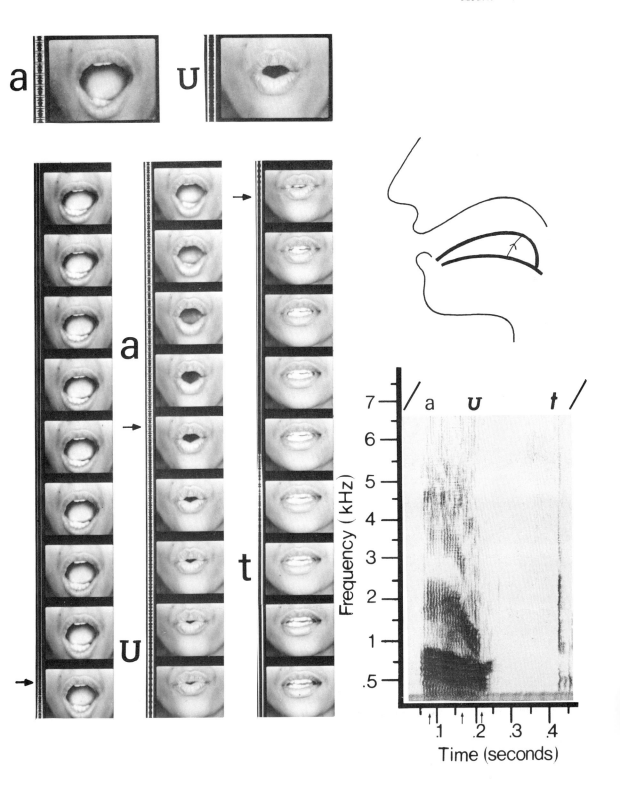

a   U

/ a   U   t /

Frequency (kHz)

7
6
5
4
3
2
1
.5

.1   .2   .3   .4

Time (seconds)

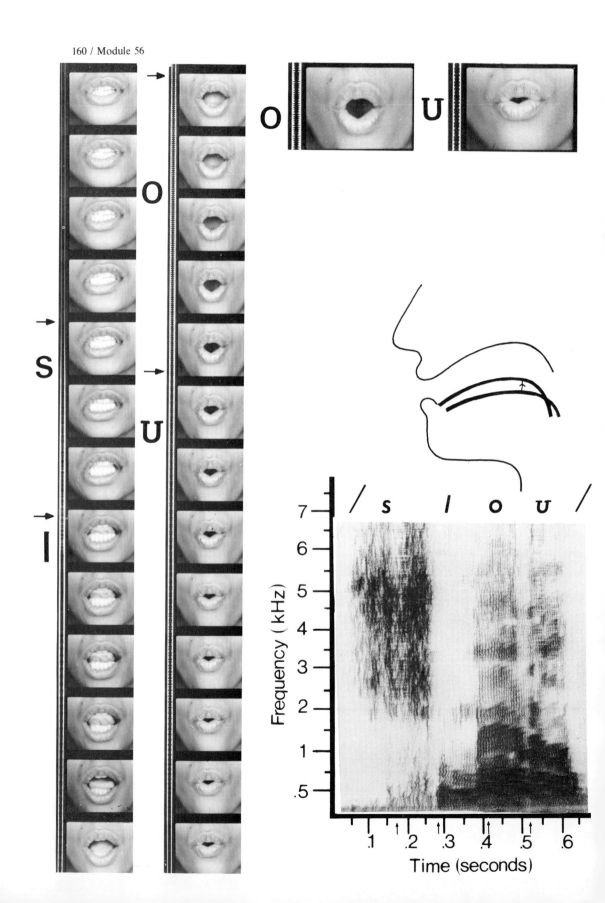

/ s l o u /

EXERCISES

Fill in the Blanks

1. In Module 17 the sound track of the film strips does not begin until frame
    _____.

2. In Module 24, although the first frame is involved in the production of the nonlabial phoneme /z/, it shows considerable amount of lip rounding because of the influence of _____.

3. In Module 40, the frames at the end of the first strip of film are involved in the production of /____/.

4. The two isolated frames in Modules 49 and 50 show that /_____/ is more rounded than /_____/.

5. The schematic diagram of the words /_____/, /_____/, and /_____/ would be similar to that of the word /bʌz/ in Module 25.

6. The schematic drawing in Module 43 shows that vowel /ɛ/ is a _____ vowel.

7. In Module 21, the schematic drawing shows the movement of the tongue from the _____ position to the _____ position and from this position to the _____ position.

True or False

____ 1. There is a great similarity between the sound spectrograms in Modules 15 and 25.

____ 2. Frames 1 through 6 in Module 6 and frames 1 through 4 in Module 35 are identical because they are all involved in the production of /b/.

____ 3. The schematic diagram of the word /tʌn/ would be similar to that of the word /nʌn/ in Module 34.

____ 4. The schematic diagrams in Modules 10 and 15 are similar.

Phoneme Identification

Identify the phonemes missing in the seven modules presented on the following pages. In each of the first five modules one phoneme is missing. The last two modules require identification of all phonemes.

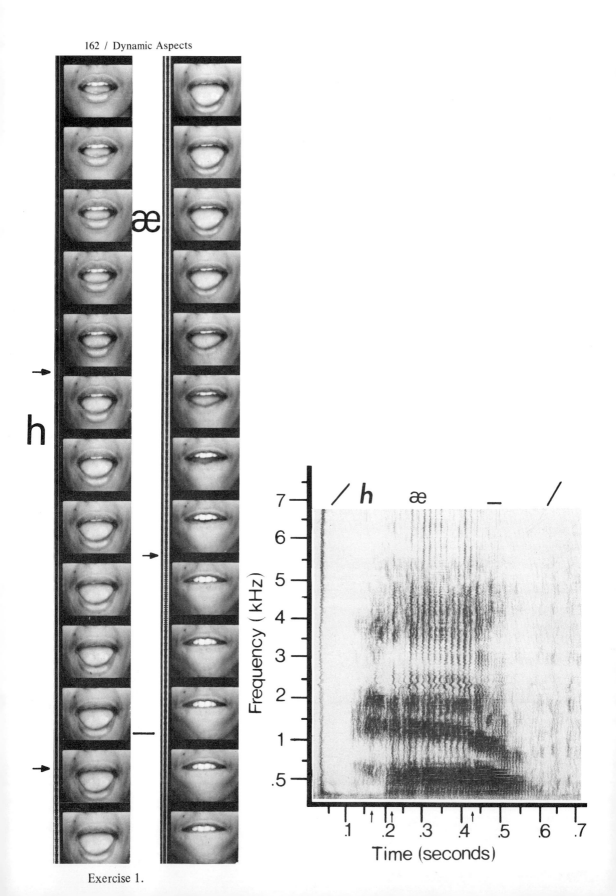

Exercise 1.

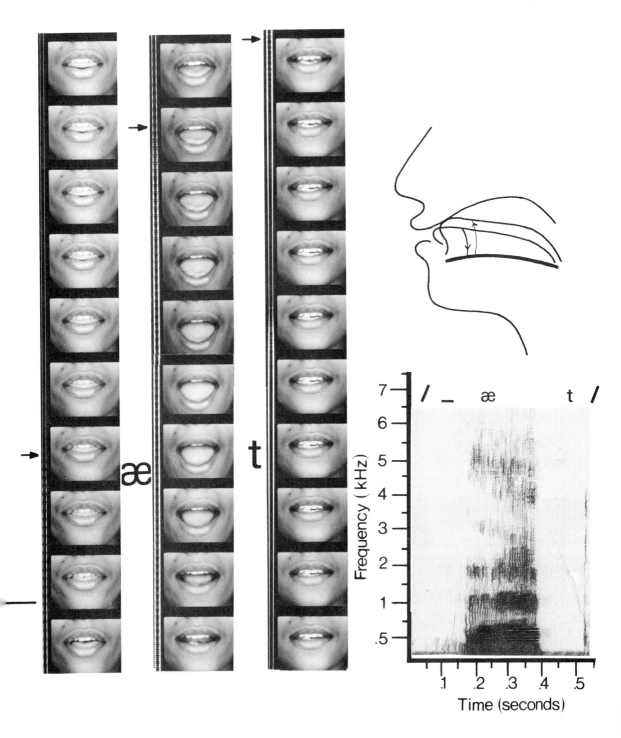

æ

t

$/ \_ \quad æ \quad t /$

Exercise 2.

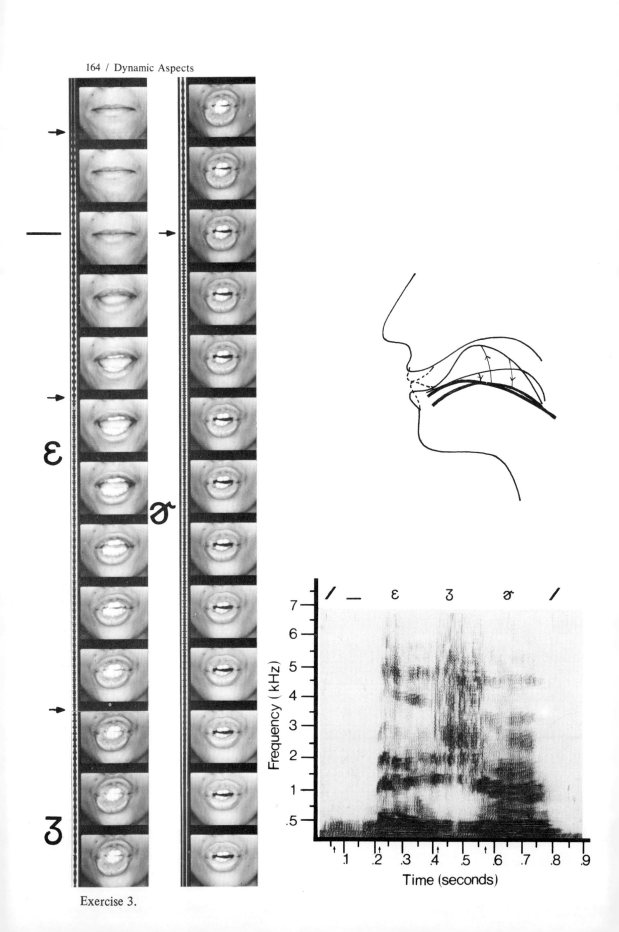

Exercise 3.

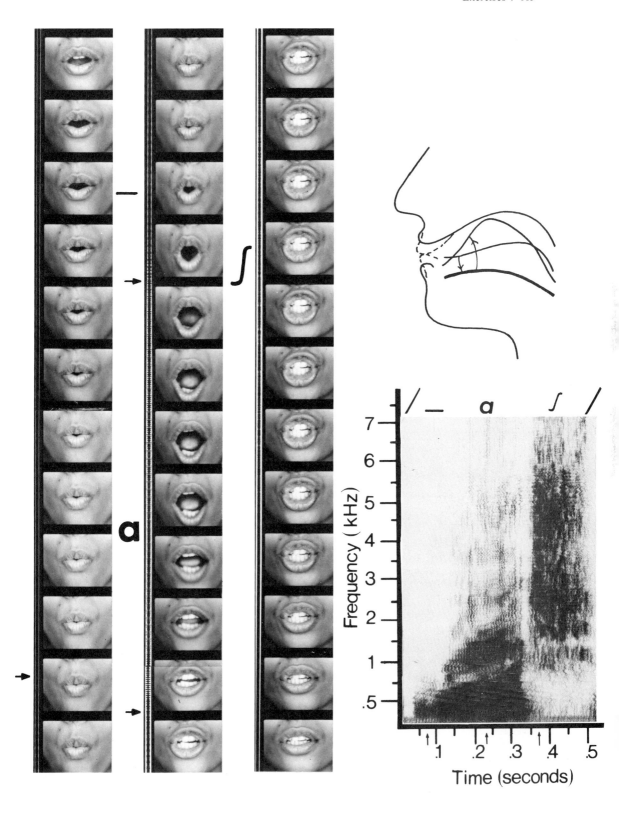

Exercise 4.

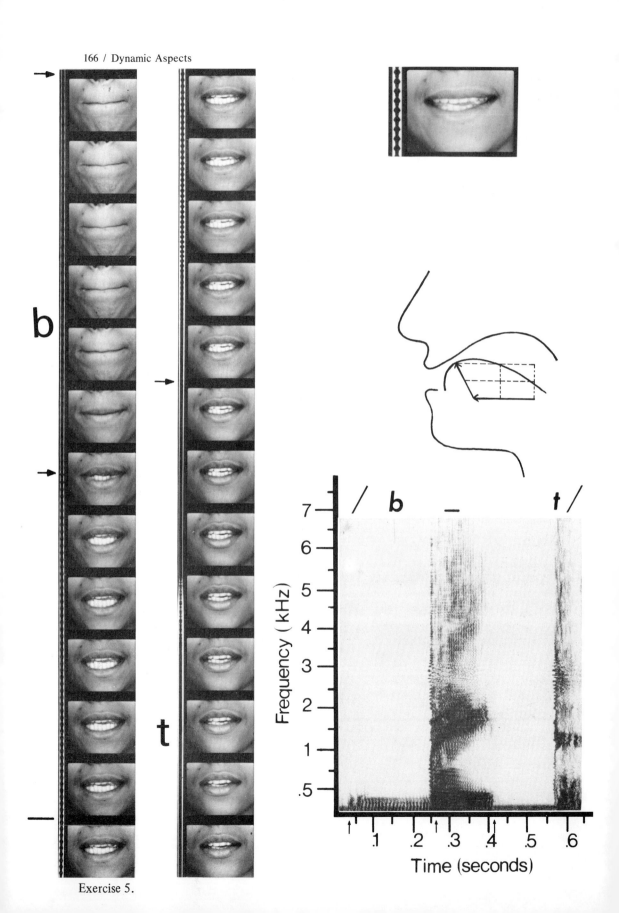

b

t

—

Exercise 5.

/ **b** _ **t** /

7

6

5

4

3

2

1

.5

Frequency (kHz)

.1 .2 .3 .4 .5 .6

Time (seconds)

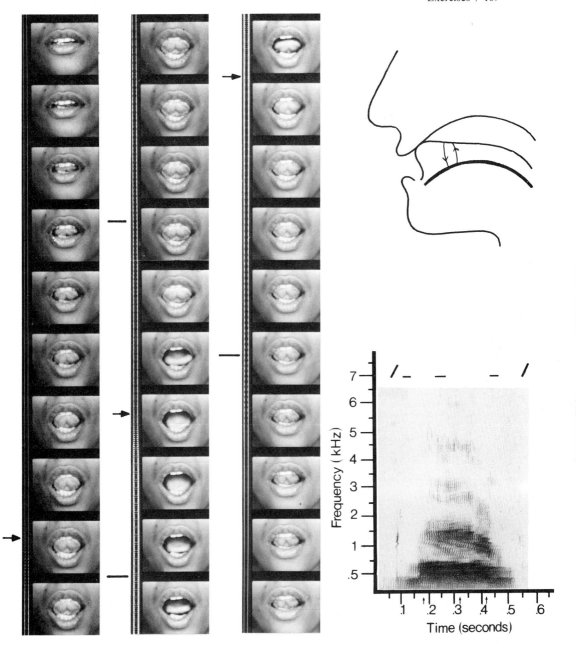

Exercise 6.

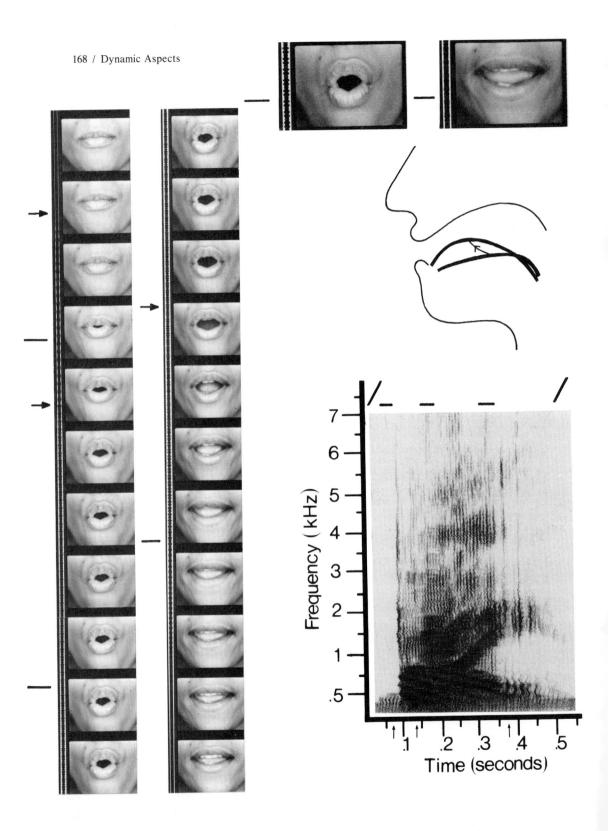

Exercise 7.

Chapter 8 SYLLABLE AND STRESS

In English, syllables can be formed either by a solitary vowel or diphthong or by combining a vowel or diphthong with one or more consonants. There are different types of syllables in English formed by the various consonant-vowel combinations.

SYLLABLE TYPES

Table 2 shows the various syllable types and provides an example for each type. The symbol *V* in this table indicates the presence of a vowel or diphthong, the symbol *C* indicates the presence of a consonant, and the repeated entries of *C* indicate the presence of more than one consonant.

Of the fifteen different syllable types noted, the last eleven types are derived from the first four. Therefore, the first four syllable types are called "simple" and the

rest are called "complex." Although the syllables contain different numbers of consonants, they always contain one and only one vowel at the word-initial position, word-medial position, or word-final position. It is for this reason that a vowel is often referred to as the nucleus of the syllable.

In certain languages, e.g., Sanskrit, modern Indian, and languages derived from Sanskrit, the syllable is the basic unit for teaching the alphabet. In English, however, children are not exposed initially to syllables but to an orthographic system that emphasizes individual sounds. A complete understanding of the structure of English syllables is important for the phonetic transcription of conversational speech. It is also important to understand other features that are superimposed on the syllable. Such features are known as *supra-*

Table 2.   Listing of different syllable types used in English, with orthographically written and phonetically transcribed examples

	Word example	
Syllable type	Orthographic transcription	Phonetic transcription
Simple		
V	a	/ə/ or /ʌ/
CV	the	/ðə/
VC	eat	/it/
CVC	sit	/sɪt/
Complex		
CCV	tree	/tri/
VCC	east	/ist/
CCVC	stood	/stʊd/
CCCVC	street	/strit/
CCCVCC	streets	/strits/
CCCVCCC	strengths	/strɛŋθs/
CVCC	sips	/sɪps/
CCVCC	treats	/trits/
CVCCC	depths	/dɛpθs/
CCCV	screw	/skru/
VCCC	asks	/æsks/

segmental features and include stress and intonation.

STRESS

The term "stress" is used interchangeably with the term "accent." It refers to the most prominent part of a syllable or a word. This prominence is considered to be caused by additional breath force. A syllable may or may not be stressed, depending on whether it is prominent or not prominent.

Stress is related to syllable nucleus and is used to denote differing degrees of prominence in words containing more than one syllable. Stress cannot be marked in monosyllabic words. It is crucially important to understand the property of stress because it relates to the different vowels, the grammatical word classes, and the types of sentences.

Using the International Phonetic Alphabet, three distinct stress levels used in the English language can be described: 1) *primary stress,* 2) *secondary stress,* and 3) *unstress.* Primary stress represents the maximal prominence of a syllable. Secondary stress indicates the second degree of prominence, and unstress shows the smallest degree of prominence of the syllable.

Notation

Polysyllabic words always contain a syllable with primary stress. A syllable with primary stress may be called a *strong syllable,* and a syllable with no stress may be referred to as a *weak syllable.* Primary stress is marked by a stroke at the upper lefthand side of the syllable, secondary stress is marked by a stroke at the lower lefthand side of the syllable, and unstress is not marked at all. For example, the word 'incapable' /ˌɪnˈkeɪpəbl̩/ contains all three types of syllable stress. The first syllable /ɪn-/ has secondary stress, the second syllable /-keɪ-/ has primary stress, and the third and fourth syllables /-pə-/ and /-bl̩/ are unstressed.

Stressing has been found to be associated with high amplitude (loudness), long duration (time), and high frequency (pitch).

Changes in Stress

Stressing is a relative phenomenon in English. Therefore, it must be studied in word context and also in sentence context. The same syllable and even the same word may be stressed or unstressed depending upon the context of a sentence and the degree of emphasis placed on a certain part of the sentence.

The words /ˌɪˈkɑnəˌmɪ/ and /ˌɪkəˈnɑˌmɪkəl/ show that the second syllable of the noun *economy* has primary stress, and the third syllable is unstressed. In the adjectival form, *economical,* primary stress is on the third syllable and the second syllable is unstressed. In the word /ˌɪˈkɑnəˌmɪ/, the vowel in the syllable with primary stress (second syllable) is /ɑ/, while the vowel in the syllable with no stress (third syllable) is /ə/. Once the stress pattern reverses, the vowel /ɑ/ becomes /ə/, and the vowel /ə/ becomes /ɑ/, as in the word /ˌɪkəˈnɑˌmɪkəl/.

In the sentence, 'I am sick,' the emphasis may be on the monosyllabic words 'am' or 'sick,' depending on meaning, and may be transcribed as /aɪˈæmsɪk/ or /aɪmˈsɪk/, respectively. Note that the nature of the vowel changes according to whether the primary stress is on the second or the third syllable.

Grammatical Changes

The examples presented on the next page show the unstressing of some of the primarily stressed English vowels. The first column on the left includes examples of primarily stressed vowels. The second column includes conditions under which the stressed vowel becomes unstressed. The third column presents the stressed vowel and its unstressed counterpart. The fourth column indicates which syllable in the example underwent the stressing change.

Primary stress	Unstress	Vowel changes	Syllable
/'sʌbsɪˌdaɪz/	/ˌsəb'sɪdiəri/	/ʌ/ ⇒ /ə/	1st
/'ɛksport/	/əks'port/	/ɛ/ ⇒ /ə/	1st
/'hæbɪt/	/ˌhə'bɪtʃjuəl/	/æ/ ⇒ /ə/	1st
/'kɑnvɪkt/	/kən'vɪkt/	/ɑ/ ⇒ /ə/	1st
/kən'sʌlt/	/ˌkansəl'teɪʃən/	/ʌ/ ⇒ /ə/	2nd
/ɪn'stɔl/	/ˌɪnstə'leɪʃən/	/ɔ/ ⇒ /ə/	2nd

The change in stress in the above examples is mainly a result of changes in the grammatical classes of the words. For example, the word /'kɑnvɪkt/ is a noun; however, when transformed to a verb it becomes /kən'vɪkt/.

Contextual Changes

Besides the changes in stress re-sulting from changes in gram-matical classes, words of the same grammatical classes may change stress according to the context of a phrase or sentence. The following are some examples showing the stressed and un-stressed versions of some English prepositions, pronouns, and mo-dals.

Stressed	Example	Unstressed	Example
Prepositions			
/tu/	/ɪn'tu ðə/ (into the)	/tə/	/tə'gou/ (to go)
/fɔr/	/wət'fɔr/ (what for)	/fər/	/fər'ju/ (for you)
/ʌv/	/'ʌv ðə θri/ (of the three)	/əv/	/'wʌn əv ju/ (one of you)
/baɪ/	/'baɪ ðə weɪ/ (by the way)	/bə/	/bə'nau/ (by now)
Pronouns			
/hi/	/wət'hi wɑnts ɪz ju/ (what he wants is you)	/ɪ/	/kʊd ɪ'du ɪt/ (could he do it?)
/hɪm/	/ɪt ɪz nɑt'hɪm, bʌt ju/ (it is not him, but you)	/əm/	/'gɛt ɪtˌfɔr əm/ (get it for 'em)
/hɚ/	/ɪt ɪz 'hɚ, nɑt mi/ (it is her, not me)	/ɚ/	/wʌnɚ 'fɪldʌp/ (wan' 'er filled up?)
Modals			
/kæn/	/'kæn ju du ɪt/ (can you do it?)	/kən/	/ju kən 'gou/ (you can go)
/wɪl/	/'wɪl ju du ɪt/ (will you do it?)	/əl/	/ju'əl 'gou/ (you'll go)

/ʃæl/	/ˈʃæl aɪ du ɪt/ (shall I do it?)	/ʃəl/	/aɪ ʃəl ˈgou/ (I shall go)
/æm/	/ˈæm aɪ əˌful/ (am I a fool?)	/əm/	/aɪmˈsɪk/ (I'm sick)

Similar examples can be given for articles, conjunctions, and verb classes of English words.

Verbs

If the final syllable of a verb contains a lax vowel followed by a single consonant, it is unstressed.

Examples: /ˈprɑmɪs/, /ˈɛdɪt/, /ɪˈmædʒɪn/

If the final syllable contains a tense vowel or a diphthong that is followed by a single consonant, it is stressed.

Examples: /əˈtʃiv/, /ɪˈreɪs/, /sɚˈmaɪz/

If the final syllable contains a double consonant cluster, it is stressed.

Examples: /ɪˈlɛkt/, /kənˈvɪns/, /əˈdæpt/

The above rules apply only to verbs. It would be erroneous to apply these rules to other lexical classes such as nouns or adjectives. According to the last example, if a word ends in a consonant cluster, the final syllable of the word is stressed. However, nouns such as /ˈirɪŋz/, /ˈstaɪpənd/, and /ˈtɛmpəst/ have stress on the first syllable, in spite of the fact that they end in a double consonant cluster.

INTONATION

Intonation is the rise and fall of pitch of voice monitored by the laryngeal movements of the speaker. It provides a sentence with a variety of meanings depending on the emphasis placed by the speaker. In addition, intonation also allows the speaker to convey his emotional state of mind. All spoken languages have inherent patterns of intonation. In some languages, such as Chinese, intonational changes are extensive. A single word in Chinese may carry several different meanings according to changes in intonation. However, there are other languages where intonational changes have only a slight effect on the meaning. American English intonation is determined to a certain extent by convention.

Intonation may be either:

1. Rising or upward intonation denoted by (⌣)
2. Falling or downward intonation denoted by (⌢)
3. Neutral intonation denoted by (→)

The sentence, "Did you do that," may be said using each of the above three intonation patterns as follows:

1) Did you do *that*? (⌣)

In this sentence the intonation pattern is rising, and the word "that" has been stressed greatly.

Such a statement made by the speaker usually means that he is surprised that you have done such an unexpectedly good or bad job.

2) Did *you* do that? (⌢➤)

In this sentence the intonation pattern is falling, and the word "you" has been stressed greatly. Such a statement made by the speaker usually means that he is surprised that you did the job.

3) Did you do that? (⟶➤)

In this sentence the intonation pattern is neutral and all words have been stressed equally. Such a statement made by the speaker usually means that he is interested in knowing if you did the job that was expected of you.

EXERCISES

Fill in the Blanks

1. In English, a _____ can be formed by combining a vowel with one or more consonants.
2. There are three different levels of stress: _____, _____, and _____.
3. The rise and fall in the pitch of voice of a speaker is referred to as his _____.
4. Intonational changes are extensive in languages such as _____.

True or False

____ 1. A syllable contains one and only one consonant.
____ 2. Maximal prominence of a syllable is represented by primary stress.

Multiple Choice

____ 1. The term "stress" is used interchangeably with the term:
    a. syllable
    b. intonation
    c. accent
____ 2. Primary stress is marked by a stroke at the:
    a. upper lefthand side
    b. upper righthand side
    c. lower lefthand side

_____ 3. Rising intonation is denoted by:

     a. (⌣⟶)

     b. (⌢⟵)

     c. (⟶)

Phonemic Transcription

Transcribe phonemically utilizing stress markers.

Primary and Unstress

1. issue _____
2. county _____
3. open _____
4. table _____
5. mother _____

6. upper _____
7. autumn _____
8. cement _____
9. process _____
10. nephew _____

Primary and Secondary Stress

11. mistook _____
12. insert _____
13. window _____
14. outline _____
15. defeat _____

16. withdrawn _____
17. enjoy _____
18. angry _____
19. insist _____
20. inside _____

Primary, Secondary, and Unstress

21. rheumatic _____
22. telephone _____
23. disorder _____
24. develop _____
25. employment _____

26. encounter _____
27. invention _____
28. utility _____
29. television _____
30. cigarette _____

Chapter 9 DISTINCTIVE FEATURE BASIS FOR THE GENESIS AND COMPARISON OF PHONEMES: CONSONANTS

Distinctive features are those indispensible attributes of a phoneme that are required to differentiate one phoneme from another in a language. For example, the phonemes /k/ and /g/ in English are differentiated by the feature voicing, which in turn is an indispensible attribute in differentiating phonemes in the English language. When two phonemes differ by only one distinctive feature, they are known as being *minimally distinct* from each other; e.g., phonemes /p/ and /b/ are minimally distinct because the only feature that distinguishes them is voicing. Similarly, /p/ and

/t/ are minimally distinct, separated by the feature labiality.

MINIMALLY DISTINCT PHONEME PAIRS

In order to understand minimal distinction between the pairs of English phonemes, it may be helpful to study Figure 13. This figure is presented so that, upon viewing, the student will be able to identify all minimally distinct phoneme pairs. For example, the phonemes /p/ and /t/ share all features except labiality, the phonemes /t/ and /k/ share all features except front/back place, the phonemes /f/ and /θ/ share all

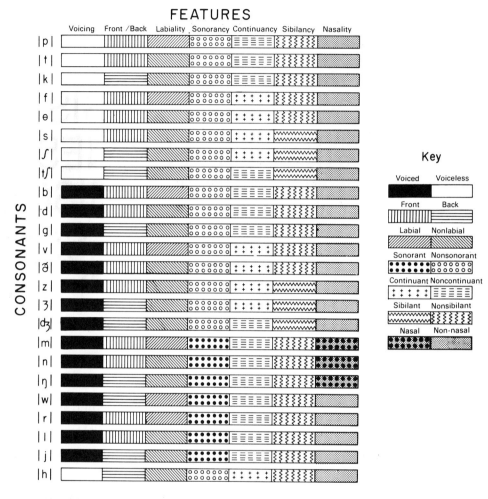

Figure 13. A visual description of distinctive feature contrast among English consonants.

features except labiality, and so on. Although the minimally distinct phoneme pairs differ by one feature, others pairs of phonemes may differ by two or more features. For example, phonemes /p/ and /k/ are different by two features, front/back place and labiality, and /p/ and /g/ are different by three features, front/back place, labiality, and voicing.

Calculating Feature Differences

On the basis of the articulatory descriptions and their acoustic correlates, a matrix has been constructed to describe speech sounds in terms of distinctive features. Table 3 presents a distinctive feature system of English consonants. In this table, the columns represent the consonants and the rows represent the features; the number *one* represents the presence of a feature in a consonant and *zero* represents the absence of that feature. The numerical values, ones and zeros, are used here instead of plus and

Table 3. A feature-by-consonant matrix showing seven distinctive features and twenty-four consonants

Feature													Consonant*											
	p	t	k	b	d	g	f	v	θ	ð	s	z	tʃ	dʒ	ʃ	ʒ	m	n	ŋ	j	r	l	w	h
Voicing	0	0	0	1	1	1	0	1	0	1	0	1	0	1	0	1	1	1	1	1	1	1	1	0
Nasality	0	0	0	0	0	0	0	0	0	0	0	0	0	0	0	0	1	1	1	0	0	0	0	0
Continuancy	0	0	0	0	0	0	1	1	1	1	1	1	0	0	1	1	0	0	0	1	1	1	1	1
Sibilancy	0	0	0	0	0	0	0	0	0	0	1	1	1	1	1	1	0	0	0	0	0	0	0	0
Front	1	1	0	1	1	0	1	1	1	1	1	1	0	0	0	0	1	1	0	0	1	1	1	0
Sonorancy	0	0	0	0	0	0	0	0	0	0	0	0	0	0	0	0	1	1	1	1	1	1	1	0
Labiality	1	0	0	1	0	0	1	1	0	0	0	0	0	0	0	0	1	0	0	0	0	0	1	0

*1, feature present; 0, feature absent.

minus in order to calculate numerically the differences between phonemes.

Using this table, all phonemes can be compared by calculating the similarities or differences among them. For example, the difference between /p/ and /s/ can be determined from this table in the following manner:

$$D\frac{/p/}{/s/} = \frac{V^0, N^0, C^0, Sib^0, F^1, Son^0, L^1}{V^0, N^0, C^1, Sib^1, F^1, Son^0, L^0}$$

$$= C, Sib, L$$

where D signifies the difference between the phonemes /p/ and /s/; V is voicing; N, nasality; C, continuancy; Sib, sibilancy; F, front; Son, sonorancy; and L, labiality. The calculation shows that the differences between /p/ and /s/, in terms of the seven distinctive features, are attributable to three features: continuancy, sibilancy, and labiality. This kind of comparison can be extended to all consonant pairs.

Application to Speech Pathology

With the phonemic comparison strategy shown above, a number of phoneme pairs can be compared to determine the differences between them. The phonemes in the /p, b/ pair differ by one feature, and the phonemes in the /p, s/ pair differ by three features. It is obvious that a three-feature difference is greater than a one-feature difference, thus implying greater possibilities of errors in the /p, b/ pair than in the /p, s/ pair. If one child makes

substitution errors within the former pair and another child makes substitution errors within the latter pair, then the second child has a more severe articulation problem than the first child. A one-feature error is called an *error of minimal distinction* and a three-feature error is called an *error of triple distinction*.

Such a feature system not only explains why two phonemes are different from each other, but also provides a numerical value to the difference. This is a scientific advancement of considerable importance in the field of phonetics.

FEATURE DIFFERENCES BETWEEN PHONEME PAIRS

Utilizing the distinctive feature system, we can describe each consonant in terms of its relationship with its probable substituting consonant(s). In the next chapter we will describe similar relationships between the vowels. Consonant clusters and diphthongs are not included because their essential properties may be explained in terms of their component consonants or vowels.

Obstruents /p, b/ and Sonorants /m, w/

The phonemes /p, b, m, w/ are produced at one end of the vocal tract and involve both lips in their production. The phoneme /p/ is perhaps the first sound that a child utters in a meaningful way. Of course, the parental feedback that a child receives is language dependent and determines the child's later language development.

/p/ may be the earliest uttered consonant because of the minimal amount of neuromuscular and respiratory constraint involved in its production. Precise placement of the teeth, gums, or tongue is not needed. Because it is a voiceless consonant, vocal fold vibration is also not needed. It is known that most very young children (less than six months old) do not have teeth. They also do not have a well developed and adequately projected alveolar ridge, and have insufficient motor control to drive the tongue precisely to produce alveolar, palatal, or velar sounds. However, the lip musculature has been strengthened by excessive use in sucking and the infant is ready to use lips in saying something like /pɑ/.

In the case of deaf infants, the /p, b/ phonemes still may be the first uttered because these two sounds are most visible. Deaf persons who are beginners in lip reading usually can lip read /p, b, m/ with relative ease but have greater difficulty with other sounds.

The phoneme /p/ is not only one of the earliest sounds learned, but it is also one of the last sounds to be lost if one loses language as a result of a neurological affliction.

The phoneme /p/ is different from /b/ by one added degree of complexity—the vocal fold vibrations. Because vocal fold vi-

brations are necessary for the production of /b/, the amount of force required for its production has to be readjusted. Physiologically, therefore, /b/ is considered a more complex sound than /p/.

The phoneme /m/ has further added complexity because lip closure and vocal fold vibrations have to be synchronized with the opening of the nasopharyngeal valve. In the production of the nasal consonant /m/, there is a division of the air pressure into the oral and nasal cavities, and, therefore, the amount and quality of the resonance is somewhat diffuse. Although the continuous air stream must pass through the nose, a certain amount of air pressure also must be channeled to the oral cavity for opening the point of constriction in the oral cavity. The /m/ phoneme is a sonorant sound because it is produced with spontaneous and smooth vibration of the vocal folds. However, because it requires closure in the oral cavity, it also may be labeled as a stop.

In articulation disorders /p/ and /b/ are two of the most stable sounds. Usually, they replace other consonants when errors are made. They are rarely replaced by other consonants. Of the three English nasal consonants /m, n, ŋ/, /m/ is considered the nasal counterpart of the oral consonants /p, b/. If there is auditory confusion or misarticulation among the labial group, the general tendency is to replace /m/ by either /b/ or /p/ and to replace /b/ by /p/. Of course, there are some cases when these substitutions may not be true. For example, a child with a short palate or a repaired cleft palate may replace both /p/ and /b/ by /m/.

The phoneme /w/ is considered labial because lip rounding is absolutely necessary for its production. However, while the lip rounding takes place in the front of the mouth, there is a vowel-like resonating activity at the back of the mouth. Therefore, /w/ has been expressed in the distinctive feature chart as being labial and back. This may seem contradictory but actually is not. The phoneme /r/ is also similarly marked. Although the phoneme /r/ is produced at the alveolar ridge, it is considered labial because lip rounding necessarily accompanies it in normal English production.

/w/ is not a widely used consonant in other languages of the world. In some languages of the Indic family, /w/ is in allophonic distribution with /b/. In English, because of its glide-like characteristic, /w/ at the final position of a word becomes a diphthong; e.g., the word 'how' is pronounced as /haʊ/. In articulation and speech perception disorders, /w/ is most commonly replaced by /b/, and in some instances by /v/, but rarely by /r/. However, /r/ is most usually substituted by /w/. With some American English speakers, /r/ and /w/ at the word-initial position are allophones of the phoneme /r/ (e.g., the word 'rush' may also be pronounced 'wush'). This is because /w/ and /r/, at the word-initial position, are best realized by lip rounding.

Obstruents

Labiodental Fricatives /f, v/

Closely behind the lips in the vocal tract is the labiodental position. The two English consonants /f, v/ are produced at this position. Both are identical in all features except voicing. They both utilize the lower lip in their production and, therefore, have the same visual advantage as /p/ and /b/. The phonemes /f, v/ differ from /p, b/ by the continuancy feature. The diagram on the next page shows the relationship of /f, v/ with /p, b/ in terms of the added complexity of the feature continuancy. In addition, whereas the production of /f, v/ involves the participation of two dissimilar organs (lower lip and upper teeth), the production of /p, b/ requires the participation of two similar organs (lower and upper lips).

The place of articulation for these two pairs of consonants is quite adjacent to each other. Actually, in the distinctive feature system presented in this chapter, the /p, b/ pair is distinguished from the /f, v/ pair only by the feature continuancy, a difference in the manner of articulation. As far as the place of articulation is concerned, both of these pairs are labials.

A two-way matrix describing /f, v/ and /p, b/ reveals the following relationships:

Manner

		Stop	Continuancy
Voicing	Voiceless	p ←————————— f	
		↑	↑
	Voiced	b ←————————— v	

The arrows indicate the direction in which the consonant features flow in misarticulation and misperception. For example, if an articulation disorder involves /f, v/, a speech and hearing therapist can analyze the substitutions by observation of the direction of the arrows. The arrows show that continuants become stops and voiced becomes voiceless. In language learning, these arrows can be interpreted in such a way that the phoneme upon which all arrows converge is the first learned and the phoneme from which all arrows move away is the last learned phoneme (on any given diagram).

These arrows indicate only the general tendency of the consonantal errors. In exceptional cases, the arrows may flow in the opposite direction. The patient whose substitution errors defy the direction of these arrows would be labeled as having a more severe problem than one whose errors are consistent with the direction of the arrows. The direction of the arrows mostly pertains to the ease in articulating the phoneme, in terms of the physiological simplicity of the target sound. On the manner continuum the stops /p, b/ have a shorter and a more abrupt duration than the continuants /f, v/. It is, perhaps, easier to explode than to sustain a steady flow of energy. In addition, /p, b/ are bilabial sounds whereas /f, v/ are labiodentals. The involvement of an added articulator (upper teeth) is an added complexity.

An examination of the acoustic display of the articulatory gestures associated with these consonants further supports the direction of the arrows established in the above diagram. The following chart shows that, in a consonant-vowel syllable, the production of /p/ does not involve the action of the vocal folds before the onset of the vowel segment nor does /p/ have a long, sustained duration. The production of /b/, however, requires vocal fold vibration before the plosive burst.

	/p/	/b/	/f/	/v/
Voicing	—	Begins before the explosion	—	Begins before the explosion
Manner	—	—	Long duration	Long duration

The phoneme /f/ does not require vocal fold vibration but does require the maintenance of a long and sustained flow of low amplitude energy. The production of the phoneme /v/, however, requires both markers of complexity described in case of /b/ and /f/, i.e., vocal fold vibration before the plosive burst and long duration.

Another reason for the simplicity of the phoneme /p/, compared with its voiced or continuant counterparts, is its flexibility resulting from allophonic variations. *Allophones* are different versions of the phonetic manifestations of a phoneme resulting from contextual constraints. The difference between a phoneme and an allophone is that a phoneme cannot be replaced by another of its kind without destroying its meaning, but the allophone can be replaced by another of its kind and the meaning remains unaltered. Usually, allophonic variations are not permitted for /f/ and /v/; thus, any digression from the ideal speech is considered an error.

Some phoneticians hold that, in the word-medial position, the phonemes /f/ and /v/ when followed by a bilabial consonant become bilabial fricatives [φ] and [β], respectively, thus forming allophones of /f/ and /v/. The allophonic variations of the voiceless stops /p, t, k/ have maximal flexibility, in the sense that the articulatory particulars required for one context may be used in another context without changing the meaning of the utterances. This kind of flexibility is reduced for the voiced counterparts of these stop consonants. For example, the initial consonants usually aspirated in the words 'pill,' 'till,' and 'kill' may be pronounced without aspiration and the meaning of the utterance remains unaltered. However, the initial consonants usually unaspirated in the words 'bill,' 'dill,' and 'gill' may be pronounced with aspiration and the meaning is altered; e.g., when the phoneme /b/ in 'bill' is aspirated, the word is perceived as 'pill,' thereby changing the meaning.

The flexibility of the /f, v/ phonemes is generally reduced to one and only one acceptable pronunciation in all contexts.

Linguadental Fricatives /θ, ð/

The next phoneme pair on the horizontal continuum of the vocal tract is /θ, ð/. These two phonemes do not have distinctive orthographic representations; they are both written by the two letters 'th' as in the words 'think' /θɪŋk/ and 'that' /ðæt/. In our experience, this pair of sounds is one of the most difficult to learn in phonetic transcription. Besides the ambiguity in the orthographic representations, there are other articulatory, acoustic, and phonological properties relating to these two phonemes that make them most vulnerable to errors. Because of these complexities children develop these sounds much later in their phonological repertoire. Perhaps because the essential articulators for the successful production of these sounds are the upper and lower teeth, /θ, ð/ undergo immense distortion if a few of the front teeth are missing or if the denture is not steadfast.

These constraints are very superficial, in that they do not relate to the true parameters of phoneme processing. However, they do play an important role in the production of /θ/ and /ð/. Fortunately, the frequency of occurrence of these two phonemes in the English language is not very high. Their reduced use in every-day conversation minimizes the probability of errors relating to them.

The relationship of the linguadentals /θ and ð/ with the neighboring labiodental phonemes /f, v/ is shown in the following two-way matrix:

Place

	Labiodental	Linguadental
Voicing	Voiceless	f ← θ́
		↑ ↑
	Voiced	v ← ð

Both pairs are continuants, hence they do not differ in their manner of articulation. The direction of the arrows shows the tendency for voiced to become voiceless and for linguadental to become labiodental.

An examination of the oral structures involved in producing these phonemes reveals that the production of the linguadentals /θ, ð/ involves the lower teeth, the upper teeth, and the tip of the tongue, but the production of the labiodentals /f, v/ requires only the lower lip and the upper teeth. The tongue as an additional agent of articulation is uninvolved. There is ample evidence in misarticulations and in certain dialects of English that /θ/ is replaced by /f/, and /ð/ is replaced by /v/, perhaps because of the relative ease in the production of /f, v/. Thus, the word 'bath' /bæθ/ is pronounced /bæf/ and 'mother' /ˈmʌðɚ/ is pronounced /ˈmʌvɚ/.

Acoustic data also support the direction of the arrows in the above diagram. Table 4 demonstrates the differing degrees of acoustic complexity involved in the production of /f, v/ and /θ, ð/. It is well known that mastering low frequency sounds with high amplitude is generally easier than mastering high frequency sounds with low amplitude. A serious acoustic deficiency that /θ, ð/ suffer from is the lack of audible amplitude. /θ/ especially is a very feeble sound, containing the smallest amount of energy of all English consonants. Table 4 shows that /ð/ is the most complex of the four sounds; it is

Table 4.   Comparison of /f, v/ and /θ, ð/ phonemes according to their acoustic components of frequency, amplitude, and voicing

Acoustic property	Phoneme			
	/f/	/v/	/θ/	/ð/
Frequency	Low	Low	High	High
Amplitude	High	High	Low	Low
Voicing	None	Yes	None	Yes

positively marked for each of the three markers of complexity—high frequency, low amplitude, and voicing.

/θ, ð/ are interdental sounds produced with the tip of the tongue between the teeth, but /t, d/ are alveolar sounds produced with the tip of the tongue behind the upper teeth (alveolar ridge). In terms of the number of oral structures involved, /t, d/ merely involve the contact of the tongue tip with the alveolar ridge, whereas /θ, ð/ involve the lower teeth, the upper teeth, and the tongue tip.

/θ/ and /ð/ do not have any permitted allophones in standard American English. In dialects of English where precision in articulation of the so-called standard form is not considered an essential part of language learning, /θ/ and /ð/ are replaced at the word-initial places by /t/ and /d/, respectively. At the word-medial and word-final positions, they are replaced by /f/ and /v/, respectively. Thus, instead of saying /ðɪs/ and /ðæt/, the speakers of certain English dialects say /dɪs/ and /dæt/. The same speakers may also say 'bof' /bouf/ for 'both' /bouθ/ and 'bave' /beɪv/ for 'bathe' /beɪð/. Because the above contextual phonetic variations are permitted by some speech communities, they therefore can be considered as the allophonic variations of the phonemes /θ, ð/ in those dialects.

The following two-way matrix maps the relationship between /t, d/ and /θ, ð/:

Manner

		Stops	Continuants
Voicing	Voiceless	t ←——————— θ
		↑ ↑
	Voiced	d ←——————— ð

This matrix shows that continuants /θ/ and ð/ become stops /t/ and /d/, respectively; and voiced /d/ and /ð/ become voiceless /t/ and /θ/, respectively.

Table 5 presents the underlying structure of the acoustic relationship between the phoneme pairs /t, d/ and /θ, ð/. The relative complexity of the above paradigm is reflected in the acoustic description of these two pairs of phonemes. While phonemes /t/ and /d/ have shorter duration and relatively high amplitude in a well defined frequency region, the phoneme pair /θ, ð/ has long duration and low amplitude, scattered in a relatively less well defined frequency region. (See sound spectrograms of /t/ and /θ/ in Modules 3 and 12 of Chapter 7.)

Table 5. Comparison of /t, d/ and /θ, ð/ phonemes according to their acoustic components of duration, frequency, amplitude, and voicing

Acoustic property	Phoneme			
	/t/	/d/	/θ/	/ð/
Duration	Short	Short	Long and sustained	Long and sustained
Frequency–amplitude relationship	High amplitude in well defined frequency region	High amplitude in well defined frequency region	Low amplitude in less defined frequency region	Low amplitude in less defined frequency region
Voicing	None	Yes	None	Yes

Alveolar Stops /t, d/

Let us now examine /t, d/ as criterion phonemes, having relationships with other phonemes that are close articulatory, acoustic, and perceptual approximations of them. Within the stop category, in front of them lies the phoneme pair /p, b/ and behind them lies the phoneme pair /k, g/. In the following two-way matrix, the direction in which the arrows point is very closely tied with the substitution errors in speech production and speech perception. In addition, the directionality of the arrows is also supported by acoustic data:

Place

	Labial	Alveolar
Voiceless	p ←	t
Voiced	b ←	d

Voicing

/t, d/ are generally quite stable in articulation and speech perception. However, if they are misarticulated, there is greater probability that they will be replaced by labial stops. In the preceding matrix the horizontal arrows indicate that alveolar becomes labial and the vertical arrows indicate that voiced becomes voiceless. This strategy is well supported by the evidence from articulatory, acoustic, and perceptual literature. Acoustically, /p/ and /b/ show low frequency concentration of energy around 1,000 Hz whereas /t/ and /d/ show mid frequency concentration of energy around 2,000 Hz.

The phoneme pair /t, d/ is of interest to phoneticians from two points of view: 1) that /t/ is one of the three most frequently used consonants in English, and 2) that both are consonants used in forming past tense in English. The /-t/ ending is added to words like 'walk' /wɑk/ to formulate the past tense 'walked' /wɑkt/. The /-d/ ending is added to formulate the past tense for words such as 'bug' /bʌg/, which becomes 'bugged' /bʌgd/.

Alveolar Sibilant Fricatives /s, z/

Similar to the phoneme pair /t, d/ the phoneme pair /s, z/ has several interesting aspects that need scrutiny. First, /s/ is one of the most frequently used consonant phonemes in everyday English conversation. Second, both phonemes are used to pluralize English words. For example, the word 'cat' /kæt/ becomes 'cats' /kæts/, and the word 'dog' /dɔg/ becomes 'dogs' /dɔgz/.

Based on acoustic and articulatory details, relationships of the phoneme pair /s, z/ may be established with the pairs /t, d/, /θ, ð/, and /ʃ, ʒ/. The selection of these pairs for determining relationships is based on the observation of errors in articulation and in speech perception. In addition, when children's phonological competence is not reached, they substitute /s, z/ with /t, d/ or /ʃ, ʒ/.

In articulatory terms, /s/ and /z/ are grooved continuant sibilant consonants that are produced by the passage of a strong flow of air at the alveolar place of articulation, resulting in a hissing sound. It is usually agreed that, although /s, z/ are not produced as far back as the center of the hard palate, they are also not produced as far front as the alveolar ridge. In counting feature differences between /s, z/ and /t, d/, the place of articulation feature is not considered, because both pairs are produced virtually at the same location. The other feature differences (continuancy and sibilancy) between these two pairs of phonemes are significant.

The phoneme pair /s, z/ has the longest duration and the greatest acoustic energy of all continuant pairs in English. /s, z/ have their energy concentration around the highest frequency region. Both lie at the extremes of the frequency, time, and amplitude continua. They have long duration and very high amplitude concentration in the high frequency regions. To the contrary, the phonemes /t, d/ have short duration and mid frequency energy concentration in a relatively well defined region. Because of their extreme high frequency nature, /s/ and /z/ are often misarticulated and are most frequently substituted by /t/ and /d/, respectively, except when /-s/ and /-z/ are used to form plurals.

In some instances, /s/ and /z/ are substituted by the phonemes /θ/ and /ð/. The only articulatory basis for this substitution is that the phoneme pair /s, z/ requires the passage of air through the groove-like opening in the mouth. However, the phonemes /θ, ð/, within the same manner category (continuant), require a flat placement of the tongue tip between the lower and upper teeth.

Palatal Sibilant Fricatives /ʃ, ʒ/

In some instances, phonemes /s, z/ are misarticulated and replaced by a slightly back phoneme pair /ʃ, ʒ/. These two consonant pairs share all articulatory features except the place feature. In the acoustic domain, the /ʃ, ʒ/ pair is slightly shorter in duration than the /s, z/ pair and has energy concentration in slightly lower and higher frequencies than the /s, z/ pair. Some children substitute /s/ by /ʃ/ and /z/ by /ʒ/.

Palatal Sibilant Stops /tʃ, dʒ/

The phonemes /tʃ, dʒ/ are considered stops by many phoneti-

cians, and sound spectrographic display (see Modules 28 and 30 in Chapter 7) of these phonemes supports that definition. Traditionally, these consonants have been called affricates. An examination of their articulatory and acoustic properties suggests that they cannot be continued after their release; this is in keeping with the definition of a stop.

Both pairs of consonants, /tʃ, dʒ/ and /ʃ, ʒ/, have energy concentration in the same frequency regions. However, although the production of /tʃ, dʒ/ is somewhat similar to that of stops, /ʃ, ʒ/ are purely continuant consonants. An inspection of the sound spectrograms of /tʃ/ and /dʒ/ phonemes shows that the initial acoustic characteristic is a complete gap, implying a stoppage of the air stream in the oral cavity, but the release of the air stream after the stoppage makes it a continuant sound. In the distinctive feature system being described in this text, /tʃ, dʒ/ are considered noncontinuants. The /tʃ, dʒ/ pair differs from the /ʃ, ʒ/ pair by the feature continuancy.

Velar Stops /k, g/

Of all the three pairs of pure English stops, /p, b/, /t, d/, and /k, g/, the /k, g/ pair shows the maximal amount of fricative-like aspiration. This may be because, at the other two places of articulation (labial and alveolar), a clear articulatory distinction must be maintained between the stops /p, b/ and /t, d/, and their close continuant counterparts /f, v/ and /θ, ð/, respectively. Such articulatory precision of stops is not required at the velar place of articulation, because in English there is no velar fricative pair that needs distinction from the velar stop pair.

The /k, g/ phoneme pair strongly resembles the /p, b/ and /t, d/ pairs. The /k, g/ consonants are replaced in articulation and speech perception errors by both /t, d/ and /p, b/. Although the articulatory approximation of /k, g/ is nearer to /t, d/ than it is to /p, b/, because of certain acoustic factors the probability of /k, g/ being substituted by either /t, d/ or /p, b/ is almost equal.

Sonorants

Nasals /m, n, ŋ/

Nasality in consonants is a universal feature and one of the features learned earliest by children in most languages. Most languages distinguish between oral and nasal consonants.

The nasal consonants /m, n, ŋ/, according to their error tendencies in articulation and speech discrimination, can be safely classified as belonging to one group. In speech production and speech perception errors, each of these three consonants has a strong tendency to be substituted by the remaining two. This tendency is perhaps a result of their "ethnic" nature. There are relatively fewer of them, and they differ in terms of their origin and nature. Consequently, they rarely cross their own boundaries when interacting with other consonants, and when they do, they become stops. Rarely do they become continuants.

The nasal consonants share an important articulatory function with the oral stop consonants, namely, closure in the oral cavity:

Oral cavity	Nasal stops	Oral stops	Continuants
Velar valve open	+	−	−
Oral closure	+	+	−

With the continuants, however, they do not share either the oral closure function or the opening of the velopharyngeal port.

Orals /r, w, l, j/

The consonant /r/ is uniquely different from all other consonants in English. In terms of its relationship with other consonants, it is considered closest to /w/ and /l/.

In traditional phonetic terminology, the consonants /r, w, l, j/ are called *glides* because of their extreme flexibility in assuming the role of either a consonant or a vowel. The phoneme /r/, for example, is mostly a consonant at the word-initial position but is usually a vowel at the medial and final positions, especially if the preceding sound is a vowel. For example, in the word 'river' /'rɪvɚ/ the initial /r/ is consonantal and the final /r/ is vocalic (vowel-like). The consonant /l/ serves the function of a consonant at the word-initial and word-medial positions, but functions as a vowel at the word-final position, especially if the word contains more than one syllable.

In many Southeast Asian languages, /r, l/ consonants are in allophonic variation. Also, in some very young children and children who have misarticulations, /r/ is one of the very commonly misarticulated phonemes. Within the same language the production of /r/ differs considerably depending on differences in the dialects of that language. In dialects of the northeastern and southern United States, /r/, when preceded by a vowel (especially neutral and back vowels), adds duration to the preceding vowel with the assimilation of retroflexion into that vowel. For example, 'car' /kɑɚ/ becomes /kɑ·/.

The distribution of /r/ in English is such that at the initial position of a word it is confused with /w/. Actually, in many instances, /r/ and /w/ at the initial position are in allophonic variation. This is because both consonants require lip rounding. At the medial and final positions, however, /r/ may become a vowel or may be confused with /l/, and in some speech disorders /r/ may be substituted by /d/.

Table 6 shows some details of the articulatory relations of /r/ with /w, l, d/. Note that, on the lip dimension, /w/ and /r/ share roundedness, but on the tongue dimension, they do not have any aspect in common. Phonemes /r/ and /l/, on the other hand, do not share similarities on the lip dimension; however, on the tongue dimension, both consonants are produced by the contact of the tongue tip with the alveolar ridge, accompanied by an opening. The phoneme /d/ does not share the lip roundedness aspect with /r/. It does share the place of articulation aspect with /r/ and /l/; however, /d/ is distinct from /r/ and /l/ because its production is not accompanied by

Table 6. Comparison of /w, r, l, d/ phonemes according to their articulatory components involving lips and tongue

Articulators	Phoneme			
	/w/	/r/	/l/	/d/
Lips	Round	Round	Flat	Flat
Tongue	Vowel-like position	Contact with alveolar ridge with smooth central opening	Contact with alveolar ridge with lateral opening	Contact with alveolar ridge without any opening

an opening between the tongue tip and alveolar ridge.

In most English dialects, the phoneme /w/ is allophonic with the phoneme /ʍ/ (wh) at the initial position of the word. For example, the words 'what,' 'which,' 'where,' etc., are produced in most dialects as /wɑt/, /wɪtʃ/, and /wɛɝ/ and in some dialects as /ʍɑt/, /ʍɪtʃ/, and /ʍɛɝ/. In several languages, the phoneme /w/ is in allophonic variation with /b/ and /v/. /r, l/ and /w, j/, despite their overall vowel-like acoustic characteristics, possess consonant-like acoustic energy concentration. For example, /w/, because of its labiality, has low frequency energy; /r/ and /l/, because of their alveolarity, have energy concentration in mid frequencies; and /j/, because of its palatal nature has two prominent energy concentration areas.

Division into Two Groups

On the basis of the above descriptions, the seven sonorant consonants /m, n, ŋ, j, r, l, w/ can be divided into two functional groups. One group includes /m, n, ŋ, l/, which can serve as "pure" consonants in words such as 'man' /mæn/, 'king' /kɪŋ/, and 'lad' /læd/.

These consonants also can serve as vowels (the nucleus of syllable) in words such as 'rope 'em,' / ropm̩/, 'button' /bʌtn̩/, 'we c'n go' /wi kæŋ gou/, and 'kettle' /kɛtl̩/. The syllabic /m̩, n̩, ŋ̩, l̩/ besides being represented by a stroke (ˌ) directly under the consonants, also can be represented by /əm/, /ən/, /əŋ/, and /əl/, respectively.

The second group is the syllabic /w, j, r/, which become entirely independent vowels. After syllabification, the phoneme /j/ becomes /i/ or /ɪ/, /w/ becomes /u/ or /ʊ/, and /r/ becomes /ɚ/ or /ɝ/. Some examples to substantiate the above rule are: 'boy' /bɔɪ/, 'bowl' /boul/, 'bird' /bɝd/, and 'father' /fɑðɚ/.

Glottal Voiceless Fricative /h/

The phoneme /h/ in English is a voiceless consonant with vocalic characteristics. It is called vocalic because it is articulated without any closure in the vocal tract. The /h/ phoneme is produced by glottal constriction and is a continuant sound. Acoustically, /h/ has high frequency energy with a very low amplitude. It is a highly intelligible consonant and is rarely confused with any other consonants.

EXERCISES

Fill in the Blanks

1. Of the seven distinctive features, the phonemes /p, z/ are separated by _____ feature(s), namely, _____
_____.

2. In the production of /m/ the lip closure and vocal fold vibrations have to be synchronized with _____.

3. Because of the lip-rounding component, /w/ is considered as having the feature _____.

4. The phoneme pair /f, v/ differs from the phoneme pair /p, b/ by the feature _____.

5. The /_____/ pair and the /_____/ pair are called labials.

6. Of the phonemes /p, b, f, v/ the phoneme _____ is the most complex in terms of articulatory and acoustic details.

7. The allophonic variations of /p/ are _____.

8. In the so-called nonstandard form of English, the phonemes /θ, ð/ are substituted by /_____/ at the word-initial position and by /_____/ at the word-final position.

9. Besides being an English consonant, the phoneme /t/ also serves the function of a _____.

10. The phonemes /s/ and /θ/ are separated by feature _____.

11. The /k, g/ pair has an equal probability of being substituted by _____ and _____ pairs.

12. The consonant /r/ becomes _____ in the word-final position.

13. The /_____/ phoneme pair is separated from the /m, n/ pair by the feature nasality.

14. In most English dialects, the phoneme /w/ is allophonic with /_____/.

15. The continuant sound produced by glottal constriction is _____.

True or False

_____ 1. A substitution error is considered more serious when the distinctive feature difference between two phonemes is great.

_____ 2. The distinctive feature system is unable to provide a numerical value to the difference between two phonemes.

_____ 3. /m/ has properties of a sonorant and of a stop.

_____ 4. /w/ does not possess the feature front.

_____ 5. In articulation and speech perception errors, /w/ is replaced by /r/ and vice versa.

_____ 6. There is a three-feature difference between the phonemes /p/ and /v/.

_____ 7. In substitution errors voiced sounds become voiceless.

_____ 8. The phoneme /b/ has three allophonic variations.

_____ 9. /f/ has two permitted allophones in English.

_____ 10. /d/ and /θ/ are minimally distinct phonemes.
_____ 11. /h/ and /ʃ/ are minimally distinct phonemes.
_____ 12. Most languages make a distinction between oral and nasal consonants.
_____ 13. Nasal consonants are rarely substituted by continuants.
_____ 14. The phoneme /h/ is rarely confused with other consonants.

Multiple Choice

_____ 1. The phonemes in the /b, m/ pair differ by:
      a. one feature
      b. two features
      c. three features

_____ 2. The possibility of speech production and speech perception errors is _____ in the /p, b/ pair than in the /p, s/ pair.
      a. lesser
      b. greater
      c. the same

_____ 3. One of the first phonemes produced by children is:
      a. /p/
      b. /k/
      c. /f/

_____ 4. The musculature that is well strengthened in children less than six months old is the:
      a. soft palate
      b. tongue
      c. lip

_____ 5. /p, b/ sounds are the most:
      a. oral
      b. visible
      c. complex

_____ 6. One of the last sounds to be lost if one loses language is:
      a. /p/
      b. /t/
      c. /k/

_____ 7. /p, b/ and /f, v/ pairs differ by the feature:
      a. labiality
      b. continuancy
      c. sonorancy

_____ 8. There exists a triple distinction between the phonemes:
      a. /p, ð/
      b. /p, θ/
      c. /b, ð/

_____ 9. The /k, g/ phonemes acoustically have a _____ energy concentration area.

        a. single

        b. dual

        c. triple

_____ 10. The phonemes /w, j, r/ possess one common property. They are all:

        a. back consonants

        b. vocalic

        c. sonorants

Phonemic Transcription

Transcribe phonemically the following minimally distinct pairs. (Answers to this exercise are not provided because of the simplicity of the transcription task.)

1. pan _____	ban _____		21. tin _____	kin _____
2. pin _____	tin _____		22. day _____	gay _____
3. pool _____	fool _____		23. dull _____	lull _____
4. bid _____	did _____		24. sue _____	zoo _____
5. ban _____	van _____		25. sow _____	show _____
6. bore _____	roar _____		26. shoe _____	chew _____
7. mit _____	knit _____		27. shirt _____	hurt _____
8. mat _____	rat _____		28. lesion _____	legion _____
9. won _____	run _____		29. chip _____	gyp _____
10. war _____	your _____		30. chain _____	cane _____
11. fin _____	thin _____		31. John _____	gone _____
12. ferry _____	very _____		32. coat _____	goat _____
13. van _____	than _____		33. cow _____	how _____
14. thigh _____	thy _____		34. guess _____	yes _____
15. thigh _____	high _____		35. sin _____	sing _____
16. thin _____	tin _____		36. sane _____	same _____
17. thank _____	sank _____		37. night _____	light _____
18. there _____	dare _____		38. rate _____	late _____
19. thee _____	zee _____		39. less _____	yes _____
20. tot _____	dot _____			

Chapter 10 DISTINCTIVE FEATURE BASIS FOR THE GENESIS AND COMPARISON OF PHONEMES: VOWELS

Vowel features are presented separately from consonant features because a vowel-consonant confusion is rare in any language. Actually, we believe that vowels and consonants utilize different sets of distinctive feature systems. For a better understanding of the nature of American English vowels, readers are referred to Modules 40 through 51 in Chapter 7.

FRONT VOWELS

/i/

/i/ is a front-high, tense English vowel. It appears in words such as 'bead' /bid/, 'treat' /trit/, 'receive' /rəˈsiv/, and 'believe' /bəˈliv/. It is used to formulate both open and closed syllables such as 'tea' /ti/ and 'need' /nid/, respectively. In most instances it is a stressed vowel.

In acoustic terms, /i/ is a vowel of longer duration than its lax counterpart /ɪ/. Its formant characteristics show an extreme low frequency F_1 and an extreme high frequency F_2. The F_2 and F_3 frequencies of /i/ are in close approximation. A low F_1 is indicative of a high vowel and a high F_2 is indicative of a front vowel.

/ɪ/

/ɪ/ is a front-high, lax English vowel. It appears in words such as 'kit' /kɪt/, 'it' /ɪt/, and 'pity' /pɪtɪ/. In most instances it is unstressed, associating itself with all the necessary functions of unstressing, namely, short duration, low amplitude, and low pitch. It is one of the two most frequently used vowels in conversational American English.

/e/

/e/ is a front-mid, tense English vowel. It occurs very rarely, only in some dialects of English, in words such as 'vacation' /ve-'keɪʃən/ and 'vacate' /ve'keɪt/. In most instances, it is assumed that this vowel takes on the diphthongized role of /eɪ/ as in words like 'cake' /keɪk/ and 'take' /teɪk/. The nondiphthongized /e/ is a short vowel with frequency characteristics in a lower range than the two high front vowels /i/ and /ɪ/. /e/ has a slightly higher F_1 and a slightly lower F_2 than the vowels /i/ and /ɪ/.

/ɛ/

/ɛ/ is a front-mid, lax English vowel with frequent occurrence in all English dialects in words such as 'head' /hɛd/, 'bed' /bɛd/, 'let' /lɛt/, and 'crest' /krɛst/. It is a stressed vowel with high amplitude and long duration characteristics. Similar to the lax vowel /ɪ/, /ɛ/ also appears only in closed syllables. The stressing of the vowel /ɛ/ may be seen in polysyllabic words like 'event' /ˌɪv'ɛnt/ and 'eventually' /ˌɪ'vɛntʃəlɪ/.

/æ/

/æ/ is a front-low English vowel with frequent occurrence in American English, especially in the midwestern and the western regions of the United States. It is a widely used variation of the standard British English /ɑ/. For example, the vowel /ɑ/ in the word 'dance' /dɑns/ in the British English is pronounced as /æ/ in /dæns/ in most speech regions of America.

However, speakers of British English use /æ/ in the same way as speakers of American English, in words like 'fat' /fæt/, 'bad' /bæd/, 'bat' /bæt/, and 'cat' /kæt/. When the vowel /ɑ/ is followed by a nasal /n/ as in 'chance' the general American pronunciation becomes /æ/ while the New England British English and the colonial English pronunciation remains /ɑ/. Examples are 'can't' /kɑnt/ which becomes /kænt/, 'dance' /dɑns/ becomes /dæns/, 'France' /frɑns/ becomes /fræns/, and 'aunt' /ɑnt/ becomes /ænt/.

The vowel /æ/ is stressed in English. It appears in stressed positions in words like 'transfer' /'trænsfɚ/ and 'intransitive' /'ɪnˌtrænzətɪv/. The acoustic characteristics of the vowel /æ/ include a high F_1, high F_2, and a relatively high F_3. The formant bandwidth is wide, with indications of the presence of high amplitude. Because /æ/ is produced with a considerable amount of mouth opening coupled with lip widening, the oral cavity works as the most effective resonator (amplifier). The large resonator size results in greater amplification in the low frequency regions.

Because of its rich acoustic

properties /æ/ is a highly intelligible vowel. However, for teachers of English as a foreign language, it is very troublesome because most non-American speakers of English use /ɑ/ for /æ/.

BACK VOWELS

/ɑ/

/ɑ/ is one of the most widely used vowels in the world. It is perhaps the most universal of all speech sounds. It is one of the earliest learned vowels by children of all languages. The convenience and facilitation of its articulatory delivery is, perhaps, the basis for its universal usage and early acquisition. It is a back-low vowel produced with considerable opening of the oral cavity. Because of this large cavity size, the F_1 and F_2 are adjacent to each other. A comparison of the formant frequencies shows that /ɑ/ has a higher F_1 and a lower F_2 than /æ/. Similar to the vowel /æ/, /ɑ/ is a vowel of long duration, high amplitude, and low pitch. As far as the articulatory effort is concerned, /ɑ/ is produced with the least amount of effort. The lips are not required to be widened or rounded because a total opening of the oral cavity provides the best quality to this vowel. /ɑ/ is a stressed vowel in English and used in words such as 'father' /fɑðɚ/ and 'hot' /hɑt/. It is not differentiated from /ɔ/ in most American English dialects.

/ɔ/

/ɔ/ is a back-mid, lax English vowel used in the stressed position in words such as 'bought' /bɔt/, 'fought' /fɔt/, 'thoughtful' /'θɔtfʊl/, and 'costly' /'kɔstlɪ/. The frequency with which this vowel appears in English is relatively low. The articulatory dimension includes slight lip rounding together with wide mouth opening. The back portion of the tongue is in the high-mid position. Thus, not unlike the vowel /ɑ/, there is a considerable amount of resonance in the oral cavity during its production. The lower two formant frequencies are extremely close to each other, indicating a great deal of speech power.

In perception, /ɔ/ is confused most frequently with the vowel /ɑ/. In some dialects of English, it is in allophonic variation with /ɑ/, e.g., 'hot' /hɑt/ becomes /hɔt/, 'shot' /ʃɑt/ becomes /ʃɔt/. This results from the articulatory overlap between these two vowels. Actually, we have found that, in some speakers of American English, the formant frequencies of these two vowels totally overlap.

/o/

/o/ is a back-mid, tense English vowel used mainly in the secondary stress position in English words such as 'rotate' /ˌroˈteɪt/ and 'shadow' /'ʃæˌdo/. Usually, the vowel /o/ is pronounced as the diphthong /oʊ/, as in 'program' /ˌproʊˈgrəm/ and 'window' /ˌwɪnˌdoʊ/, although some speakers may not diphthongize the vowel, thus resulting in the words /'proˌgræm/ and /'wɪnˌdo/. The articulatory uniqueness of the vowel /o/ lies in the maximal rounding of the lips. This phenomenon is reflected in the acoustic representation of the formant frequencies of this vowel. Because of the primary role of lip rounding, F_1 and F_2 frequencies are both low.

/ʊ/

/ʊ/ is a back-high, lax English vowel used mostly in the position of secondary stress, as in words like 'input' /'ɪnˌpʊt/ and 'thoughtful' /'θɔtˌfʊl/. It is a frequently used vowel in the English language. For example, the suffix /-fʊl/ is utilized in a number of words such as 'youthful'/'juθˌfʊl/, 'joyful' /'dʒɔɪˌfʊl/, and 'mouthful' /'maʊθˌfʊl/. One-syllable words such as 'should' /ʃʊd/, 'could' /kʊd/, and 'put' /pʊt/ further increase its frequency of utilization. Its first two formants are low. A low F_1 is indicative of a high vowel and a low F_2 is indicative of a back vowel.

Lip rounding is an added feature of /ʊ/. In perceptual confusions, /ʊ/ is most frequently confused with the mid-central neutral vowel /ʌ/. It is seldom confused with the vowel /u/, although /ʊ/ and /u/ are adjacent to each other on the vowel diagram (see Figure 7).

/u/

/u/ is a back-high tense English vowel. Comparing it with /i/, it is different only because of the advancement component. /u/ and /ʊ/ are different in terms of the amount of articulatory tension involved. /u/ appears at the stressed positions of a word. Because of its tenseness it appears in both open and closed syllables. Thus, we have words like 'boot' /but/ and 'shoes' /ʃuz/ as well as words like 'shoe' /ʃu/ and 'true' /tru/. The stressing of this vowel can be exemplified by words such as 'prudent' /'prudənt/ and 'moonlit' /'munlɪt/. The acoustic representation of /u/ shows low F_1 and F_2 frequencies and a high F_3. The tongue is at its highest position and is farthest back in the mouth, and the lips are maximally rounded.

CENTRAL VOWELS

/ʌ/

The vowel /ʌ/ is a central-low stressed English vowel used in words such as 'trust' /trʌst/, 'but' /bʌt/, and 'cut' /kʌt/. Besides the fact that /ʌ/ is a lower vowel than /ə/, /ʌ/ has longer duration and higher amplitude characteristics than /ə/.

/ə/ or Schwa

The vowel /ə/ is an unstressed neutral English vowel. Its neutrality indicates that the tongue is at its rest position on both the advancement and the height continua. It is used most frequently in English in words such as 'again' /ə'gɛn/ and 'about' /ə'baʊt/. Because the tongue advancement and tongue elevation are neutrally located in the production of the vowel /ə/, the F_1, F_2, and F_3 are ideally at uniform distances from each other.

/ɚ, ɝ/

/ɚ/ and /ɝ/ are unstressed and stressed retroflex vowels, respectively. Their locations are neutral on the vowel diagram. Actually, for all practical purposes, /ɚ/ can be expressed as the vowel /ə/ plus the consonant /r/, written as /ər/, and similarly /ɝ/ can be expressed as the vowel /ʌ/ plus the consonant /r/, written as /ʌr/. Although these expressions do not violate any principle involved in vowel production, they simplify the phonological description of the vowels in the sense that one need not mark the retroflexion feature for the vowels. At the present time, however, in phonetic transcription /ɚ/ is most often used in unstressed words at the word-final position, e.g., 'father' /ˈfaðɚ/, 'mother' /ˈmʌðɚ/, and 'either' /ˈaɪðɚ/. The long duration, high amplitude stressed vowel /ɝ/ most usually occurs in the word-medial position as in the words 'bird' /bɝd/ and 'hurdle' /ˈhɝdl̩/.

It is believed by some phoneticians that the unstressed neutral vowels /ə/ and /ɚ/ are not independent phonemes but are allophones of all other English vowels in certain unstressed positions.

EXERCISES

Fill in the Blanks

1. In analyzing formant frequencies of vowels, a lower F_1 is indicative of a _____ and a lower F_2 is indicative of a _____.
2. In most instances the vowels /e/ and /o/ in the word-final position take on the role of a _____.
3. The lax counterpart of the vowel /o/ is the vowel _____.
4. Vowel unstressing is usually related to _____ duration, _____ amplitude, and _____ pitch.
5. _____ is a low, front English vowel.
6. /ɔ/ is a _____, _____, _____ vowel in English.
7. The tongue is at its highest position and is farthest back in the mouth during the production of the vowel _____.
8. /ɚ/ differs from /ə/ in that /ɚ/ is _____.

True or False

____ 1. A vowel-consonant confusion is rare in any language.
____ 2. /i/ is a central-high tense vowel in English.

_____ 3.   The vowel /æ/ is one of the earliest learned by children all over the world.

_____ 4.   In the word 'bought' the vowel used is /o/.

_____ 5.   Most American English speakers pronounce the vowel /o/ as the diphthong /aʊ/.

Multiple Choice

_____ 1.   Acoustically, the formant characteristics of /i/ show a _____ F_1.

        a.   high
        b.   low

_____ 2.   For the vowel /æ/, most non-American speakers of English use:

        a.   /ɔ/
        b.   /ɑ/
        c.   /e/

_____ 3.   The back-high, lax vowel of English is:

        a.   /u/
        b.   /ʊ/
        c.   /ɔ/

_____ 4.   In the production of vowel /ə/, the distance between the F_1, F_2, and F_3 formants is:

        a.   uniform
        b.   greater between F_1 and F_2
        c.   greater between F_2 and F_3

Orthographic Counterparts

Write orthographic representations for the following minimally distinct pairs.

1.	/bit/ _____	/bɪt/ _____		15.	/pɪn/ _____	/pɛn/ _____
2.	/mit/ _____	/mɪt/ _____		16.	/tɪn/ _____	/tɛn/ _____
3.	/hit/ _____	/hɪt/ _____		17.	/kɪn/ _____	/kɛn/ _____
4.	/lip/ _____	/lɪp/ _____		18.	/bɪn/ _____	/bɛn/ _____
5.	/tin/ _____	/tɪn/ _____		19.	/wɪn/ _____	/wɛn/ _____
6.	/sin/ _____	/sɪn/ _____		20.	/pɪt/ _____	/pɛt/ _____
7.	/kin/ _____	/kɪn/ _____		21.	/sɪt/ _____	/sɛt/ _____
8.	/bin/ _____	/bɪn/ _____		22.	/mɪt/ _____	/mɛt/ _____
9.	/win/ _____	/wɪn/ _____		23.	/tɪl/ _____	/tɛl/ _____
10.	/slip/ _____	/slɪp/ _____		24.	/mɪl/ _____	/mɛl/ _____
11.	/nit/ _____	/nɪt/ _____		25.	/nɪl/ _____	/nɛl/ _____
12.	/ʃip/ _____	/ʃɪp/ _____		26.	/sɪl/ _____	/sɛl/ _____
13.	/nil/ _____	/nɪl/ _____		27.	/nɪk/ _____	/nɛk/ _____
14.	/it/ _____	/ɪt/ _____				

28. /sin/ _____ /sen/ _____
29. /kin/ _____ /ken/ _____
30. /tim/ _____ /tem/ _____
31. /lin/ _____ /len/ _____
32. /min/ _____ /men/ _____
33. /ʃip/ _____ /ʃep/ _____
34. /kip/ _____ /kep/ _____
35. /it/ _____ /et/ _____
36. /bit/ _____ /bet/ _____
37. /mit/ _____ /met/ _____
38. /hit/ _____ /het/ _____
39. /fit/ _____ /fet/ _____

40. /et/ _____ /æt/ _____
41. /bet/ _____ /bæt/ _____
42. /met/ _____ /mæt/ _____
43. /ken/ _____ /kæn/ _____
44. /men/ _____ /mæn/ _____
45. /kep/ _____ /kæp/ _____
46. /het/ _____ /hæt/ _____
47. /fet/ _____ /fæt/ _____

48. /men/ _____ /mɛn/ _____
49. /met/ _____ /mɛt/ _____
50. /get/ _____ /gɛt/ _____
51. /bet/ _____ /bɛt/ _____
52. /ken/ _____ /kɛn/ _____
53. /let/ _____ /lɛt/ _____
54. /pen/ _____ /pɛn/ _____
55. /wen/ _____ /wɛn/ _____
56. /tel/ _____ /tɛl/ _____
57. /mel/ _____ /mɛl/ _____
58. /nel/ _____ /nɛl/ _____
59. /sel/ _____ /sɛl/ _____

60. /ful/ _____ /fʊl/ _____
61. /luk/ _____ /lʊk/ _____
62. /pul/ _____ /pʊl/ _____

63. /pul/ _____ /pol/ _____
64. /mun/ _____ /mon/ _____
65. /nun/ _____ /non/ _____
66. /blu/ _____ /blo/ _____
67. /θru/ _____ /θro/ _____
68. /kru/ _____ /kro/ _____
69. /flu/ _____ /flo/ _____
70. /ʃu/ _____ /ʃo/ _____
71. /kun/ _____ /kon/ _____
72. /tu/ _____ /to/ _____
73. /mu/ _____ /mo/ _____

74. /bʊl/ _____ /bɔl/ _____
75. /lʊk/ _____ /lɔk/ _____
76. /pʊl/ _____ /pɔl/ _____
77. /ʃʊk/ _____ /ʃɔk/ _____
78. /kuʃən/ _____ /kɔʃen/ _____
79. /pʊt/ _____ /pɔt/ _____
80. /fʊt/ _____ /fɔt/ _____

81. /bɔl/ _____ /bol/ _____
82. /tʃɔk/ _____ /tʃok/ _____
83. /bɔt/ _____ /bot/ _____
84. /nɔt/ _____ /not/ _____
85. /gɔt/ _____ /got/ _____
86. /mɔl/ _____ /mol/ _____

Chapter 11 NONPHONEMIC SOUNDS CLOSELY RELATED TO ENGLISH PHONEMES

The preceding sections of this book describe the phonemic system of normal English speakers. Speech, hearing, and language clinicians, as well as teachers of English as a foreign language, must familiarize themselves with some additional symbols that are not phonemic in normal English usage. Such symbols are frequently necessary when transcribing the phonemic systems of children with deviant articulation patterns and of young children who are in the process of acquiring normal articulation patterns. In addition, persons learning English as a second language may experience interference by the phonemic system of their first language. In such instances, a knowledge of such additional symbols would help them to understand the basis for some of the differences.

The following descriptions of the production of each phone will help the student of phonetics gain mastery of these symbols and become a versatile transcriber. *Phone* is defined here as a nonphonemic sound used by a speaker. Examples provided for each phone will aid in learning the sounds and their associated symbols. For example, the phoneme /p/ may have the sounds [ɸ], [p], and [ʔ] as closely related phones. The phone [ɸ] is described as a voiceless, bilabial fricative. It is shown here as occurring during the pronunciation of the word 'paper,' in which the phoneme /p/ is substituted by [ɸ]. The phone [ɸ], although not phonemic in the English lan-

205

guage, is phonemic in other languages, such as German. Thus,
a native German speaker may
experience interference of this
phone when learning the English
phoneme /p/.

Phoneme	Phone	Manner of production	Example	Language in which the phone is allophonic or phonemic
/p/	[ɸ]	Voiceless, bilabial fricative	paper [ɸeɸɚ]	German
	[p̪]	Voiceless, bilabial, palatal stop	pen [p̪ɛn]	Russian
	[ʔ]	Glottal stop	apple [æʔl]	German
/t/	[t̪]	Voiceless, interdental stop	today [t̪ʊd̪e]	French
	[ʈ]	Voiceless, alveolar, retroflexed stop	potato [pət̪et̪o]	Marathi
	[t̪]	Voiceless, alveolar, palatal stop	tomato [t̪əmet̪o]	Russian
	[ʔ]	Glottal stop	tiger [ʔaɪɡɚ]	German
/k/	[χ]	Voiceless, velar fricative	baking [beɪχɪŋ]	German
	[ʔ]	Glottal stop	uncle [ənʔl]	German
/b/	[β]	Voiced, bilabial fricative	baby [βeɪβɪ]	Spanish
	[b̪]	Voiced, bilabial, palatal stop	beat [b̪it]	Russian
	[bʰ]	Voiced, bilabial, aspirated stop	boy [bʰɔɪ]	Hindi
/d/	[d̪]	Voiced, interdental stop	David [d̪eɪvɪd̪]	French
	[ɖ]	Voiced, alveolar, retroflexed stop	door [ɖor]	Marathi
	[d̪]	Voiced, alveolar, palatal stop	day [d̪eɪ]	Russian
	[ɖʰ]	Voiced, alveolar, retroflexed, aspirated stop	soda [soʊɖʰa]	Marathi
	[đ]	Combination of /d/ and /ð/	modern [mɔđɚn]	Spanish
/g/	[ɣ]	Voiced, velar fricative	buggy [bʌɣɪ]	German
	[gʰ]	Voiced, velar, aspirated stop	garage [gʰərɑdʒ]	Marathi
/f/	[f̪]	Voiceless, labiodental, palatal fricative	father [f̪aðɚ]	Russian
/v/	[ɣ]	Voiced, labiodental, palatal fricative	very [ɣɛri]	Russian
/θ/	[t̪ʰ]	Voiceless, interdental, aspirated stop	bath [bɑt̪ʰ]	Marathi
	[tʰ]	Voiceless, retroflexed, aspirated stop	three [tʰri]	Hindi

Phoneme	Phone	Manner of production	Example	Language in which the phone is allophonic or phonemic
/ð/	[d̪ʰ]	Voiced, interdental, aspirated stop	this [d̪ʰɪs]	Marathi
	[ḍʰ]	Voiced, retroflexed, aspirated stop	those [ḍʰoʊs]	Hindi
/s/	[ş]	Voiceless, palatal, slit fricative	some [şʌm]	Russian
	[s̪]	Lateral lisp	soap [s̪oʊp]	
/ʃ/	[ʃʲ]	Voiceless, palatal, groove fricative	shore [ʃʲor]	Russian
/z/	[ts]	Combination of /t/ and /s/	zebra [tsibrɑ]	Russian
/r/	[ř]	Tongue tip trill	train [třen]	Marathi
	[ʀ]	Voiced, uvular trill	cigarette [sɪgəʀɛt]	German
	[ɾ]	One tap	Roy [ɾɔɪ]	Hindi
/l/	[ḷ]	Retroflex	calling [kɔḷɪŋ]	Tamil
	[λ]	Lateral palatal	lady [λeɪdɪ]	Spanish
/w/	[β]	Voiced, bilabial fricative	west [βɛst]	German
/m/	[ɱ]	Labiodental nasal	mommy [ɱɑɱɪ]	Italian
/n/	[n̪]	Interdental nasal	no [n̪o]	Hindi
	[ɳ]	Retroflexed nasal	money [mʌɳɪ]	Tamil
	[ɲ]	Palatal nasal	onion [ʌɲən]	Marathi
/tʃ/	[t̪ʃ]	Voiceless, alveolar affricate	match [mæt̪ʃ]	Marathi
	[t̪ʃʰ]	Voiceless alveolar, aspirated affricate	chair [t̪ʃʰɛr]	Marathi
	[tʃʰ]	Voiceless, aspirated affricate	chess [tʃʰɛs]	Hindi
/dʒ/	[d̪ʒ]	Voiced, dental affricate	George [d̪ʒɔrd̪ʒ]	Marathi
	[d̪ʒʰ]	Voiced, dental, aspirated affricate	fudge [fʌd̪ʒʰ]	Marathi
	[dʒʰ]	Voiceless, aspirated affricate	jump [dʒʰʌmp]	Hindi
/h/	[χ]	Voiceless, velar fricative	house [χaʊs]	German
	[ɦ]	Voiced	home [ɦoʊm]	Hindi
/i/	[y]	Lips rounded	eat [yt]	French
	[ɨ]	Central	cheese [tʃɨz]	Russian
	[ʝ]	Voiced, palatal fricative	hear [hʝɚ]	French

continued

Phoneme	Phone	Manner of production	Example	Language in which the phone is allophonic or phonemic
/e/	[ø]	Lips rounded	bay [bø]	French
/ɛ/	[œ]	Lips rounded	sell [sœl]	French
/u/	[ʉ]	Central	cool [kʉl]	Norwegian
	[ɯ]	Unrounded	two [tɯ]	Russian
/ɪ/	[ʏ]	Lips rounded	win [wʏn]	German

Chapter 12 DIACRITIC MARKERS

Diacritic markers are arbitrary signs used to represent those phonetic variations of a phoneme that cannot be accounted for by the phonetic symbols. These markers allow a much greater approximation of the individual's speech production than is possible with broad phonetic transcription. Be- cause it is the tool for a narrow phonetic transcription, the words transcribed with the aid of these markers are always placed in closed brackets. Proficient use of diacritic markers is especially important to students interested in studying the variations and de- viations of phoneme production.

[:] *full lengthening* This mark, when placed to the right of a phoneme, indicates that the duration of the phoneme has been increased considerably (almost doubled); e.g., /ɛg/ becomes [ɛ:g].

[·] *half lengthening* This mark, when placed to the right of a phoneme, indicates that the duration of the phoneme has been somewhat increased (not as much as for full lengthening); e.g., /tɔk/ becomes [tɔ·k].

[~] *nasalization* This mark, when placed above a phoneme, in- dicates that the phoneme, usually non-nasal, has become nasalized; e.g., /tɔp/ becomes [tɔ̃p].

[̥] *devoicing* This mark, when placed below a phoneme, indicates that the phoneme, usually voiced, has become devoiced; e.g., /beɪbɪ/ becomes [b̥eɪb̥ɪ].

[ˇ] *voicing* This mark, when placed below a phoneme, indicates that the phoneme, usually voiceless, has become voiced; e.g., /sup/ becomes [ṣup].

[ʻ] *aspiration* This mark, when placed at the top right side of the phoneme, indicates that the phoneme, usually unaspirated, becomes aspirated; e.g., /tek/ becomes [tekʻ].

[ʼ] *unaspiration* In American English, this mark, placed at the top left side of phonemes /p, t, k/ in the word-initial position, indicates that the phonemes, usually aspirated, become unaspirated; e.g., /pɑt/ becomes [ʼpɑt].

[◡] *labialization* This mark, placed directly below the phoneme, indicates that the phoneme, usually nonlabial, becomes labialized; e.g., /nouz/ becomes [n̮ouz].

[◠] *nonlabialization* This mark, placed directly below the phoneme, indicates that the phoneme, usually labial, becomes nonlabial; e.g., /wɪθ/ becomes [w̠ɪθ].

[–] *dentalization* This mark, placed directly below the phoneme, indicates that the phoneme, usually not linguadental, is produced at the linguadental place of articulation; e.g., /tɪtʃ/ becomes [t̠ɪtʃ].

[˙] *palatalization* This mark, placed directly above the phoneme, indicates that the phoneme, usually nonpalatal, becomes palatalized; e.g., /zu/ becomes [żu].

[.] *closing of vowel* This mark, placed directly below the vowel phoneme, indicates that the phoneme is produced with greater closing than normally required for its production; e.g., /edʒ/ becomes [ẹdʒ].

[ˌ] *opening of vowel* This mark, placed directly below the vowel phoneme, indicates that the phoneme is produced with greater opening than normally required for its production; e.g., /ˈenˌdʒəl/ becomes [ẹ̦nˌdʒəl].

[⊥] *tongue raising* This mark, when placed to the right of the vowel phoneme, indicates that the phoneme is produced with more than usual tongue raising; e.g., /ðe/ becomes [ðe⊥].

[⊤] *tongue lowering* This mark, when placed to the right of the vowel phoneme, indicates that the phoneme is produced with more than usual tongue lowering; e.g., /blu/ becomes [blu⊤].

[+]   *tongue advancement*   This mark, when placed to the right
or   of the vowel phoneme, indicates that the phoneme is produced
[˔]   with more than usual tongue advancement; e.g., /tu/ becomes
       [tu+].

[−]   *tongue retraction*   This mark, when placed to the right of
or   the vowel phoneme, indicates that the phoneme is produced
[˕]   with more than usual tongue retraction; e.g., /tʃik/ becomes
       [tʃi−k].

[ɔ]   *lip rounding*   This mark, when placed at the top right side of the
       vowel phoneme, indicates that the phoneme is produced with
       more than usual lip rounding; e.g., /ʃit/ it becomes [ʃiᵓt].

[ᴄ]   *lip spreading*   This mark, when placed at the top right side of the
       vowel phoneme, indicates that the phoneme is produced with
       more than usual lip spreading; e.g., /sun/ becomes [suᴄn].

[-]   *vowel centralization*   This mark, when placed across the vowel
       phoneme, indicates that the phoneme, usually noncentral,
       becomes centralized; e.g., /it/ becomes [ɨt].

[ˌ]   *consonant syllabification*   In American English, this mark is
       placed below the consonants /m, n, ŋ, l/ when these consonants
       perform the function of the nucleus in a syllable; e.g., /bɔtəl/
       becomes [bɔtl̩].

EXERCISES

Fill in the Blanks

1. Diacritic markers are used in _____ type of phonetic
   transcription.
2. The diacritic marker for nasality is _____.
3. In American English the diacritic marker ['] placed at the top left side of
   the phoneme applies only to phonemes _____ in the
   word-initial position.
4. If the final phoneme in the word 'let' were produced with aspiration, its
   phonetic transcription would be _____.
5. If the word 'do' is transcribed as [d̈u], it indicates that the phoneme /d/
   has become _____.
6. Vowel centralization is indicated by the diacritic marker
   _____.

True or False

_____ 1. Diacritic markers allow a much greater approximation of the individual's speech production.

_____ 2. The diacritic marker [:] indicates the half lengthening of a phoneme.

_____ 3. When a usually labial phoneme becomes nonlabial, the diacritic marker used is [ᵕ].

_____ 4. [ẹ] is an especially close vowel.

_____ 5. The diacritic marker [+] placed to the right of the phoneme is a marker of tongue raising.

_____ 6. More than usual lip spreading during vowel production is indicated by the diacritic marker [ᴄ].

Multiple Choice

_____ 1. Half lengthening of a phoneme is marked by:
   a. [··]
   b. [:]
   c. [·]

_____ 2. The diacritic marker [₀] placed below a phoneme, indicates that the phoneme has become:
   a. unaspirated
   b. devoiced
   c. palatalized

_____ 3. The diacritic marker for dentalization is:
   a. [ᵕ]
   b. [ₙ]
   c. [ᵛ]

_____ 4. The vowel centralization diacritic marker is placed _____ the phoneme.
   a. above
   b. below
   c. across

_____ 5. The diacritic marker [.] indicates that the vowel affected is produced with more than usual:
   a. tongue lowering
   b. opening of vowel
   c. lip rounding

_____ 6. An example showing the use of the diacritic marker for labialization is:
   a. [douz]
   b. [douz]
   c. [douz]

Chapter 13 RELATIONSHIP OF PHONETICS TO OTHER FIELDS

Phonetics is related to a number of fields: speech pathology, audiology, linguistics, anthropology, engineering, education, communication sciences, teaching of foreign languages, theater and drama, and education of the deaf and other communicatively handicapped. This final section studies the relation of phonetics to these disciplines.

SPEECH PATHOLOGY

A speech pathologist: 1) tests and diagnoses speech problems, 2) provides the covert treatment, and 3) measures the success of treatment. A thorough knowledge of phonetics is necessary to execute these functions successfully.

Approximately eighty percent of all speech-handicapped school children in the United States have articulation problems. Two factors considered crucial in the testing, diagnosis, and treatment of articulation problems are: 1) the target or model utterance, considered the standard for the patient's age and socioeconomic background, and 2) the actual utterance that the patient displays in speaking. To compare the target utterance with the actual utterance, the speech pathologist uses phonetic transcription as a tool and phonetic principles as guides for making accurate judgments. Phonetic transcription assists in determining the explicit nature of the problem, and the knowledge of phonetic principles assists in establishing the relative severity or the magnitude of the problem.

For example, if a ten-year-old child says 'baftub' for 'bathtub,' it is evident that he has substituted 'f' for 'th.' If the child speaks standard American English, this substitution indicates that he lacks the distinction between 'th' and 'f' in

213

his phonetic repertoire. Using the principles of articulatory phonetics, speech pathologists can determine the severity of this substitution. The sound pair 'th' and 'f' is one of the closest of all sound pairs in the English language. The relationship between this pair of sounds is analogous to the relationship between identical twins who share all features commonly used to distinguish one person from another. Sometimes a simple cue that distinguishes a pair of identical twins may get masked and the differentiation may disappear. Similar is the case of the 'th' and 'f' distinction. In the phonetic repertoire of many children with marginal articulatory problems, this distinction does not register. However, children who say 'babtub' for 'bathtub' have a problem of a much greater magnitude since 'b' and 'th' share few distinctive features. To understand the underlying phonetic system of speech defective individuals, a speech pathologist must have a thorough knowledge of phonetics.

AUDIOLOGY

Audiology is the science of hearing. One of the predominant functions of an audiologist is to assess the ability of hearing-impaired persons. This assessment involves the measurement of the phonetic parameters of the sounds of speech. Although some audiologists may limit their probe only to the person's hearing of

phonemes, the most realistic assessment of the ability of hearing-impaired persons is in terms of the processings of the distinctive features (mini-interpreters) of phonemes.

READING

Learning to read is very closely related to the sound patterns of a language. Reading ability very much depends on knowledge of the sounds and lexical items of the language. Whereas writing depends on the orthographic system, reading directly relates to the phonetic parameters of speech. Therefore, in order to better understand the dimensions of reading, it is important to have a good understanding of the phonetic system of a language.

LINGUISTICS

It is important here to understand the difference in the application of phonetics to linguistics, and to speech, language, and hearing pathologies. A linguist utilizes phonetics to describe the speaking behavior of the normal user of a language, and a speech and/or hearing pathologist strives to utilize this knowledge to enable a deviant speaker and/or listener to meet the minimal standards of acceptable speech and hearing habits of a given community.

Phonology, a branch of linguistics, is the study of the relationships between speech sounds of a language. Because the construction of the phonological rules of a language is based on the phonetic interpretations of its speech sounds, a uniform set of symbols becomes necessary. The task of a linguist would be difficult if he had to base phonological rules on standard written letters (orthographic units) only. This becomes clear when one attempts to write a rule for the fact that in the English language 'o' in 'do' is pronounced differently from the 'o' in 'go,' 'so,' and 'no.' Some languages, however, are phonetically sound in their orthography; i.e., their written system directly represents the spoken system.

Semantics, also a branch of linguistics, deals with meaning. It is known that words differ in meaning as the sounds in them are replaced. Changes in sounds signal changes in meaning. The words 'bat' and 'pat' are inherently different in meaning because the sounds /b/ and /p/ in these words are different. Semantics, at least to some extent, depends on the understanding of the system of sounds in a given language.

ANTHROPOLOGY

Anthropology involves the interpretation of the cultural heritages of different peoples of the world. Therefore, anthropologists study a culture in the past, present, and projected future. Most pioneer American linguists were by train-

ing anthropologists or missionaries involved in understanding the cultures of the world. Historically, it is known that some of them became linguists and phoneticians, motivated by their need for understanding the unknown cultures in their totality. A culture cannot be studied in depth without knowing the code or the communication system utilized by its people. Anthropologists had to know the language of the people in order to know the people, their religion, living habits, marriage habits, emotions, feelings, and their interactions among themselves.

The language learning process involved is very methodical. For example, if a native informant points to a stallion and says 'ghora' and then points to a mare and says 'ghori,' the anthropologist receives a clue that perhaps the '-a' ending signifies the masculine gender and the '-i' ending denotes the feminine gender of animate objects. A number of other examples may be used to verify this rule. Such a language learning process depends on obtaining a *corpus* (speech sample) of a native speaker and transcribing it phonetically so as to derive phonological rules. Phonetics cannot be ignored as the basis for this entire process.

ENGINEERING

The only aspect of engineering science that directly relates to phonetics is the one concerned with the sending, receiving, and transmitting of the speech signal. Telephone engineers, for example, are concerned with communication because speech sounds must be picked up by the microphone, transmitted via the systems for on-line transmission, and received by the speaker.

Space scientists also must be familiar with the physical properties of speech sounds and their relative degree of importance in speaking and listening behavior. In communication between Earth and space, the knowledge regarding how robust or how vulnerable certain speech sound properties are in the presence of space noise is immensely useful for enhancing the quality of the signal transmitted and received. The knowledge of the acoustic properties of speech sounds is greatly responsible for such improvements. For example, if one discovers that some noise in space intervenes specifically with the /s/ sound in a message so that /s/ sounds like /f/, then the high frequency components of the sending and receiving systems need to be improved. This tip is provided by phonetic research that clearly indicates that /f/ has prominent components in the relatively low frequencies, whereas /s/ has prominent components in the high frequencies.

Manufacturers of communication devices such as telephones can benefit a great deal from the knowledge of phonetics. Over the telephone, at least sixty percent of the time, people hear our name as *F*ingh instead of *S*ingh. This may be because the telephone system is designed in such an economical way that the extensive quality of speech transmission and reception has been sacrificed. The frequency range in most telephone systems is between 250 Hz and 3,000 Hz, a relatively poor range for transmitting all speech sounds. For example, the critical frequency domain of /s/ does not belong in this frequency range. It is the input from articulatory, acoustic, and perceptual phonetics that enables the engineer to develop the kind of circuits that are necessary for minimal, if any, errors in transmission.

EDUCATION

Teachers sometimes develop biases about children just because of the way they talk. Teachers would be more compassionate and would have a better understanding of children's speech if they were students of phonetics and were aware of the variables that influence speech. Children who "talk differently" need a positive bias, if any at all. Sociolinguistic variables, pathologies of speech and hearing, language problems, or a combination of these factors may be involved in the speech differences detected by the teacher. It is evident that, in the schools of the black ghettos of America, teachers are confronted with a serious problem if they want all students to speak "correct" English. In sociologically mixed neighborhoods, serious problems result when a teacher is unable to understand the language environment of a child. If teachers have not had a basic training in descriptive phonetics, they may assume automatically that the child's speech will be similar to their own. This assumption negatively affects the teacher's approach to the students, in turn affecting the students' interaction with the teacher, as well as with the total process of learning.

In order to avoid such problems, a teacher should have a working knowledge of language development and of the developmental and sociological aspects of phonetics. The knowledge of phonetics provides a means for determining the quality of the difference in speech when the target word 'with' is pronounced as 'wif' by a number of persons in a community. Teachers with an adequate perspective will understand that this difference relates to a dialectal difference and not to a speech defect. Thus, they will be descriptive rather than prescriptive in evaluating speech differences.

LANGUAGE DEVELOPMENT

The science of language development deals with the study of the process by which language is learned by normal children and also by children who have developmental language problems. It is an important field of study for students of speech and hearing because it helps to distinguish a child whose articulation is characteristic of normal language development from another child whose articulation is characteristic of a developmental language problem. It is the study of phonetics that enables one to chart the development pattern of a child's phonemic system.

EXERCISES

Fill in the Blanks

1. A child who says 'baftub' for 'bathtub' has substituted the speech sound _____ for the speech sound _____.

2. A linguist utilizes phonetics to describe the behavior of a normal user of a language, but a speech and hearing pathologist utilizes the knowledge of phonetics to describe the _____.

3. Phonology is a branch of study in the field of _____.

True or False

_____ 1. A speech pathologist uses phonetic transcription to determine the explicit nature of articulation problems.

_____ 2. In evaluating articulation errors, speech pathologists must use their own speech as the model utterance.

_____ 3. Semantics is a branch of the study of phonology.

_____ 4. Classroom teachers without a basic knowledge of descriptive phonetics may assume automatically that every child's speech will be similar to their own.

Multiple Choice

_____ 1. Audiology is the science of:
   a. speaking
   b. seeing
   c. hearing

_____ 2. Assessment of a hearing problem in terms of distinctive features would be quite:
   a. realistic
   b. unrealistic
   c. unnecessary

_____ 3. A study of relationship between speech sounds is:
   a. sociolinguistics
   b. psycholinguistics
   c. phonology

_____ 4. Semantics is the study of:
   a. meaning
   b. pronunciation
   c. orthography

_____ 5. Phonetics is related to communication engineering in the manufacturing of devices such as:
   a. automobiles
   b. clocks
   c. telephones

_____ 6. Classroom teachers, when confronted with a speech pattern different from their own, should be:
   a. prescriptive
   b. descriptive
   c. instructive

ANSWERS TO EXERCISES

CHAPTER 1

Fill in the Blanks

1. speech organs
2. phonetics
3. consonants
4. phoneme
5. non-nasal sounds
6. vocal folds
7. acoustic
8. frequency, time, amplitude
9. speech discrimination
10. International Phonetic Alphabet, or IPA

True or False

1. T
2. F
3. T
4. T
5. F
6. T
7. F
8. T

Multiple Choice

1. b
2. b
3. a
4. a
5. c
6. b
7. a
8. b

CHAPTER 2

Fill in the Blanks

1. International Phonetic Alphabet
2. orthography; speech
3. spoken
4. /æ/; /ə/
5. /ə/; /ɑ/

6. loose; two; blue; flew; shoe
7. for; paw; tall; George
8. 19; 24
9. International Phonetic Alphabet
10. phonetic; phonemic
11. [pʰæn]
12. /pæn/
13. narrow, broad
14. postvocalic
15. postvocalic; intervocalic
16. intervocalic
17. /dɔg/; prevocalic; postvocalic
18. /v/; /f/
19. /ðɪs/; /ð/
20. /mæθ/; /θ/
21. /suzi/; /s/, /z/
22. /sɪzɚz/; intervocalic, postvocalic,
23. consonant cluster
24. /ð, dʒ, ʃ, θ, tʃ, ʒ, ŋ/

True or False

1. F
2. T
3. T
4. T
5. T
6. F
7. F
8. T
9. T
10. F
11. T

Multiple Choice

1. b
2. c
3. d
4. a
5. c
6. c
7. b
8. b

Phonemic Transcription

1. /steɪʃən/
2. /zu/
3. /bɪzɑr/
4. /tæksɪ/
5. /sɛz/
6. /sɔsɚz/
7. /trɛʒɚ/
8. /kuʃən/
9. /kritʃɚ/
10. /tʃiz/
11. /dʒɔɪ/
12. /bædʒ/
13. /mʌnɪ/
14. /neɪmɪŋ/
15. /ɪŋk/
16. /roud/
17. /mɛrɪ/
18. /lɑlɪpɔp/
19. /wægən/
20. /kɑubɔɪ/
21. /ju/
22. /jʌŋ/
23. /haɪ/
24. /haus/
25. /ohɑjo/
26. /θri/

Orthographic Counterparts

1. wish
2. make
3. believe
4. tough
5. need
6. they
7. come
8. also
9. added
10. source
11. face
12. hall
13. women
14. phonetics
15. politician
16. degree
17. young
18. gentle

19. request
20. tables
21. winter
22. pull
23. county
24. T.V.
25. ease
26. lunch
27. budget
28. Wednesday
29. editor
30. love
31. two or too
32. eight
33. Monday

CHAPTER 3

Fill in the Blanks

1. vocal folds
2. voiceless
3. larynx
4. larynx
5. vocalis; vocal
6. nasopharynx, oropharynx, laryngopharynx
7. nasopharynx, oropharynx
8. epiglottis
9. lips; cheeks; hard and soft palate; tongue
10. bilabial
11. back of tongue; soft palate
12. manner
13. stop
14. /t, d/; /s, z/
15. slit
16. consonantal
17. vowels
18. nucleus
19. sibilancy
20. parallel
21. voicing

True or False

1. T
2. T
3. F
4. F
5. T
6. F
7. T
8. F
9. T
10. F
11. T
12. F
13. F

Multiple Choice

1. c
2. c
3. b
4. a
5. a
6. c
7. d
8. b
9. c
10. b
11. d
12. b
13. c
14. b
15. b
16. a
17. a
18. b

Phonemic Transcription: Place

Some of the vowels may vary depending on the different regions of the United States.

1. /pɛnsəl/
2. /ʃip/
3. /eɪp/
4. /pipəl/
5. /æpəl/
6. /pɪg/

7. /bɛd/
8. /əbaʊt/
9. /kæb/
10. /boʊt/
11. /ræbət/
12. /nɑb/

13. /mɪlk/
14. /kəmænd/
15. /ðɛm/
16. /snoʊmæn/
17. /laɪm/
18. /mʌŋkɪ/

19. /wɑtʃ/
20. /wɑk/
21. /həwɑjɪ/
22. /tɑwɚ/
23. /wʊd/

24. /fork/
25. /ɛləfənt/
26. /dʒɪræf/

27. /fʊl/
28. /raɪfəl/
29. /laɪf/

30. /væləntaɪn/
31. /rɪvɚ/
32. /lɪv/ or /laɪv/
33. /neɪtɪv/
34. /vaɪjəlɪn/
35. /ɪvɛnt/

36. /θri/
37. /θɪn/
38. /hɛlθɪ/
39. /pæθ/
40. /bæθrum/
41. /boʊθ/

42. /mʌðɚ/
43. /ðæt/
44. /rɪð/
45. /smuð/
46. /fɑðɚ/
47. /ðoʊz/

48. /toʊz/
49. /teɪp/
50. /dɪtɛkt/
51. /tɝdəl/
52. /ɪt/
53. /pɛt/

54. /daɪm/
55. /bɝd/
56. /dudəl/
57. /dʌk/
58. /hɛd/
59. /bɪdɪŋ/

60. /nɪkəl/
61. /ɑksən/
62. /poɚkjupaɪn/
63. /bənænə/
64. /noʊz/
65. /bənænzə/

66. /sæntə/
67. /sæləd/
68. /sɪstɚ/
69. /pæsɪŋ/
70. /hors/
71. /wɔlrəs/

72. /zɪpɚ/
73. /zu/
74. /roʊzɪz/
75. /reɪzɚ/
76. /sɪzɚz/
77. /aɪz/

78. /reɪr/
79. /roʊz/
80. /kærət/
81. /bɝamɪtɚ/
82. /feɪɚ/
83. /kɑr/

84. /lɪlɪ/
85. /leɪk/
86. /æləgeɪtɚ/
87. /seɪlboʊt/
88. /dɔl/
89. /kul/

90. /tʃeɪɚ/
91. /tʃɝtʃ/
92. /kætʃ/
93. /mɑrtʃɪŋ/
94. /mætʃɪz/
95. /nɑtʃ/

96. /dʒeɪl/
97. /dʒʌdʒ/
98. /dʒulaɪ/
99. /ɔrəndʒ/
100. /dɑdʒɪŋ/
101. /dʒʌdʒmɪnt/

102. /ʃuz/
103. /ʃeɪr/
104. /neɪʃən/
105. /mɪlkʃeɪk/
106. /dɪʃ/
107. /fɪʃ/

108. /mɛʒɚ/
109. /vɪʒən/
110. /beɪʒ/
111. /dɛkopɑʒ/

112. /jɛs/
113. /junɪvɝs/
114. /jɛloʊ/
115. /joʊjoʊ/

116. /kændɪkeɪn/
117. /kʌp/
118. /stɑkɪŋ/
119. /tækəl/
120. /klɑk/
121. /bæk/

122. /gʌn/
123. /gɪft/
124. /əgɛn/
125. /taɪgɚ/
126. /dɔg/
127. /pɪg/

128. /dɔŋkɪ/
129. /sɪŋ/
130. /silɪŋ/
131. /θæŋkju/

132. /hi/
133. /hɪt/
134. /hæm/
135. /biheɪv/
136. /ɪnhɛrənt/

Phonemic Transcription: Manner

1. /pɛnsɪlveɪnjə/
2. /oupən/
3. /ʌp/

4. /bɔɪ/
5. /labstɚ/
6. /rab/

7. /tɛksəs/
8. /kɛntʌkɪ/
9. /bæt/

10. /dɛləwɛɚ/
11. /ɪndɪjænə/
12. /bɝd/

13. /kæləfornjə/
14. /pɪkɪŋ/
15. /sæk/

16. /gɛt/
17. /bʌgɪ/
18. /lɔg/

19. /florɪdə/
20. /tɛləfon/
21. /skarf/

22. /vɚdʒinɪjə/
23. /sɝveɪ/
24. /karv/

25. /θrɛd/
26. /nʌθɪŋ/
27. /mæθ/

28. /ði/
29. /brɛðrɪn/
30. /beɪð/

31. /sɛlərɪ/
32. /kænzəs/
33. /kæps/

34. /zum/
35. /bɪzaɚ/
36. /bʌz/

37. /ʃaɪn/
38. /kruʃəl/
39. /liʃ/

40. /trɛʒɚ/
41. /dɪsɪʒən/
42. /gəraʒ/

43. /haus/
44. /ɪnhɛrɪt/
45. /nuhæmpʃɚ/
46. /ohaɪjo/

47. /jutɑ/
48. /juθ/
49. /nujɔrk/

50. /reɪz/
51. /məzurɪ/
52. /tar/

53. /læp/
54. /æləbæmə/
55. /kæməl/

56. /wɪskansɪn/
57. /ajowə/
58. /stounwɛɚ/

59. /mɪʃɪgən/
60. /lɛmən/
61. /kʌm/

62. /norθ kærolaɪnə/
63. /ʌnjʌn/
64. /klaun/

65. /rɪŋɪŋ/
66. /sɔŋ/

67. /si/
68. /mɪsɪsɪpɪ/
69. /bʌs/

70. /zirou/
71. /ɛrəzonə/
72. /snuz/

73. /ʃor/
74. /waʃɪŋtən/
75. /puʃ/

76. /prɑɪʒən/
77. /liʒɚ/

78. /tʃeɪs/
79. /kætʃɚ/
80. /hætʃ/

81. /dʒordʒə/
82. /dʒʌdʒɪŋ/
83. /bægɪdʒ/

84. /mɛrɪlənd/
85. /bʌmpɚ/
86. /neɪm/

87. /nəvædə/
88. /ɪlɪnɔɪ/
89. /meɪn/

90. /hʌŋgrɪ/
91. /lɔŋ/

Orthographic Counterparts: Voicing

1. puppy
2. paper
3. tatoo
4. potato
5. cake
6. clock
7. funny
8. suffer
9. thirsty
10. bathtub
11. sesame
12. street
13. slush
14. sugar
15. choice
16. munch
17. baby
18. bubble
19. daddy
20. door
21. gamble
22. gigantic
23. very
24. voice
25. they
26. lather
27. zebra
28. zoology
29. lesion
30. rouge
31. jump
32. porridge

Phonemic Transcription: Consonant Clusters

1. /sɪksθ/
2. /ɛksplod/
3. /kənsɪst/
4. /θɪŋks/
5. /skru/
6. /strɔŋ/
7. /mɪspɛl/
8. /dɪstrækt/
9. /spɪn/
10. /kræk/
11. /sʌmwʌn/
12. /frɔstɪ/
13. /snou/
14. /spaɪdɚ/
15. /skeɪts/
16. /strɔbɛriz/
17. /klaun/
18. /treɪn/
19. /glæs/
20. /flauwɚz/

CHAPTER 4

Fill in the Blanks

1. front, central, and back
2. high, mid, and low
3. tense and lax
4. tense, front-high
5. central-mid
6. diphthong
7. /ɔ/; /ɪ/

True or False

1. F
2. F
3. T
4. T
5. F

Multiple Choice

1, c
2. b
3. c
4. c
5. a

Phonemic Transcription: Advancement

1. /itʃ/
2. /it/
3. /mit/
4. /lin/
5. /hi/
6. /ki/

7. /ɪt/
8. /ɪnsaɪd/
9. /bɪg/
10. /rɪdʒɪd/

11. /edʒ/ or /eɪdʒ/
12. /ekɚ/ or /eɪkɚ/
13. /beʒ/ or /beɪʒ/
14. /gez/ or /geɪz/
15. /le/ or /leɪ/
16. /ðe/ or /ðeɪ/

17. /ɛg/
18. /ɛnd/
19. /pɛt/
20. /hɛd/

21. /æt/
22. /æpəl/
23. /bæt/
24. /ðæt/

25. /əgɛn/
26. /əbaʊt/
27. /tɛləfon/
28. /pəteɪtə/
29. /trænsətɪv/

30. /ʌp/
31. /ʌs/
32. /bʌt/
33. /kʌp/

34. /ɚbeɪn/
35. /ɚθlɪ/
36. /kɚs/
37. /nɚs/
38. /bʌtɚ/
39. /taɪgɚ/

40. /ɝk/
41. /bɝ/
42. /fɝ/
43. /bɝd/
44. /ʃɝt/

45. /uz/
46. /ups/
47. /kul/
48. /frut/
49. /blu/
50. /ʃu/

51. /fʊt/
52. /pʊt/

53. /owesɪs/
54. /opən/
55. /modɚ/
56. /roteɪt/
57. /to/ or /toʊ/
58. /go/ or /goʊ/

59. /ɔfʊl/
60. /ɔl/
61. /kɔt/
62. /bɔl/
63. /strɔ/
64. /lɔ/

65. /aɚ/
66. /aɚgju/
67. /hat/
68. /kat/
69. /spa/
70. /mama/

Phonemic Transcription: Height

1. /it/
2. /istɚ/
3. /sim/
4. /bit/
5. /si/
6. /fri/

7. /ɪndʒɚ/
8. /ɪmpasəbəl/
9. /sɪstɚ/
10. /fɪst/

11. /umlaut/ or /ʌmlaut/
12. /ulɔŋ/
13. /ful/
14. /rum/
15. /flu/
16. /tru/

17. /bʊk/
18. /ʃʊk/

19. /endʒəl/ or /eɪndʒəl/
20. /enʃənt/ or /eɪnʃənt/
21. /sel/ or /seɪl/
22. /trel/ or /treɪl/
23. /se/ or /seɪ/
24. /me/ or /meɪ/

25. /ɛndʒɪn/
26. /ɛnvɪ/
27. /bɛd/
28. /sɛt/

29. /ənaʊns/
30. /ənʌðɚ/
31. /dʒɛlətɪn/
32. /təmeɪtə/

33. /ɚdʒɪnt/
34. /ɚdʒ/ or /ɝdʒ/
35. /kɚɪ/ or /kərɪ/
36. /sɚvənt/ or /sɝvənt/
37. /faðɚ/
38. /sɪstɚ/

39. /ɝθ/
40. /hɝd/
41. /əkɝd/

42. /ozoʊn/ or /oʊzoʊn/
43. /omɪt/ or /oʊmɪt/
44. /dop/ or /doʊp/
45. /rop/ or /roʊp/
46. /no/ or /noʊ/
47. /ʃo/ or /ʃoʊ/

48. /orɪndʒ/ or /oʊrɪndʒ/
49. /orgən/ or /oʊrgən/

50. /fɔt/
51. /θɔt/
52. /pɔ/
53. /klɔ/

54. /ænt/
55. /æd/
56. /bæk/
57. /pæk/

58. /ʌntaɪd/
59. /ʌnwɔntəd/
60. /kʌt/
61. /ʃʌt/

62. /ɑnsɛt/
63. /ɑlɪv/
64. /nɑt/
65. /hɑrθ/

Orthographic Counterparts:
Tenseness

1. economy
2. heat
3. knee
4. ache
5. nail
6. ballet
7. ashamed
8. about

9. earning
10. surgeon
11. mother
12. oodles
13. boot
14. grew

15. okay
16. cope
17. flow

18. ignite
19. kiss

20. edge
21. bet

22. earn
23. clerk

24. look
25. awesome
26. tall
27. saw

Orthographic Counterparts: Retroflexion

1. August
2. necessary
3. often
4. frequent
5. associate
6. column
7. suffice
8. attorney
9. adverse
10. allege
11. allied
12. aloof
13. Havana
14. Iowa
15. diphtheria

16. together
17. incubator
18. other
19. rather
20. daughter

Phonemic Transcription: Diphthongs

1. /aɪs/
2. /aɪz/
3. /aɪ/
4. /aɪl/
5. /daɪm/
6. /taɪm/
7. /daɪs/
8. /baɪt/
9. /kaɪt/
10. /taɪ/
11. /saɪ/
12. /laɪ/
13. /paɪ/
14. /aʊns/
15. /aʊtʃ/
16. /aʊtsaɪd/
17. /aʊl/
18. /əbaʊt/
19. /haʊs/
20. /maʊs/
21. /praʊl/
22. /klaʊd/
23. /kaʊ/
24. /haʊ/
25. /naʊ/
26. /plaʊ/

27. /eɪs/
28. /eɪd/
29. /eɪk/
30. /eɪm/
31. /eɪt/
32. /teɪp/
33. /seɪf/
34. /beɪt/
35. /leɪt/
36. /preɪ/
37. /deɪ/
38. /beɪ/
39. /streɪ/
40. /oʊk/
41. /oʊr/
42. /oʊt/
43. /toʊz/
44. /boʊt/
45. /koʊt/
46. /θroʊt/
47. /goʊl/
48. /sloʊ/
49. /bloʊ/
50. /moʊ/
51. /ɔɪstɚ/
52. /ɔɪntmɪnt/
53. /ɔɪl/
54. /əvɔɪd/
55. /tʃɔɪs/
56. /hɔɪst/
57. /pɔɪz/
58. /bɔɪ/
59. /tɔɪ/
60. /dikɔɪ/

CHAPTER 5

Fill in the Blanks

1. acoustic
2. sound spec-
   trograph
3. frequency, time,
   amplitude
4. formant fre-
   quency
5. /v, ð, z/
6. vowels
7. high
8. oral cavity
9. antiresonance

True or False

1. F
2. T
3. F
4. F
5. T

Multiple Choice

1. c
2. a
3. a

CHAPTER 6

Fill in the Blanks

1. electronic
2. continuancy,
   sibilancy
3. former

True and False

1. F
2. T
3. F
4. T

Multiple Choice

1. c
2. a

CHAPTER 7

Fill in the Blanks

1. twenty
2. the following
   vowel /u/
3. /w/
4. /u/; /ʊ/
5. /pʌs/, /pʌn/, /mʌd/
6. front-mid vowel
7. interdental;
   front-low vowel;
   alveolar

True or False

1.	T	3.	T
2.	F	4.	F

Phoneme Identification

1.	/v/	4.	/w/	7.	/bɔɪ/
2.	/ð/	5.	/i/		
3.	/m/	6.	/lʌl/		

CHAPTER 8

Fill in the Blank

1. syllable
2. primary, sec-
   ondary, unstress
3. intonation
4. Chinese

True or False

1. F   2. T

Multiple Choice

1. c   3. a
2. a

Phonemic Transcription

1. /'ɪʃju/
2. /'kaʊntɪ/
3. /'oʊpən/
4. /'teɪbəl/
5. /'mʌðɚ/
6. /'ʌpɚ/
7. /'ɔtəm/
8. /sə'mɛnt/
9. /'prɑsɛs/
10. /'nɛfju/
11. /ˌmɪs'tʊk/
12. /'ɪnˌsɝt/ or /ˌɪn'sɝt/
13. /'wɪnˌdoʊ/
14. /'aʊtˌlaɪn/
15. /ˌdɪ'fɪt/
16. /ˌwɪθ'drɔn/
17. /ˌɛn'dʒɔɪ/
18. /'æŋˌgrɪ/
19. /ˌɪn'sɪst/
20. /ˌɪn'saɪd/
21. /ˌru'mætɪk/
22. /'tɛləˌfoʊn/
23. /ˌdɪs'ɔrdɚ/
24. /ˌdɪ'vɛləp/
25. /ˌɛm'plɔɪmənt/
26. /ˌɛn'kaʊntɚ/
27. /ˌɪn'vɛnʃən/
28. /ˌju'tɪlətɪ/
29. /'tɛləˌvɪʒən/
30. /ˌsɪgə'rɛt/

CHAPTER 9

Fill in the Blanks

1. four; voicing, continuancy, sibilancy, and labiality
2. the opening of the nasopharyngeal valve
3. labiality
4. continuancy
5. /p, b/; /f, v/
6. /v/
7. [pʰ], [p], [p⁻]
8. /t, d/; /f, v/
9. morphophoneme
10. sibilancy
11. /p, b/, /t, d/
12. vocalic
13. /r, l/
14. /ʍ/
15. /h/

True or False

1. T
2. F
3. T
4. T
5. F
6. F
7. T
8. F
9. F
10. F
11. T
12. T
13. T
14. T

Multiple Choice

1. b
2. b
3. a
4. c
5. b
6. a
7. b
8. a
9. b
10. c

CHAPTER 10

Fill in the Blanks

1. high vowel; back vowel
2. diphthong
3. /ɔ/
4. short; low; low
5. /æ/
6. back, mid, lax
7. /u/
8. retroflexed

True or False

1. T
2. F
3. F
4. F
5. F

Multiple Choice

1. b   3. b
2. b   4. a

Orthographic Counterparts

Homophones (two or more words that are pronounced the same, but whose spellings and meanings are different) are acceptable answers. For example, either beat *or* beet *is correct for the first part of question 1. Other homophones occurring in these answers include: ate-eight, seen-scene, tale-tail, blue-blew, mane-main-mein-Maine, etc.*

1. beat; bit
2. meat; mit
3. heat; hit
4. leap; lip
5. teen; tin
6. seen; sin
7. keen; kin
8. been or bean; bin
9. wean; win
10. sleep; slip
11. neat; knit
12. sheep; ship
13. kneel; nil
14. eat; it
15. pin; pen
16. tin; ten
17. kin; Ken
18. bin; Ben
19. win; when
20. pit; pet
21. sit; set
22. mit; met
23. till; tell
24. mill; Mel
25. nil; Nell
26. sill; sell
27. Nick; neck
28. seen; sane
29. keen; cane
30. team; tame
31. lean; lane
32. mean; main
33. sheep; shape
34. keep; cape
35. eat; ate
36. beat; bait
37. meet; mate
38. heat; hate
39. feet; fate

40. ate; at
41. bait; bat
42. mate; mat
43. cane; can
44. main; man
45. cape; cap
46. hate; hat
47. fate; fat
48. main; men
49. mate; met
50. gate; get
51. bait; bet
52. cane; Ken
53. late; let
54. pain; pen
55. wane; when
56. tale; tell
57. male; Mel
58. nail; Nell
59. sale; sell
60. fool; full
61. Luke; look
62. pool; pull

63. pool; pole
64. moon; moan
65. noon; known
66. blew; blow
67. threw; throw
68. crew; crow
69. flew; flow
70. shoe; show
71. coon; cone
72. too; toe
73. moo; mow

74. bull; ball
75. look; lock
76. pull; Paul
77. shook; shock
78. cushion; caution
79. put; pot
80. foot; fought

81. ball; bowl
82. chalk; choke
83. bought; boat
84. not or nought; note
85. got; goat
86. mall; mole

CHAPTER 12

Fill in the Blanks

1. narrow
2. [~]

3. /p, t, k/
4. [lɛt‘]

5. palatalized
6. [−]

True or False

1. T
2. F

3. F
4. T

5. F
6. T

Multiple Choice

1. c
2. b

3. b
4. c

5. b
6. a

CHAPTER 13

Fill in the Blanks
1. 'f'; 'th'
2. deviant speaker

3. linguistics

True or False
1. T
2. F

3. F
4. T

Multiple Choice
1. c
2. a

3. c
4. a

5. c
6. b

Index